Ma & Me

Also by Dr. Thomas "Billy" Byrom

Nonsense and Wonder:
The Poems and Cartoons of Edward Lear

The Dhammapada:
A Translation of The Sayings of the Buddha

The Heart of Awareness:
A Translation of the Ashtavakra Gita

Ma & Me
The Story of an Apprenticeship

Thomas "Billy" Byrom

KASHI
Kashi Publishing
Sebastian, Florida

© 2023 Kashi Foundation, Inc.

Copyright ©2023 by Kashi Publishing
All Rights Reserved

No portion of this book, except for brief reviews, may be reproduced, stored in a retrieval system, or transmitted in any form or by any means—electronic, mechanical, photocopying, recording or otherwise—without written permission of the publisher. For information, contact Kashi Publishing.

First Edition: December 2023

Published by Kashi Publishing
11155 Roseland Road
Sebastian, Florida 32958

Edited by Swami Matagiri Jaya
Additional Editing and Translations by Devadatta Kali
Cover and Book Design by Laurie Douglas

Printed in the United States of America
ISBN: 979-8-9894657-0-5

This book was published after the author's death in 1991. Descriptions of Kashi Ashram and surroundings were as he experienced them at that time.

Ma Jaya's quotes, River poem, and images from *Bones and Ash* are used with permission from The Ma Jaya Bhagavati Trust.

Quotes from Thomas "Billy" Byrom's unpublished manuscript of *The Third Wish* are used with permission from The Ma Jaya Bhagavati Trust.

Every effort has been made to credit the owners of all copyrighted material. Kashi Publishing welcomes communications from readers who may have knowledge of additional material to be credited.

For Ma and Ganga—
One Heart Never Apart

Praise for *Ma & Me*

Mixing elements of autobiography, biography, memoir, and spiritual reflection, Byrom often allows Ma to tell her story in her own words, and her rough Brooklynese stands in stark contrast to his evocative literary prose. The stream-of-consciousness narrative is a rich mosaic of personalities, events, and contemplation, all conveying the story of two seemingly disparate lives and how they came to be intertwined. Whenever Ma's experiences veer dangerously close to the limits of credibility, the author interposes quotations from the likes of St. Teresa of Ávila, Thomas Merton, Rumi, and Ramprasad to show that Ma is in very good company indeed. Thanks to his extensive knowledge of the world's religions and philosophies, Byrom is able to demonstrate time and again that true spirituality is spontaneous, unpredictable, and often paradoxical.

—*Devadatta Kali*
Musician, translator, author of several books on the Goddess

An affectionate and intimate portrait of a devotee's guru, as told through her first student, a stiff Oxford don who, in searching for a teacher, finds her in the holiest of holy places: Brooklyn, N.Y. Thomas Byrom, or Billy as he was called, follows his restless heart into hilarity, death, and deep stillness as he follows Ma Jaya on a journey that will last his lifetime.

Through his eyes, observing, and experiencing nature in all of its seasons, we follow his own emotional life with every descriptive sentence and verse of poetry. Billy writes beautifully, and his observations of those devotees who soon joined him are spot on. When I arrived on the scene in 1974, he was the disciple whose devotion to Ma was one I tried unsuccessfully to copy. With perfect diction he could explain to me in one impeccable sentence what Ma was about. I loved him like the older brother I never had.

—*Yoga Acharya Swami Laxman Das*

Billy (Thomas Byrom) and I became friends in the late 1980s, when I met Ma during her visits to California to work with people who were HIV+. We never met in the flesh, but we clicked through messages and letters—we had a shared background and a parallel reaction to Ma: she crashed through our lives that were filled with books, but also with death, bringing us life in a chaotic, lively, loving form we hadn't experienced elsewhere.

Byrom's fine translations of spiritual texts—the *Dhammapada* and the *Ashtavakra Gita*—are still among the best for both these famous works; he knew not only the languages and the cultures behind them, but he understood their most important messages. He thus did something not many can—he used his learning and intelligence as vessels to lead to spiritual growth, rather than for their own sakes. *Ma & Me* is his story of how an intelligent man falls toward illness and death, and discovers the perfect teacher—Ma Jaya, who was full of the life and joy he so needed.

—*Dr. Paul G. Antinello*
Jungian psychoanalyst, Senior lecturer in music at Newcastle University UK

I had the opportunity to collaborate with Billy and others to start the River School on Ma Jaya's ashram in Roseland, Florida. Billy was teaching Latin declensions, I was teaching beginning reading; somehow Oxford, Harvard, and the traditions of Australian grammar schools blended with Maria Montessori and Rudolf Steiner. Service and compassion were the roots as students learned how not to fear the unknown and how to have humble confidence. We all learned that through service we can grow, become more aware, and touch a deeper self.

Billy's bench sits underneath a southern live oak tree on Kashi Ashram, not far from the dock on the St. Sebastian River. If you ever get the chance to sit there, listen and you will hear the story of the river.

—*Anasuya Carson, Ph.D.*

Billy continually discovers that the formless God he is seeking is actually everywhere, in every form—and most recognizably in the children. Thus evolved the basis of our River School curriculum: to nurture the heart of each child as we helped equip him or her to live fully in this difficult world. Ma was very proud of her school, and we were blessed with both Ma's and Billy's guidance. For me, Billy helped us maintain our balance between academic excellence, service, and, above all, Love.

Ma & Me is much more than a memoir; it is an authentic, totally honest look into the soul of a deeply committed seeker.

—*Swami Anjani, River School Principal*

Contents

Prologue vi

PART 1 FINDING 1
   1   Tirza the Wine Bath Girl 2
   2   Breath and Appetite 19
   3   The Flower by the Breastbone 40
   4   The Old Man in the Blanket 69
   5   Summer Snow 107
       Photos 133

PART 2 UNFOLDING 147
   6   River Song 148
   7   Grandma Lulu Breaks Her Silence 180
   8   Wild Cotton 205
   9   The Last Degree of Love 225
  10   The Betrayal of Joseph Tillman 253
  11   Anna's Holiday 283

About the Author 313
Endnotes 314

Prologue

I never got my breath back. I never recovered my senses. But who will understand?

And how shall I ever find words to describe the fire and the silence which provoked this absurd and bewildering life of seeking? One evening, an evening like any other, in the dead time between winter and spring, I stand at the open glass doors of my living room. My eyes fall on the stubble of an empty field, and three black birds rise one by one into the air; and with them there arises in my heart a single, startling movement of complete understanding, a flight of absolute passion, leaving me breathless and dazed. I know for the first time that all my life I have been in love, crazed with love, drunk with love. And now for the first time I understand the desolation I have always endured, every day of my life, beyond despair! And that night and the next day the feeling does not desert me, though I hold the doors open, but only deepens till I am able to calculate, with all my senses on fire, that I shall have lived my life, when it ends, in two halves, the first asleep and the second, into which I have just now awakened, *awake!* Awake, and burning....

Burning with a single flame, the flame which burns in the silence of the heart, and at the crown of the head, where all desires and all fears are consumed, in whose blazing even the fear of love is burned to ash, and with it the desolation of the separate self. But who is there to understand? "Love has ten degrees," the Sufi proverb goes. "The ninth is silence, and the first, flight from people." Tongue-tied, ashamed, stumbling, on fire, like an adolescent fresh to passion, I hid my love from family and friends, and yet it leaked out of me, in sudden intemperate remarks or abrupt and rowdy silences or aimless chatter, or in unfinished fits of mutinous laughter, making me foolish and impossible. Everything I said sounded self-serving or inflamed, and my mother and my father, my brothers and sisters, all my friends, remained unalterably angry or distressed on my account, and certain that I was making it all up or putting on grotesque airs.

Yet it really did happen! Though I haven't the words for it, it really does happen! So St. Teresa promises her novices. And so crazy St. Catherine protests to her impatient Beloved, "My heart is breaking but cannot break for the hungry longing it has conceived for you!" This is my calamity—I fell in love. That's all. I fell in love with the love which had been burning in my heart, unacknowledged, all my life. And every day my love grew more foolish and complete, exceeding its own folly, exhausting its own fulfillment. And no one would listen to me. I did not know how to talk, or where to put myself, or whom to embrace.

Until I found You.

Part 1
Finding

1
Tirza the Wine Bath Girl

After I brought the car around to the gate to pick Ma up, I found I had half an hour to spare, so I walked down to the river through the pine flatwoods and the grove of old live oaks. I made my way through the brambles to the end of the little spit by the collapsed boat dock. I sat for a spell above the lip of the current, a thick quiver of willows between me and the climbing sun. Then a fat wind came suddenly around the southern bend, stalled in a stand of red bay where a hammock of oak and palm scythes into the stream, in a moment recovered and brushed the last smoke of morning mist out of the backwaters, lifting and freshening the air.

Who is happy? Who is afraid?

This morning I heard these questions on the wind—out of the wind's silence—as the wind lifted the heavy and sweet wetness from the air.

We drive into town, Ma at the wheel, Yashoda and I crouched in our seats, protesting at every lurch and swerve. But Ma is unperturbed by the terror she provokes. And it is small comfort that she always talks her way out of tickets either with a pugnacious innocence or by beguiling the officer's manhood with her wholly bewildering purity, as if she were both the girl of his dreams and his mother. Today we end up astride County Road 510 in Wabasso directly under a red light, blocking all westbound traffic.

She will not take the least criticism.

"Don't tell me how to drive or youse can both get out here."

"But Ma," I choke, "back up at least and let the truck…"

"Truck? What truck!" (Her language is a good deal rougher than I care to represent it.)

A lorry with several tons of Indian River grapefruit looms at the right window. From here I can see the rifle latched above the dash. The light changes, and Ma surges forward, savagely cutting off a tow truck. Ma has always been a formidable driver. Savage but impeccable, she drives with flawless mastery and complete abandon.

As her passenger for the best part of twenty years, I am sometimes given to wonder, after my professorial fashion (I was once a professor of Old and Middle English), if there is a particular theology to her driving. If so, it is all grace and no doctrine. It must be a lawless theology of absolute presence, in which all attention is miraculously gathered into the present moment. Only a driver fully abandoned to the here and now, the sanctity of the actual and immediate, could ever escape alive and unscathed by such wildness. And for that matter only a passenger safely buckled into an eternal present could ever ride willingly at her side without an overwhelming panic of the kind that overtakes me now, provoking flurried thoughts about first and last things.

As we hurtle south toward Vero Beach through the dense orange groves, pumping in the sudden heat before spring the gorgeous perfume of their blossoming, I notice the whites of my knuckles on the door handle, and wondering where God is now, I reflect with misplaced and improvident calm, born of deep panic, that it was a car crash which landed us in Florida—in this mess, this sublime mess—in the first place. Not that it was her fault. She has truly never hurt a soul.

But it's a long story. A long and scarcely credible story how Christ came to her and how her hands bled on Good Friday and again on Easter Sunday when she was trying to serve spareribs to her family in spite of the blood trickling down her forehead; how he told her to turn her back on everything and walk away and share her love for God—that crazy, impatient, blaspheming God, so full of tricks and tall stories, who never stopped bothering her, pulling at her sleeve, tripping her up with unannounced ecstasies, filling her house in Brooklyn with spiritual riffraff, bankers and druggies, professors and gun molls, priests and whores; how her husband Sal, whom she loved to distraction, fell apart in a motel in Montauk, and the judge broke down when she sang in court; and how, swerving to avoid some newlyweds in front of her on the highway, she flipped the van over on the Long Island Expressway, striking her head on the dash; how after three years of trying to share it all and keep her family, of giving it all away even to people who didn't want it, she hopped on a plane to Miami, alone and battered, and Sam at the car rental tried to take her home to Coconut Grove and have his wife patch her up—"Lady, you ain't going nowhere like that!"

A long story, and who would believe it?

But not for now. Now the cool musk of the blossoming oranges drenches our minds and our senses.

"Don't tell me how to drive!"

"Did I say anything?" Yashoda protests. "Did I say anything?" She is sitting cowered in the backseat, the cooler on her lap for a buffer, her face as white as orange blossoms, the bright floss of her blond hair shocked with fright.

A few miles south of Wabasso, between the Indian River and US 1, there is a wild orchard. Passing by a month ago I saw a road gang of county prisoners buckhorning the trees where a hard frost in February had burned them back. Now to my astonishment the stumps are already sprouting, and around them the healthy trees are full, heavy, and fragrant. Most of their blossoms will fall chastely to the ground. But from an abundant few the infant fruit will soon issue.

A southeast wind sweeps across from the beaches and the barrier island, runs through the orchard, and spills the pregnant musk of its blossoming onto the roadway, flooding the car.

THOMAS "BILLY" BYROM

We are late for Ma's appointment.

* * *

This is the story of a holy person, but from the start I should make it clear that I am not writing about someone who pretends to be particularly good or wise. Though I once believed in the refining of such qualities, and even in the possibility of their perfection, I have come to believe that the refinement of virtue is almost always a presumption, and that perfection of any sort—intellectual, moral, spiritual—is not a human property. And since it is not human, it cannot be divine either, and to hearken after it is a kind of folly. Even Christ was troubled and afraid and angry, and though you wouldn't know it from the Gospels, I am sure he played tricks on people and told tall stories and laughed. And where there is fear and trouble and laughter, there cannot be perfection, or the affectation of goodness and wisdom. If we seek perfection we should look to that supremely confident and credible fellow who tempted Christ in the wilderness. He never laughed or faltered. His performance was perfect. If anything is truly evil, it is the plausible clarity of such perfection, which proceeds from a limitless pride and denies the infinite humanity of God. Instead of perfection, I have come to believe in the possibility of fulfillment—and that is quite another thing. It is less a matter of goodness and wisdom than of joy—of that fulfillment of our natural capacity for happiness which Christ promised John: "That my joy may be in you, and that your joy may be made full."

Ma was always very full, and full of joy, and entirely without scruples. She was always happy and bad and passionate. From the start I saw that she was wild, that she would stop at nothing, that she had her own rules and always broke them. I saw that there would never be an end to her tricks and her makebelieve and her show. Her language would make a sailor blush—a talent she learned from her mother Anna, who had also instructed her at an early age to "talk all day but say nothing" and to "never leave well enough alone."

From the moment I met her I have never known her to give a direct account of herself or of any of the amazing consequences of her wildness and her crazy love. Everything has to be blown up and embellished, even when it is already beyond the bounds of belief. Everything, that is, this side of her silence.

Whenever she falls silent, the world stops, and with it all her show, and then she can never keep a straight face. In the end, she gives herself away. She always gives herself away. But she could be very rough, and I, as an Oxford don whose life had been sheltered from the criminal world (though I had encountered the peculiarly base criminality of the High Table), I was often and for a long time shocked by Ma's happy savagery. She had been brought up in poverty, in a cellar on Brighton 8th Street, under the Boardwalk, and on the back streets of Coney Island and Brighton Beach. She had joined a gang when she was ten, quit school at fifteen, and married at fifteen into a Sicilian family. Before she was out of her teens, every door in Redhook and Green Point was open to her.

She sold seconds and closeouts in her garage, and in order to inflame the demand she promoted her goods as hot off the trucks. At one time she had forty-five women working for her. Everyone adored her. No one messed with her, ever.

Her father Harry was a gambler, and after her mother died, when Ma turned thirteen, she was pretty much on her own. So she was streetwise, tough, a law unto herself.

"You have to eat everything and everyone life puts in your way," she has always said, and she lived this cannibalism. Seeing her consume the bigotry of southern sheriffs, I understood where she had learned to make the offal of their hatred delicious—in her savage childhood, on the other side of the law. She once hauled me in front of one such constable, a man who made Rod Steiger in *The Heat of the Night* look tame. He was standing by the pool of a Florida Holiday Inn, a steel pistol on each hip, a bandolier of bullets for a belt, the regulation deep shades, broken yellow teeth, a smile like a pit bull, and in every troubled gesture a thinly-veiled criminal rage. Pushing me forward, she told him, "He's scared of you. In fact he's terrified. Look, he's shaking! But I'm not scared of you," Ma announced brightly. "I think you're cute!" And she laughed in his face.

"She loves everyone," I stammered, scrambling to excuse this provocation of the law, choking, pulling at Ma's sleeve, and looking around for a means of escape. "Really, she does."

He looked at me again, as a man looks at a snake the moment before he shoots its head off. Then he turned to meet Ma's eyes. At first he couldn't; they dazzled him, and I thought we were lost. But when he looked a second time and held her gaze, he saw something there he understood, and broke slowly into a crooked, remorseless smile. And I saw that what he understood, he also loved.

The next moment we were out the door and into the car, Ma at the wheel, pulling away before the deputy had time to recover his official composure. Ma knew from the streets when to stand and when to run.

But that only tells part of it. There is another story, among hundreds, which goes deeper and better expresses the nature of Ma's savage abandonment. It is the story of Tirza the Wine Bath Girl, and since Ma loves to tell a story and tells her own stories best, and has no patience with anyone else telling them, here it is in her own words.

*　*　*

When I was about seven, my father rented this hot corn stand in Coney Island and right across from it was the back door of Tirza the Wine Bath Girl. And he got her to babysit me in between her acts.

She was in her forties and she had a body like you never saw before. And for ten cents she would take this wine bath, on a little stage in the window where they sell knishes now, just up from Nathan's. She'd get all nude, and she'd go in the wine bath, and she'd shimmy and shake, and go Da-da, da-da Boom, da-da, da-da Boom!

And I'd go home and every night I'd take off my clothes in the bathroom and I'd practice—Da-da, da-da Boom! This was my major thing, my main ambition.

And there used to be a wino under the boardwalk and I says, "Look, you gotta give me your wine."

He says, "Ain't you too young?"

I felt terrible, but I stole his wine, and I left him a dime. And I dumped it all in my bathtub and I came out smelly, and Tirza never smelled. I really smelled and everything burned. Then one day I go to Tirza's, and her son was preparing the bath—and he put in food coloring!

I cried for days. I wouldn't stop crying. I hid in the house. And Tirza begged me to come back and she said, "It's not what it seems to be. All of life is an illusion." (This is the first time that Ma has ever heard this.) "And another thing—Tirza does not go naked." It turns out she had this flesh-colored bodysuit, and I started screaming because I thought she was peeling off her skin. "It's not what you suppose. Remember that!" And then she said, "Now you go out on the stage and you play Tirza." And I was a big girl though I was still flat as a board, and I fitted into her bodysuit.

I did her shimmy and shake, and I slipped right into that bathtub— Da-da Boom, da-da Boom!

It was the greatest moment of my life.

* * *

If I had any sense, I would let this story stand by itself. Though Ma loves a strong moral, she never tells a story to make a point. She just likes the people in it, and she likes to tell it. But I was an English professor when I was still respectable, before we got into this mess, this sublime mess; and you will know something of the confusion that arises constantly between me and her if I persist in my profession and put a gloss on her words though I know it would be better to leave them alone.

Tirza's story is not just about why Ma is wild. Her disillusionment explains, at least partly, her impatience with the artifices of reality and the folly of its shifting forms. The water was not wine! There was no transubstantiation! The skin was just a bodysuit! There was no transfiguration! No wonder Ma was compelled, in the depth and purity of her nature, to live outside the law.

But she is more than just wild. She is abandoned, hopelessly abandoned, and full, shamelessly full, full of a crazy joy. And in the story she does not walk away; in her disillusion there is not the least disaffection. No, she shimmies and shakes and goes *Da-da Boom!* and slips into the water. It's all in the *Da-da, da-da Boom!* She abandoned herself to the illusion, and joyfully.

She became a stripper herself, a *real* Coney Island burlesque queen, though her chest was still flat as a board. She fell into the heart of the whole wonderful sham. And she was a triumph. In one miraculous instant, slipping naked into the wine bath, she mastered the illusion. She consumed it, swallowed it whole. And then—and here's the point—*she* became the show, and found herself in the theatrical emptiness of her own fullness and joy. It was a triumph of illusion, a triumph of passion and of her savage abandonment. And ever since, Ma has been going *Da-da, da-da Boom!* Not just to southern sheriffs but to every love-hungry misfit who strays across her path.

She performs for all of us. Some love the show immediately and end up hating it. Some hate it and end up loving it. And some, the most purely crazy, have loved it from the beginning. But Ma doesn't care. For her the show goes on regardless, implacably, in the ashes of the artifices of reality. She is always up there in the storefront window, next door to the knishes, shimmying and shaking and shining, and splashing the red wine over her naked body.

She has no shame. *Da-da, da-da Boom, da-da, da-da Boom!*

You who tell the truth about me,
tell lies about me.

For I am knowledge and ignorance.
I am shy and bold.
I am shameless; I am ashamed.
I am tough and I am terror.

I am present in all fears,
and I am strength in agitation.

—The Thunder, Perfect Mind

* * *

When Ma was eighteen, her hair turned completely white. Every few weeks she has the roots dyed blue-black. Today she sits quietly in the chair while Jan fixes her braid. Ma is a very beautiful woman. Once, talking of her childhood on the streets and under the boardwalk, she told me, "That's all I had—my looks and my mouth."

Jan threads a single thick braid, then swivels the chair around for us to admire her handiwork. Yashoda starts putting the diamonds back in Ma's ears, nine in the right, six in the left. There is another diamond in her nose, and on each arm she wears a mass of gold bangles. This is a particular scandal to pious Indians, who warn against *kanchankamini*, "women and gold," as well as a general provocation of suspicion or outrage in the skeptical or the righteous, the boldest of whom sometimes demand to know why a woman with a calling, a holy woman, flaunts her wealth and her beauty.

I have never heard Ma defend herself from these charges. And why should she, when her show is so brazen and the charges are so false?

Her ostentation is a kind of test, and those who pass it soon discover to their confusion that she is indeed poor, and not only modest but uncommonly shy.

Like many shy people, she has a big mouth, and her bragging is one of the arts of the street, a Brooklyn braggadocio which she needed in her childhood just to survive. But it is also a snare for the proud and the humorless. People who are stuck up usually lack a sense of irony, at least regarding themselves, and just as they are the first to be nettled by Ma's constant boasting, so they are the first to find themselves suddenly outwitted and humbled by the dangerous artlessness of her show. Ma shakes her bangles and complains like a child that Yashoda is taking too long. A blue-rinsed matron in the chair next to her scowls and looks away. But across the salon a plump lady in violet who is having her nails done transfixes Ma with a look of happy amazement, and when Ma turns to meet her gaze, they exchange a wonderful smile, like little girls.

"Hi!" Ma shouts across to her. "You're a hell of a nice lady!" The blue-rinsed matron flinches.

"So are you," the plump lady chirps back, her hands held captive by the manicurist, but her eyes flying all around Ma like a startled bird. Ma turns away and talks to Jan because such sudden joy, such unaccountable love, is hardly social—indeed, it is subversive, and it must be contained or at least distracted. Ma is often this way with strangers, bold but secret, easily abashed, and her shyness, the mark of a love so freely shared, helps explain her brashness, her brazen show, with which in every new encounter she at once provokes purity and exposes impurity.

The lip of the blue-rinsed matron curls.

But Ma is examining herself in the mirror, a profile that could be Indian, Hebrew, Egyptian, Arab, Native American, Romany, Tibetan, her eyes dark and gentle and lustrous, her face strong yet fine, and profoundly soft. "All I had was my looks and my mouth."

Ma is a mirror. If you come to her with pride and affectation, she gives you back a reflection of your showy self. Come to her humbly, and you find yourself with someone infinitely open. There is nothing tendentious in her teaching: it is entirely without design, strategy, or intention. It arises from an absolute emptiness. She is as empty as a mirror. So when she goes out to have her hair dyed, she wears a mask of wealth and beauty, and reflects the world with all its swagger and material insolence. At home, in the privacy of her own room, she at once discards the excess of makeup and jewelry; and only then, with all the veils removed, is it possible to see her true beauty. Then she is like a child, not an ordinary child, but somehow very ancient, even primitive—a child who has been here from the very beginning, and who has always been a child.

Then she is completely simple, and the strangest thing is, there is nothing around her eyes. When many years ago I first noticed this about her, I realized to what degree my own eyes—and everyone else's—are always pinched. Even children acquire at an early age invisible crow's feet. We are all guarded when our eyes meet, and forever glancing away. There is an ancient Sanskrit scripture which asks, "Who is lazier than the master? He has trouble even blinking!" In Ma's eyes, and around them, I see the same sublime indolence, the supreme laziness of God. At home and stripped of her war paint, she never seems to blink; and around her eyes, though she has creases of age and laughter and pain, there is a complete relaxation, a depth without a surface, a fathomless openness.

Then it seems she sits alone in the forest, at the beginning of time.

Sometimes her eyes are black. Now, as she turns from the mirror and scolds Jan for leaving a shadow below the hairline, her eyes are a very light brown, almost transparent.

"Can I go home now?" The matron looks at her sharply again, with contempt. But the lady in violet is sitting very still, caught up in a quiet and sudden happiness. She looks both composed and astonished, and every now and then she steals a glance at Ma. How often I have seen Ma dispense these small ecstasies, describing rings of quietness around how many startled strangers. How many astonished faces I see now looking after her, as the years separate and she passes through. "I told them you were coming," Jan whispers to Ma, a little ashamed.

"*Who* did you say was coming?" I ask.

"Well, you know—a guru. A beautiful guru, a real guru. They've never seen one before, you know."

"Not a *real* guru," I help her out.

"There you are! Not a *real* one."

"You better believe I'm real," Ma says quietly but with a savage brightness, "or we're all in a hell of a lot of trouble." And she turns to the proud matron with blue hair and smiles a boundless smile, effortlessly commanding, wholly innocent, full of happiness and understanding. "Don't worry, lady," she says. "I'm just faking it!"

Confounded by the scandal of this confession, and shamed by such uncritical love, the matron shrivels, and her pride seems to rise out of her in a thin black fume. She cannot meet Ma's eyes, and instead hangs onto her own reflection in the mirror. I follow her startled gaze, and I see that for a moment, beneath the shame and fear, she looks young and free and beautiful, like a child.

> *Inside the seed, light! Fill yourself*
> *With the light in the seed, your own light ...*
> *Or you are lost.*
> *I'm forever tangled in her wild hair,*
> *Wave upon wave, wild and alive and unfurling.*
> *In her company whoever is proper or sensible*
> *Is truly crazy!*
>
> —*after Rumi*

* * *

I remember the moment clearly.

I had escaped from my sisters, over the rocks and around the point. Above me, a rough escarpment of boulders singing in the early heat, at my feet a rock pool of perfect, inviolable stillness, and beyond, the blue vastness of the South Pacific. There was no other living creature. I was by myself, barefooted, a child of seven, tipped between the sea and the sky.

As I squatted there, watching the reflection of the wind in the unrippled pool, hearing its exhilaration high above me in the bright emptiness of the sky, I became aware for the first time of awareness itself. I had no name for it, but I could almost feel it—as if it had substance, like the cold water in the rock pool, now warmed by the sun, or breath, like the shouting wind.

I saw that I was entirely by myself in a boundless ocean of awareness. In the same instant I understood that awareness is the single mystery of life, that it enfolds all other mysteries, even the secret of the separate self. I was indelibly astonished, and I knew that all my life, whenever I remembered this moment, I would be pinching myself and asking, what is awareness? Nothing else could ever command my attention so completely. How could it? For nothing else mattered next to the constant pressure, the single compulsion of this mystery.

A quarter of a century went by. I was teaching at a small college in Southern Vermont. My life was words and books and bright, angry pupils. The moment by the rock pool was deeply buried, trodden under by the necessary artifices of reality, and I was buried with it, compelled to live this mystery without understanding its constant pressure around my heart.

And then one evening in my thirty-second year, in the dead time between winter and spring, I stood at the open door of my house and looked out over the stripped fields toward the flanks of a low mountain which Trappists farmed, and all at once I saw three blackbirds rise one by one from the empty stubble, and with them there arose in my heart a single, startling movement of complete understanding, a flight of absolute passion, leaving me breathless and dazed. And I knew for the first time that all my life I had been in love, crazed with love, drunk with love. And all that night and the next day the feeling did not go away, though I held the door open, but only deepened, till I was able to calculate, with all my senses on fire, that my life would be lived in two halves, the first asleep, and the second, into which I had just awakened, *awake!*

Awake, and burning…

Burning with a single flame, the flame which burns in the silence of the heart, and at the crown of the head, where all desires and all fears are consumed, in whose brightness even the fear of love is burned to ash, and with it the desolation of the separate self.

This was my calamity: I fell in love. That's all. I fell in love with the love which had been buried in my heart, unacknowledged, all my life, since that moment by the rock pool on the rim of the South Pacific when I first felt myself enfolded in Your breathless, blazing silence, one with the water and the shouting wind. And every day my love grew more foolish and complete, exceeding its own folly, exhausting its own fulfillment. And no one would listen to me, and I did not know how to talk, or where to put myself, or whom to embrace.

Until I found You.

> *I am foolish and I am wise. …*
> *I am the one called law,*
> *and you have called me lawless.*
> *I am one you pursued,*
> *and I am one you seized.*

MA & ME

I am one you have scattered,
and you have gathered me together.

Draw near to childhood,
and do not despise it because it is small and insignificant.

—The Thunder, Perfect Mind

* * *

Not long after I met Ma, she took me and a few others out to Brooklyn to look for Tirza. But the storefront was gone, and there was no sign of her.

We bought knishes and walked round the corner toward the beach. The parachute jump was broken, but on the sidewalk across from it there was a freshly painted Hammer of Champions—you know, you wallop a stud and the ball shoots up the barometer and the bell rings. It was manned by a battered and road-worn derelict with only a couple of teeth left in the front, and a nose blown out and blackened by drink and the streets.

"Say, did you ever hear of Tirza?" Ma asked him, on the off chance.

He looked at her strangely, then nodded.

"Well, where is she? Where's my Tirza?"

"Living in Saint Pete."

"How do you know?"

"I'm her son."

Ma screamed and fell into his arms, and he was frightened until she pulled his ear and said, "It's me, Joyce! Don't you remember me?" He hesitated, ashamed of how he looked, and he shuffled. But then he knew her—they had played together as children—and he lit up, though shyly, and could not turn her aside. "Yeah, Joyce! How you doin'? Been a long time."

Ma was triumphant. "See, what did I tell you? And youse didn't believe me, Billy."

"I did, I did believe you," I protested. "I did."

"Nah, you never believed me. My Tirza!" And she belted me over the head for not believing her, though of course I believed her all along. I have always believed her, even when I knew she was making it all up. *Da-da, da-da Boom!*

I take the wheel driving home. Ma is too close to God, too gone, gone beyond sense or rapture, drawn into a deep silence. I am a bad driver too, but not from lawless abandon, nor am I distracted by her dangerous God. I am simply inattentive.

The midday sun has sucked up into the sky the fragrance of orange blossoms, and a high hot wind carries it everywhere, soaking the groves and the railroad tracks and the small Black community of Gifford. Ma is silent, far beyond sense or rapture, far beyond my reach.

Who is happy? Who is afraid?

I hear these questions on the wind as it sweeps across from the beaches and the barrier island, as it runs through the wild orchard, releasing a sweet thick rain of fragrance, flooding the roadway with the gorgeous scent of oranges. The flower of the orange impregnates itself. The wind shakes pollen onto the sticky petals and it falls down the stamen into the swollen heart of the flower. Of a hundred blossoms, of a thousand, only one bears fruit. Glancing across at Ma, dangerously composed in the passenger seat, nowhere to be found, I remember the words of an ancient scripture, speaking of one who touches God: "His mind is cool and drenched with nectar." I sense that Ma's whole being is cool and drenched. But it is not the wind off the barrier island and the river which cools her, nor is it the ambrosia of the blossoming orange trees which soaks her every cell. It is her own breath, her own nectar, released in that ineffable union which, like the flowering of the orange, is entirely single. In her dangerous chastity I sense the mystery of desire and renunciation, of appetite and breath, of life and death. The light in the seed is carried into the heart of the flower. But which of her blossoms will bear fruit?

Though Ma embraces all paths to God, she teaches her own way, the way of the Mother, which requires each of us to become a child and to keep our childhood, once we have regained it.

And beyond that keeping, she takes us even farther back, into a deeper silence, to a moment before the child is begotten. As Mother Julian of Norwich says in her *Revelations*, we live in the womb of Christ, "Our true mother in whom we are endlessly born and out of whom we shall never come."

There, where love and awareness are one, we become what we already are, before the first breath is ever spilled, the light in the seed, ready today to fall into the heart of the flower, today to bear fruit.

2
Breath and Appetite

It is a cool spring, days bright and dry, wind out of the northwest with a faint smell of snow, nights bearing the memory of frost. Every afternoon at about four a brilliant red cardinal, masked like a thief, feasts at the feeder I have hung from the jacaranda in my back garden. His song is a sweet chirping, and his wife, a small drab creature, watches shyly from the higher branches. By the third week of April the grass is usually bustling and fat, but this year it is holding its breath. This year everything awaits the colossal wet heat of summer hanging just over the horizon, a great tide held back only by the unseasonal constancy of the north wind.

When the wind falls, I can hear it, between breaths, a vast hush in which everything will soon drown, and flourish. In the middle of the ashram there is a large pond, excavated from a grove of scrub oak and slash pine by our neighbor who sold us the land. Then it was all mud and powdery sand. But we scooped the banks to drain the ground, put down Saint Augustine sod, planted weeping bottlebrush and willow, red and silver maples, water oaks, laurel oaks, and a long crescent of queen palms, struck a small dock out over the water, floated a pontoon for swimming, and roughly in the middle set a makeshift fountain with three plumes. And everywhere there are beds of plumbago, firethorn, crimson bougainvillea, violet salvia, purslane, and petunia.

The pond is our *tirtha*, which means "ford" or "crossing" in Sanskrit. For many thousands of years it has been the custom in India to go on pilgrimages to these holy ponds, which represent the sacred river Ganga. Dipping in her waters, the seeker makes his final passage across the river of life and death, surrendering himself to Shiva, the destroyer of desire and pride and fear, of all the attachments of the little self.

Tirtha also means "teacher" and "teaching," "spiritual opportunity," and "the right place at the right moment." Such has our pond been for us: a place and occasion for Ma's teaching, a chance to dip in the waters of the Ganga, and to find an untroubled crossing. It is the place and moment of our seeking.

I caught up with Ma just before ten this morning, walking around the pond with Yashoda, the water always on her right. This is another ancient custom. The spiritual heart, the sacred heart of Christ, is to the right of the physical heart in the center of the body, so the seeker who circles a pond or a temple or a mountain walks with the heart nearest it.

But Ma is also walking on her doctor's orders, to build herself up after seven weeks in the hospital. Somehow her autonomic nervous system does not obey the ordinary rules, and she has been very sick. Seven circuits of the lake is a mile, according to the three pedometers clipped to her yellow pants.

"Tell him to get his shit together," she is instructing Yashoda, when I catch up with them. "Does he want me to be nice? Or does he want the truth? Tell him I'm not nice. Tell him there's no such thing as truth."

"Did you ever know me to be nice?" she asks me.

"No, Ma."

At the moment we have a score of guests of all ages and occupations: a painter of tormented landscapes, a reformed banker and a bankrupt broker, an opera singer with a faltering range, a psychic who has lost her gifts, an FBI undercover agent (we are the subject of his investigation), a German film director, a Turkish spy, a fisherman, two Franciscan brothers in retreat, a carpenter, the mayor of a small town in Iowa, an Ivy League oceanographer, a tinker between carnivals, and even an Indian chief—a desperate character in a leather skirt and rustic bodice who calls himself Walking Bear.

Who is happy? Who is afraid?

Most of our guests have flown in, but Walking Bear has paddled up the Sebastian River in his canoe, landed on the crumbling boat dock, and found his way through the live oaks and the partridge pea and the derelict orchard to our houses around the pond. He waits for us with artful indifference under the weeping bottlebrush, a large Bowie knife sheathed at his waist.

"*Hi!*" he hails us as we come around, his smile uncertain, his eyes smoky and miserable. He is a picture of leafy self-sufficiency, a weekend Thoreau, desperately stuck in his pose, and though he does not know it, his need is genuine and touching. In fact, he is just like the rest of us, who all arrived at Ma's door spiritually disheveled, fixed in one shabby affectation or another, all needing to be disabused, and held.

"Hi, son! Who are you?" Ma breaks her stride. He pretends he has happened upon us quite by chance, as if we lived far beyond the pale instead of three miles from Highway One. His conversation is brief and intrepid. He has turned his back on the softness of civilization. A real trapper, he gives nothing away. It is a sad and fretful show, and I have little patience for it. But Ma listens to him as if spellbound, welcomes him with uncritical love, and sends him off to the kitchen to be fed.

"He needs fattening up," she says as we walk on. "Feed everyone" has always been Ma's first command, as it was always the first undertaking of her guru Neem Karoli Baba, whose counsel was simple and constant: "Feed everyone, love everyone." As with any mother, especially a Jewish mother, this is the first and last expression of

Ma's love. As with any holy person, when she offers you food, she takes in return your fear or anger or pride. She takes as much of your distress as you are willing to give up, and offering it to God, she releases it. This is the meaning of *annadana*, the gift of food, and of *prasad*, the food taken from the hand of the teacher. It is also the original meaning of the Host, which Christ invested with the power to take our folly and our suffering. When Ma feeds her guests, in her submission to Christ she satisfies a spiritual hunger. She quenches a deeper thirst.

It is all in the fattening up. When the love-hungry seeker sits down at God's table, his appetite is at first magically stoked, as the burden of his distress is taken from him, and then when he is truly ravenous, he is fed till he becomes full, full of life, fat with love. And this is not just a mystery. It is a matter of fact. It is not merely figurative, it is literal.

It is the physical truth of Christ's communion, when he breaks the bread and says, "This is my body, which is given for you." So Ma brings us to his table and feeds us, stoking our appetite for life, and satisfying it.

Besides, she could never abide a poor eater. In her estimation, whoever turns aside his plate cannot enjoy sex or love or life itself. And if the seeker does not enjoy life, he has nothing to give back to God. If he cannot sit and be served, he cannot sit and serve. And without the full heart which comes from a full belly, without gratitude for God's prasad, how—when the time comes—can he give up the pleasure of sensation for the ecstasy of service?

* * *

God comes to the hungry in the form of food.
—Attributed to Mahatma Gandhi

When I first met Ma, I was an indifferent eater. Most of my appetite was in my head, and Ma made it her business to bring it down into my belly where it belonged. We were still living in New York, and she would take a party of us, before and after meditation classes, to a diner in Queens, the Shalimar, and there we would set about consuming enormous quantities of cheesecake, dripping in sauce, till we were fit to burst. Shah Jehan and all his court could not have outdone us.

After a while this feasting had an unexpected, indeed an astonishing, effect on me. I began to feel really hungry, and perhaps for the first time in my life I began to notice what I ate, and to eat with gusto, as if I had never been fed before, as if I had been starving. And I found at the same time that my senses became sharper and fuller and my perceptions clearer. I felt altogether more awake and looser, less pinched and meager. With every marbled slice of chocolate cheesecake I felt the loosening of old constraints. And our feasts were not only grand, they were comical. I came away from them feeling carefree, reckless.

But most surprising of all, since it is entirely without scriptural precedent, which always prescribes fasting before sitting, I found that whenever I sat in meditation, gorged on sugar and sauce and cake, my mind was suddenly empty and quiet. Ma's method, if there was truly any method in these mad feasts, was an exact contradiction of the timeless wisdom of every religious culture—and yet it worked. The fuller I felt, the deeper the silence into which my meditations led me.

"I'm just fattening you up," Ma told me when I expressed my astonishment. I think it was then I understood for the first time, with feelings of terror and joy, that I was not just the guest at her table, I was also the meal. And I came also to understand, little by little, not just how self-denial is almost always self-serving, but how God comes to the hungry in the form of food, and how he fills us, and how fully.

The red bird swings on my feeder under the jacaranda. The first pale green fans of April are sprouting from its branches. When the heat floods us, next week or the next, the leaves will darken and unfold. Quicker than the eye, like a blushing burglar, the cardinal snatches his meal of sunflower and millet seed, and then, his appetite gorged, he chirps brightly on the bare sleeve of the jacaranda. The chirping is bright, a spark struck from stone—bright, happy and perfectly empty. In the suspense of appetite—a breath, a spark of song, a moment of perfect emptiness.

"O Sadhu! God is the breath of all breath."
—*Kabir*

* * *

It wasn't just Ma's driving that got us into this mess, this sublime mess. It was food, too. Ma always loved to eat. All her appetites were large—for family, for people, for laughter, for risks, for all the hot goods of life lived to the full. But her largest appetite by far was for food. The day I met her, Friday, March 22, 1974, she weighed two hundred and thirty pounds, wore green leotards, a mask of green and black mascara, and false eyelashes an inch long, extravagantly curled. She had a figure like an hourglass, a large hourglass but perfectly proportioned, and you could tell from the way she held herself, with the poise of the eternally slender, that she thought she looked wonderful. And she did. Well, I could have done without the eyelashes and the heavy makeup. But that was Flatbush rococo, an aesthetic of painted abundance among all the families of Mill Basin and Georgetown, as sacred as all the other Sicilian displays of the *passagiata*, an idea of beauty that you didn't mess with.

Anyway, in my shabby, patrician view, Ma looked gorgeous, vulgar, and—I quickly discovered—the only forbidden word in her lexicon was "fat" or "heavy" in the wrong context. There she sat on the couch in Hilda's apartment, daring everyone with every lustrous dipping of her eyelashes to think the unthinkable. And somehow she was right.

THOMAS "BILLY" BYROM

She was not fat, nor was she vulgar. Her real beauty shone through the painted surface.

She was as lovely and as noble as she knew herself to be. That day Hilda had invited a few of her students to meet Ma. Except for a group of Jesuit seminarians, we were her first class. And it happened that her first teaching was about food—about the nature of appetite and breath. Hilda singled out for special praise a cadaverous young man in his early twenties who had trimmed himself out in the costume of a rustic ascetic—tattered overalls, matted hair, wild eyes. He looked like Walking Bear without the leather, an urban hermit rather than a trapper. He had lived on berries in the woods for years, even as he walked the streets of Manhattan.

"He's been fasting, dear," Hilda told Ma, proud but also a little worried that he had been overdoing it. Ma took one look at him and sighed. "You from Minsk or Pinsk?" she demanded. "What is this bullshit? Don't mess with me, kid."[1]

And she described in some detail the large breakfast he had just put away in the White Tower over on Broadway. I remember it clearly: two pancakes with maple syrup, eggs over easy, strawberry malted, a double order of fries, apple pie à la mode. Spelling it out, Ma ate every mouthful over again with shameless relish. To his credit the scarecrow blushed deeply, all the wildness went out of his eyes, and he broke down. It was not the exposure which undid him, nor the loving detail, but having to declare for Minsk or Pinsk, and

---

[1] A reference to a classic joke: Two rival businessmen meet in a railway station.
"Where are you going?" asks one.
"To Minsk" was the answer.
"What a nerve you have! I know you're telling me you're going to Minsk because you want me to think that you're going to Pinsk. So I know you really are going to Minsk. So why are you lying to me?"

In her memoir, Ma recounts that her Russian grandmother would quiz her childhood friends, "Minsk or Pinsk?" If they answered wrong, they were banished from the apartment—for lying, as there is no possible "right" answer.

the ferocity with which Ma assured him that a hearty breakfast is nothing to be ashamed of.

Before he had time to recover she swept him into her ample arms, kissed him loudly, and threw him out.

"Never try to con a con, or fool a fool," she shouted after him, with love and pride, as if dismissing a prodigal favorite.

And in this way Hilda's shining example turned out to be altogether cautionary, as most shams and shows do around Ma. "I could see right into his stomach," Ma bluffed like a nine-year-old child showing off after a magic show, challenging our credulity. "I have X-ray vision," she added solemnly. "But you must *never* use the power of suggestion!"

Just as my mind was trying to make logical sense of this brazen disjunction, she swept away my calculation and my easy judgment with unanswerable force: "And never do as I do," she said brightly. "Just do as I say."

With these two forbidding commands as the uncertain moral ground of her instruction, I found myself drawn into a teaching that was to turn my life upside down; and it is certain—the only certain thing that I know—that from that day I was never the same, never wholly composed or sure of myself, never again confidently moral or safely contained, never brave or steady or judicious, never sensible, never reliable.

All she did that first day, after dismissing her phony faster, was show us a very easy breath, in and out to a simple count, and yet without doubt it was the day of my greatest calamity, the day I ate my own brain, the day I lost my breath and my senses and my wits once and for all, the day of all happiness and despair, the day I was done for, the day I folded and threw in my hand, the day of final abandonment. An easy breath, in and out freely to a simple count, never forced, without purpose: until the windows fly open and the wind blows out the guttering candle of the mind, and the breath, your own breath, floods the heart, God's heart, your own heart, the heart of all awareness.

It was *the day I found you*, the day you first introduced me to the mastery of desire, and the mystery of breath, and told me the story of how Christ came to you, and you knew he was God.

Here's the story in Ma's words.

*　*　*

In all the years we were married, my husband, my Sal, never once called me fat. Not once! And boy did I eat! But even when I shot up to 250 pounds, he always thought I looked terrific, and so did I. I always thought I was God's gift to the world, you see. I was always my favorite person. But I was smart. I'd lay out these big Italian dinners for my man and my three kids—the sauce, the bread, the lasagna or the scungille calamari, and the salad floating in oil. And every night they would eat away, but I would take just a little zupp. I would pile more and more on their plates, and I would peck like a little bird, 'til they were all stuffed. Then they would all go downstairs to the basement with the dogs and watch television, and I would make like I was clearing up. But what Sal didn't know was I had stashed away two loaves of Italian bread, not the thin kind but a special fat kind I had the baker bake for me. I showed him how to bake them for me, special. And I stashed them behind the toilet in the upstairs bathroom, and I would sneak up there with the salad bowl swimming in oil, and lock the door, and have a real feast. And boy, was that bread delicious!

Well, one day I got too cocky. I was serving lasagna, and Sal was really hungry and he asked me for more bread. But all I had was the two loaves I had stashed away for myself.

So I said, "Gee, Sal, I'm sorry, we're all out." And he said, "Never mind, Babe." And they all finish up and go downstairs to watch some police show, and for some reason I get too cocky. I clear the table and I fetch the loaves from behind the toilet, and instead of staying up there I come down and sit at the table with the bowl of oil, and right then and there I start noshing away. Well, about ten minutes later Sal suddenly comes upstairs during the commercial to get the TV Guide. And he sees me at the table, me who was before pecking like a little bird, eating so dainty and not touching this or that. There I am with my mouth stuffed, drooling oil, my fingers dripping. So Sal freezes and he doesn't say, "Hey, I thought there was no more bread, Joyce." No, he looks at me kind of sad, and for the first time in all the eighteen years we were married he says, "Eat a little, Babe, why don't you." Just like that.

And he turns around without the TV Guide and goes back down to the police show, the dogs and the kids. "Eat a little, Babe, why don't you." Just like that. So then I realize I had better lose weight. I must have been at 250 pounds and I start looking around. First I go to Dr. B. on Avenue M. He was giving shots of pregnant women's urine. All my girlfriends swore by it. You could eat as much as you wanted, and the shots took off all the weight. But I couldn't afford it, it was $75 a shot. So I do a deal with his nurse. I get the shots for $25 and I sell closeouts and seconds in the office to drum up trade for him.

Soon his office is humming, and I am getting the shots for free. But what do you know, I don't lose a pound. In fact I gain ten, and I'm up to 260!

So then I go down to Trim Away. This is a place on Nostrand Avenue where they wrap you up like a mummy, and all my girlfriends were there already. They said you could eat as much as you wanted, and the bandages took off all the weight. But after a couple of months all that happens is I have these very high love handles. Everything sort of moved up, but nothing came off, and now I'm at 265! So after that I go to Weight Watchers, and they said you can eat as much lettuce and grapefruit as you like, and I swear I was the only person ever to put on weight with lettuce and grapefruit. I ate them all day, I never stopped. And then you were asked to stand on the stage and give your testimony, and I got up there and they couldn't get me off. So they asked me to leave.

So I left. Fuck 'em, I thought. And I was still at 265. Then one day, just as I was going to give up—I was selling the closeouts in my garage, forty-five girls working for me—and in walks Maria, who used to be like a horse and is now like a toothpick! She was like a toothpick! I swear! And I said, "How did you do it?" And she said, "I take yoga at Jack LaLanne's down on Flatbush."

Yoga, I thought. I mean, that's pretty weird. Who knows from yoga? But I thought, what have I got to lose, only a hundred pounds. So I go straight down and enroll. And there's another toothpick called Sandy teaching the class. And we all go through the exercises, and I'm doing OK until the end when they all sit around in a circle and go "Om, Om," and I start cracking up because it sounds like the dumbest shit I ever heard, and I'm laughing so loud they couldn't shut me up. And they threw me out! Imagine! I got thrown out of my first yoga class! But Maria showed up in the garage the next day, still a toothpick, and I was still at 265. So I go down and apologize to Sandy, and she lets me back in, and pretty soon I'm doing all these different asanas, and even making up my own in front of the mirror, and everyone starts doing my asanas, though God knows where they were coming from, but they were better than the usual ones. But it wasn't the asanas which ruined everything, and ended my marriage, and got me in this incredible mess—it was the breath!

Sandy taught us a breath. You know, breathe in, count five, breathe out for ten, or some shit like that. And she says, "You do this for fifteen minutes a day, and you'll lose five pounds in a week."

So I immediately think, fifteen minutes, five pounds, that's twenty pounds in an hour. Why, I could lose the whole hundred pounds in one night! I rush home, I feed the family, I lock up the dogs, and when Sal's asleep I sit at the foot of the stairs and I start to breathe. And I am sure I am going to take it all off in one night, and that when Sal gets up in the morning there I'll be at the foot of the stairs like a toothpick. Or maybe I'll take off a couple of pounds anyway. So I breathe and breathe, just like Sandy says, only I don't stop. I breathe for an hour. Then two, then three.... And then when I'm going on four hours, I open my eyes, and I see this man coming up the stairs from the foyer, and I think, O shit!

He's wearing a white robe and carrying a cross. He has black hair, a black beard, black eyes, and he's carrying a cross, and his skin is darker than mine, and he's wearing sandals. And obviously this isn't for real! But somehow at the same time I am not at all scared, and I know at once who he is, who he really is. And I says to him, "Hey, Buster Brown, you got the wrong house, I'm Jewish."

But my voice is shaking, I hear my voice shaking from a thousand miles away, and the house is very dark, but inside the dark there is this very bright brightness, and his eyes, black eyes, and so much love I can't even tell if it's love there's so much, and then I know I'm not meshugah and I'm not scared even though my voice is shaking, and I know who he really is, and I'm really scared. Well, I got up so fast I must have lost the hundred pounds already, and I run upstairs and jump into bed with Sal, and I send him downstairs to get the kids and the dogs, and I make them all get into bed with us, I'm so scared, though somehow I'm not scared at all. And we all lie there, Sal, me, the three kids, Wanda the Shepherd and Brutus the Neapolitan Mastiff, and the bed's starting to give way. And I tell them what happened though they're half asleep and could care less, except for Sal. "Joyce," Sal says, "I'll call a priest."

"A priest!" I says. "What good is a priest? I've got the main man down there!" I knew at once it was really Christ because I felt this tremendous love. Like I never felt anything before.

I tell youse, no woman ever loved her husband or her kids like I loved mine. My Sal was my life. But the love I had for them—it was nothing next to the love I had for my Christ.

THOMAS "BILLY" BYROM

I'd never known love as a substance. I'd never known love inside my blood. I'd never felt love in my teeth, in my eyes, in the roots of my hair.

And Sal says, "You dumb Jewish bastard! I told you don't breathe like that!" And I lay there with the dog drooling on top of me, and all I could think was, he must be a prophet like my Isaiah. Here he was walking up the stairs carrying the cross like on the road to the Hill of Skulls and I was suddenly madly in love. I was in love like a woman, like a mother, like a daughter, like everything. I was a mad woman. But I made Sal get up again and lock all the doors and put all the lights on, and I kept all my kids and my dogs in the bed, and I held tight to them, but they didn't pay much attention because they were so used to their mother being crazy.

"You're sure you don't want a priest?" Sal kept asking.

"Are you kidding?" I said, only my language was maybe worse. But the next day first thing on the way to work Sal stops by Mary Queen of the Sea and has them send a priest over. I open the door after breakfast and Father starts flinging water all over the place, and I says, "Not on the tile, Father, I just got through mopping the fucking tile!" I sit down at the foot of the stairs where I started the breath, and I watch the priest messing up the tile, and I'm thinking, this doesn't make any sense—to begin with, I'm Jewish, for Christ's sake! And then I think, "Christ, that's some breath!" I mean I was trying to lose weight because my Sal caught me with the loaves and he said, "Eat a little, Babe, why don't you?" I mean, that's all he said. And now I'm madly in love, and I can't get the thought of him out of my head, like a fourteen-year-old girl, but a thousand times worse. And all I can think is, when will I see him again? Will he come back? And I am still feeling him, and tasting him, and breathing him in, and I don't know what to do. And then, sitting there and watching Father fling all that water around, I suddenly have a great idea! This is my chance to get my kids into Catholic school! So I go straight down to St. Edmund's on Ocean Avenue and I tell the nuns about my vision of Christ, and at first they don't want to hear it; they're real nervous, like what if it were real and they denied it. Then they'd be

in serious trouble with the main man. I can see them thinking, this is all bullshit. And then again they're thinking, now what if it isn't? You know, what if Christ really did come to her?

But I can't wait all day for them to make up their minds. I have to get Sal's lunch on the table. So I slip the head nun a gold cross I got at a closeout for Denise's confirmation, and that clinches it. Two days later my kids are all out of public school and into Catholic school. But all I can think is, When will I see him again? Will I see him again? Will he come back to me?

> "Rabbi, eat!"
>
> But he said to them, "I have meat to eat of which you do not know...
>
> My food is to do the will of him who sent me, and to accomplish his work."
>
> —John 4:31-34

* * *

Here in Florida it is cowdust time, just after sunset. Behind the magnolia tree and the thirsty water oaks the light is failing, now everything green deepens, the canna lilies and the rosewood and the parched wisteria deepen and disappear, and before long all we can see as we take our evening walk around the pond is the sky fading in the water and the white petals of the petunias, the ghosts of the drought.

In India the cows are herded home at dusk from the fields, raising the dust along the roads lined with tamarind trees, and there is never enough rain, or too much. The light has gone now from the sky, and as we walk on, the opening verses of *The Ascent of Mount Carmel* by St. John of the Cross come to mind and flood me.

> *On a dark night,*
> *Kindled in love with yearnings—oh, happy chance!—*

I went forth without being observed,
My house being now at rest.

In darkness and secure,
By the secret ladder, disguised—oh, happy chance!—
In darkness and in concealment,
My house being now at rest.

Never tiring of hearing about Ma's encounters with Christ, I ask her, "So when did he come again?" Ma's story continues in her own words.

* * *

I waited for a few days. I was so scared. But I was so much in love, soon I couldn't wait any longer. On the third night I waited 'til Sal and the children were all asleep, and everything was quiet. I went halfway up the stairs, and I started to breathe. And suddenly there he is again, carrying his cross, and I was terrified. And he says, "Don't be afraid. You know who you are to me?"

And I says, "Who?"

And he says, "You're my child. You're my mother." Mother and child! Just like that! And I was fresh because I was scared, and I says, "And you're Mickey Mouse!" I was real fresh, and I says, "And where do you send your clothes to the cleaners?"

Well, he just laughed and told me not to be afraid.

"Hey, who's afraid?" I says, but of course I was shaking.

And at first that's what he talked about, my fear. I was afraid because I knew he was real, and because of how much I loved him. I was terrified of the love I felt. I never knew there could be such love. He was inside my head, in my teeth, in my eyes and in the roots of my hair. He was even in my breath, and I was breathing him in and out. And I already know that I was going to lose everything because of him....

And then I see he has a thumb missing, his right thumb, and I says, "This is because I'm Jewish, right, that you have a piece of you missing?"

And he laughed again, and says, "I'm Jewish too!"

By now I'm really shaking hard, and I says, "So what! And we're the chosen people, I suppose."

And he says very quietly, "I was chosen. You are chosen. Everyone is chosen. No one is ever left out."

And that was when I got the courage to start poking him. I was poking him in the arm, in the shoulder. You see, he wasn't a vision. He was solid, he was flesh. And every time I poked him, he starts cracking up. Really, he thought everything was a big joke.

Then his mood changed. He talked about happiness and fear. He said that's the main thing between God and man—fear. And he told me about his mother. He talked a lot about Mary, how he loved her. He told me about fear and happiness and love. And that's everything there is.

And he said he would come to me two more times, and then he left me, and I sat there 'til dawn, and I wasn't afraid anymore. And I felt him in my blood and my bones, like I had never felt anything before. And I was burning up like a mad woman, I loved him so much. I was crazed!

* * *

In the happy night,
In secret, when none saw me,
Nor I beheld aught,
Without light or guide, save that which burned in my heart.

—St. John of the Cross

"And the third time?" I ask. "What happened?"

* * *

I was still real fresh. The moment he showed up, it was just after Christmas, I says, "So what's it like being born in a manger?"

He just looks at me with his black eyes—he's even better looking than my Sal—and he says, "What's it like being born in a drawer in Brighton Beach?" Touché! What could I say?

Then he starts talking about my kids, and I realize he knows how I bribed the nun with the hot gold cross to get them into Catholic school. And I start turning red, and I says, "You're Catholic, aren't you?" And the bastard couldn't stop laughing. And I was getting so mad I almost forgot to be scared.

"No," he says, "I'm not a Catholic. I'm not even a Christian. I'm not an anything. I'm everything. I am all paths. And you must teach all ways, because all ways are mine."

"Teach?" I says. "Hey buster, I didn't finish ninth grade. I'm not teaching anything!"

And then he is real quiet, and it was very bright, though we were in the dark, and for a long time we were just sitting there together, and I can feel my fear going away when I look into his eyes. He was eating all my fear.

* * *

> *This light guided me*
> *More surely than the light of noon day,*
> *To the place where he (well I knew who!) was awaiting me—*
> *A place where none appeared.*
>
> —St. John of the Cross

* * *

Then he told me all about Luke. He told me to read Luke's Gospel because that was the truest. He said Luke made up a lot of it as he went along but that was all right with him because the heart of it was true. He said, that's all you need. And that night, which was the third time he came to me, he talked a lot about Luke, and he said the worst thing in life is a dry heart.

And when he went away I cried. I cried I loved him so much. He was in my hair and I could taste him. And I sat there in the dark 'til it was nearly morning.

* * *

Oh, night that guided me,
Oh, night more lovely than the dawn,
Oh, night that joined Beloved with lover,
Lover transformed in the Beloved!

Upon my flowery breast,
Kept wholly for himself alone,
There he stayed sleeping, and I caressed him,
And the fanning of the cedars made a breeze.
—St. John of the Cross

"And the last time?" I ask. "What happened?"

* * *

As soon as he shows up, I give him a good poke, but this time he doesn't laugh, he says, "Cut it out, Ma!"—Ma, he calls me—and he is very quiet and very serious. He tells me how much he loves me and how much I love him, which is true, and how for such love you have to give everything up. "But don't worry," he says, "what happens is that everything gives you up."

THOMAS "BILLY" BYROM

And he asks me what I really care about, and when I say I care about everything, he says, "You don't even care about food."

"Are you crazy?" I says. I laugh in his face. "Who are you kidding? I'd fucking kill for food, and you know it!"

"You don't even care about sex," he says.

This time I know he's crazy, and for a moment I lose my fear of him completely. "I'm not giving up sex," I says, "not even for you!"

And he says quietly, "You already have."

"Listen," I says, "I'll give up sex and you show me the universe." Only my language is a little rougher, you know. I got a big dirty mouth from my mother.

"I already have," he says, even quieter.

And that shuts me right up, because I know that when I'm looking at him, I am looking at the universe. I know he is everything. That's all he is—he is everything....

"But there's still one thing you must give up," he says.

"What's that?" I ask, and now I'm scared again.

"Your family. You will have to turn your back on them and walk away."

This time I'm not laughing. "Just like that?" I says.

"They will come back to you. But it will take a long time."

"How long?" I says.

"That depends on them. But one day soon, next year or the next, because they do not understand, you will have to walk away from them."

"Over my dead body," I says. But I know he's telling the truth. Then he told me about my two best friends, how they would both get cancer, and one would live but the other would die. And that's what happened. And he said that I would have to suffer too, but he didn't say how, and I didn't ask.

But I asked him again why his thumb was missing. And he said, "You'll find out."

Then came the moment I dreaded most.

"I have to leave you," he said.

"Okay, so leave," I says. I'm really mad at him and I'm panicking. I says, "You got someone else to call on?"

He laughed and just looked at me.

"How can you leave me now? Everyone thinks I'm crazy."

And he said, "You have me. You will always have me. I have taken everything from you, and I have given you myself."

And then he was gone! Just got up and walked out on me. But I was too crazy to be mad at him. I was like a crazy woman, I was in love and I felt him in every part of me. I was completely crazy....

* * *

I remained, lost in oblivion;
My face I reclined on the Beloved.
All ceased and I abandoned myself,
Leaving my cares forgotten among the lilies.

—St. John of the Cross

THOMAS "BILLY" BYROM

The light has gone from the sky and the water, and as we turn under the balcony the wind lifts, stoking the embers of the night blooming jasmine where it is bursting the lattice. We walk on in silence. The branches of the rosewood rustle in the night wind, and bend.

3

The Flower by the Breastbone

Sometimes on these long light evenings of early summer, I stop on my way over to Ma's house and sit by the pond for a few moments of recollection. I am always so ahead of myself that it helps to sit without waiting, free of the least anticipation. Then instead of watching, I am happy just to see. Instead of listening, happy just to hear. Instead of doing, happy just to be. For those few moments, simply to be.

Tonight the children are splashing in the shallows over by the steps, bossy as nesting birds, tirelessly inventing games of trouble and danger. I see them through the spray of the fountain when the wind from the southwest shuffles its skirts. They are so bright and brave, they never falter. Nothing can undo their heroism. From here I cannot catch their words, only bits of their broken treble. The rest is a dumb show, muffled by the wind in the shifts of the fountain. They thrash in the water, then climb up onto the bank, declaiming to each other with a terrible, gracious violence. The wind rises suddenly, and I can hear nothing. I see them through a shower of silence, our brilliant kids, caught up in a great drama of their own making, one that God Himself could never unmake. Yet here come Kali and Tara to haul them all inside and bathe them, and at once they are no longer gods but a little rabble, in open rebellion against sleep.

The fountain showers me with its silence. At my feet, on the marshy lip of the pond, a green heron is picking at the stippled bass under the water lilies. He ruffles his black crest feathers and, seeing me, freezes for a long moment. His neck is a dull purple, his back green and black, throat and wings dipped in white, his bill a dark green spike. But I know him by his yellow stockings, which were first brought to my attention some years ago by a backwoodsman with metal teeth called Homer Cato, who wore a stainless steel revolver at his waist and who delighted in stepping out from behind the saw palmettos in the flatwoods down by the river, scaring the wits out of me with his terrible junkyard smile. But Cato called the heron a green egret, or fly-up-the-creek. The bird stabs and misses, tucks in his head, then flies off to his nest in a thicket behind the pink mimosa. I stretch, they are waiting for me. And still it has not rained, the longest drought since the twenties, when Cato was a young man and the hammocks and wetlands around us were still untouched. Everything still awaits the tidal heat of summer. You can hear it when the wind falls, between breaths, a vast hush in which everything will soon drown, and flourish.

* * *

Was not our heart burning within us, while he spake to us in the way?

—*Luke 24:32*

It happened all at once. And yet it happened also over a number of years, in the quiet shifts of the seasons, while my head was too distracted to notice their passage and the change they were working in me.

About twenty years ago, as I was finishing my doctoral studies at Harvard, I suffered a kind of withdrawal or contraction or gathering inward—I really don't know how to describe it. I started to lose interest in things. People, places, ideas which had once given me pleasure or stirred my imagination became stale, sometimes little by little, sometimes abruptly. I became tongue-tied and awkward, even among friends, I who had never been at a loss for words or particularly shy. My hands and my ankles felt heavy, my head light, and often my heart seemed to hesitate or stick in my throat. I felt at the same moment intensely self-conscious and completely invisible.

And I think I might have gone a little out of my mind, had it not been for another, even stranger shift in my feelings. My sense of humor changed. I am not sure, even now, how such a thing is possible. Laughter is so radical in our character. How we laugh, what we laugh at—these are such spontaneous, instinctive, deeply reflexive things, fixed in us from the earliest moments of our awareness. Anyway, it happened that I was preparing a dissertation on nonsense poetry, and in the course of reflecting a good deal about the nature of humor, both the tendentious kind which depends upon judgment, and the absurd kind in which all forms of criticism are transcended, I became aware that humor grounded in judgment no longer amused me in any of its forms. This was not by choice or will or from an intellectual or moral determination. It was not that I judged judgment or scorned the uses of ridicule. On the contrary, in those Vietnam years it seemed very important to me to hold lightly up to the light all the corporation spooks and quislings who spent their summer vacations patching up or hiding racism and neofascism in Asia. But the critical animus had gone out of me, and in its place I felt a strange exhilaration. The borders of my world seemed to draw together, but with this contraction there was a dilation of humor or joy, and with a few friends who shared this experience I found myself laughing at the most improbable things, laughing on the inside, that is, more and more quietly, with a strange and gathering intensity. Together we discovered that the world is really very absurd: that human relations are a kind of play, comically transparent and innocent at heart; that most art is a form of self-importance, its beauty an accident of the perfection to which it aspires; that no one suffers except at his own hand and that we are ourselves the source of whatever troubles weigh us down; that nothing has substance, that everything is composed of light, and the nature of every living being is fulfilled in happiness.

It seemed a complete and perfect picture of the world. But my real world was not as large or happy. Like a young tree infested with scale, I had too fat a mulch of books at my roots. I was out of touch with the natural world, smothered in words, stuffed with literature. I was laughing on the inside, and strangely quiet, and on fire—but more and more constrained on the outside. And I knew from these first fits of silence and laughter that my world was hollow and so, when I looked, was my heart—hollow, but full of an odd, pointless contentment.

That my joy may be in you, and your joy fulfilled.
—John 15:11

I felt caught between a mean contraction and a marvelous dilation, and I realized that if I was to continue to make sense, even of nonsense, I needed to break away. And so I applied for a job at a small liberal arts college in Vermont. On my way up there for an interview I was stuck between buses in a snowstorm in Pittsfield in the Berkshires. While waiting I sent my friends a telegram: *We are in love with God.* It took me half an hour to compose, and I hardly understood what I had written. It was the first time I thought of what was happening to us in that way. It was the first time God came into it.

In Vermont I taught poetry to bright, rich kids. They were warm and angry, lazy and creative, arrogant and enquiring, and free with sex and drugs. The prevailing code was a utopian, self-regarding liberalism, but no one minded it very much. The teachers were too busy assassinating each other, and the students were too spoiled to really care—they took over the administration building in season, then forgot why when the term ended, and they went off to Georgetown or Lausanne or the Cape. The professor for whom they struck, a physicist opposed to nuclear power in the state, was not renewed.

In one way this disappointed me deeply, and in another it hardly touched me. Instead I put myself in my own company, and by degrees I grew quieter. I became acutely aware, just as St. Teresa explains her Prayer of Recollection to her novices, of gradually withdrawing within myself, and I found that the sense of absurdity which had been swelling in me was already part of this practice — not yet meditation, but a kind of prayer, in St. Teresa's sense of a studied yet natural state of attention or inward concentration. Looking back, I have found her account of spiritual unfolding, both in her letters to her confessor and also in *Las Moradas* (the book she wrote to help her novices, which at that time I had never heard of), very helpful in explaining my own first steps. She has a word for the contraction I felt—*encogimiento*—which fits very well.

And there I was, broken away, in my own company at last, gathered gradually inside, and led in quiet and unannounced ways to the open glass door of my living room, where I stood one evening in the dead time of the year between winter and spring, looking out across the black thawing fields. There I stood, and for a long unmeasured moment I watched three blackbirds picking at the stubble, half in the snow and half out of it. All at once they rose one by one, and with them there arose in my heart a single, startling movement of complete understanding, a flight of absolute passion, leaving me breathless and dazed. And then I knew for the first time that all my life I had been in love, crazed with love, drunk with love, and for the first time I understood the desolation I had endured, every day of my life, beyond despair.

And when the birds were gone, I went on watching the fields, though they were empty and nothing stirred in them. I watched them for a long time, hardly drawing breath, and slowly I became aware of something out there in the earth—a force, a presence, a power, an awareness—something unseen but almost tangible, something rising up in the earth and filling the sky above it, something already fulfilled seeking to express itself. I had no word for it, but

I recognized that this astonishing thing was rising up in me also, as if I were of the same breath or substance as the cold fields, or filled with the same light as the sky, and that this unhurried rushing upwards was a flowering of the silence and the laughter and the strange passion which had gathered me inward, season by season, for the last few years.

As I say, it came slowly, and yet all at once—this understanding, this flight of the heart, a gift of the seasons and of the moment; and all that night and the next day the feeling did not go away but only deepened, till I found myself calculating, with all my senses on fire, that my life was to be lived in two halves, the first asleep, and the second, into which I had just awakened, awake. Awake at last to a love which had no sound or surface, no self to reflect, a love which was its own silence, its own assurance, its own certainty, its own truth. And though I was dazed, I felt such a quiet, familiar confidence that everything else in my life seemed shadowy and full of hesitation and childish distress. There was just a steady, silent assurance in the heart, grounded in the earth, broadcast in the sky.

It was as if someone had commanded me, with arms outstretched, "Hold me!" *As I am holding you.* Had I known then that out of this absolute fulfillment there would come an absolute longing, and as absolute a responsibility, perhaps I might have turned away. But I was already lost, the moment I stood at the door and, looking out across the fields, felt my heart burning in the fire of Your silence, the silence in which You have enfolded me every moment of my life.

There was no turning away. I was already lost, and from that moment when I first felt the beauty of his presence in the natural world, I loved God and I could think only of him, and how to love him more.

※ ※ ※

The night after Christ left her, Ma put her family to bed as usual and waited on the stairs, though she knew he would not return. She did not even bother to practice the breath. She just sat and waited, tasting him in her blood, feeling him in the roots of her hair, on fire with a longing beyond her understanding, beyond her nature, and yet the fruit of everything she had ever comprehended, a passion consuming all passions she had ever felt, a mystery which emptied and filled her completely.

She sat and waited many nights. But she knew he would not return. She had only her waiting, an intolerable, burning patience.

One night, feeling restless and drawn away from her vigil, she went upstairs to the bathroom. When she opened the door, there to her astonishment was an enormous dark-skinned man sitting with his legs crossed on her toilet.

"He had the lid down," she told us later, "and all he was wearing was a giant diaper."

"Who the *hell* are you?" she demanded.

He said nothing.

He stared at her with great sternness. His bearing was majestic, austere, impenetrable. His massive body shone in the darkness.

"*Where's my Christ?*" Ma asked, desperate, furious. "Bring him back to me!"

He looked at her without blinking. His eyes were like stone, stone without a surface, a depth cut into solid rock, completely still and soundless.

"Can you bring him back to me?" she pleaded, choking back her anger. He nodded once.

"Then who *are* you?" But he said nothing. "So what's the matter? You leave your clothes at home or something?" she taunted him, hoping to provoke him, and too embarrassed to look at his diaper, which was the Indian *sadhu*'s conventional *kaupin* or *langoti*.

"Cat got your tongue, mister?" But he only ignored her. And he continued to ignore her despite all her provocations. Try as she might, she could not get him to talk to her. His silence was a great cliff on which she could find no foothold, a fort with walls a hundred feet thick. And his eyes were rock or water without surface, deep and soundless. For hours, through the night, she tried to draw his attention, but he would not acknowledge her again. A little before dawn she gave up and sat down in the bathtub in her flannel nightgown, and there she stayed until it was light, and he was gone.

The next night it was the same, except that she knew better than to try to break his silence. Instead she accepted it and sat in it, drawing from her longing a desperate patience. She knew that though her uninvited guest's silence was unimaginably more powerful than anything she had ever known, it was not stronger than her desire for Christ. She sat and waited, feeling him in the roots of her hair, in her blood, drawing him in with every breath and holding him, knowing that in the end she would defeat the silence of the strange yogi who sat above her, his body burning in the dark.

For nearly three months she sat through the night at his feet while her family slept, Ma in her nightgown in the bathtub, soaked in his silence, the old man in his loincloth on the toilet with the lid down....

And he never said a word until one night early in summer. Ma knew her moment had come. By some instinct deeper than her own nature, she fell on her knees and begged him to bring Christ back to her.

"*Jaya*, if I speak to you, you must heed my words."

The moment he spoke all the silence went out of him into her.

"Who are you?" Ma asked him quietly. She no longer had any need to taunt him.

"*Nityananda*," he thundered, and Ma, feeling drawn into his depths, sharing his silence, needed no further explanation, and asked for none. When he spoke her name, she knew him, and knew for certain that he would bring her back to Christ, to her Beloved.

> *With all its heart the rain-bird longs for the shower of rain.*
> —Kabir

How Ma ever submitted to his instruction I find it hard to imagine, knowing how fiery, stubborn, talkative, and impudent she is. But from that night in June, every night for a year, she sat and listened while he taught her about fear and happiness, the mastery of appetite, the mystery of breath, and about deeper mysteries still—of chastity and dispassion, of love and detachment, of surrender and freedom.

Her submission was the measure of her longing, and of the silence in which he had disciplined her for so many nights.

He took her hand and led her into the children's rooms. There on each bed she saw a small heap of ash. Then he took her into her own bedroom, and instead of seeing Sal asleep, she saw another heap of ash.

"The body is nothing," he said. "The world is all inside you—your children, your family, everything you love. The whole universe is here inside you." And he tapped her lightly between the breasts. And as Christ had done, he told her that her attachment to her family had already fallen away.

"You love your husband. You love your children. But what is this love? *My* husband, *my* children, *my* home—this is not love, this is possession, attachment. If you wish them to be everything to you, know that they are already nothing to you. Know that the Christ for whom you long came with a sword to turn father against son, mother against daughter. Walk away, into his arms, and after a while they will follow you into a far deeper love where nothing separates you from them, where everything is one."

Ma knew his words were true. It only mattered that she loved her Christ, and that in the light of her desire for him she was able to see her family for the first time freely, without attachment.

"I am your teacher. I am your friend, I am not your Christ. If you listen to me, he will return," Nityananda said.

"And who am I to you?" Ma asked him.

"Once, in another life, you were given to me as a young girl to teach you and prepare you for your husband. A long time ago, in the mountains." His eyes were like stone, his words were cut into the stone face of his silence. He never laughed, and he was without pity.

Ma at once remembered the mountains, and how he had raised her. But she could not remember her husband. The moment he spoke, except when he spoke of her husband, she understood. He awakened in her a knowledge that was already complete. "I cannot teach you what you already know," he told her. "I can teach you nothing. I can only remind you. But you must listen so you can teach. I am preparing you. Many will soon be drawn to you. You will teach them for a while, and then you will not teach them anymore. You will just share yourself. You will open and fill their hearts."

He told her about the opening of the heart, and the rising of the Mother, and about discrimination, and about *chidakash*, the clear, deep sky where love and awareness are one. "You are the fullness of the Mother," he told her, "and her rising. You are the sunrise in the sky of the heart. And you are never more than the least of those whom you seek to serve."

"But when will he come back?"

But his eyes were like stone.

In every religious culture, on every path to God, there are different figures for the secret stairway by which St. John of the Cross ascended in contemplation to meet the Bridegroom.

In Indian *raja yoga*, the royal way of oneness, the images are especially vivid. In the invisible body which clothes the physical body there are seven *chakras*—wheels or spheres—from the tailbone to the crown of the head, running up the spine. At the bottom the Mother, Shakti, sleeps in the form of a coiled serpent, *kundalini*. The serpent awakens, uncoils, and rises upward. The flower opens, and the serpent passes upward until it reaches the seventh center at the crown of the head. There Shakti, the Mother, unites with Shiva, the Father, the female with the male, and as they become one, the seeker is at last free.

In other traditions the flower and wheels are seen as discs, fountains, gardens, ladders, the rooms of a castle—the figures shift from faith to faith. But in all traditions—in Hinduism, Buddhism, Taoism, Sufism, Christianity, Hasidism—there is only one inner way, and though the maps differ in their detail, the way is straight and the same.

I recall sitting once with a pupil of Gurdjieff, who had travelled many paths. Describing the spheres of the subtle body from a Sufi viewpoint, he illustrated with great simplicity how the way is always one and the same, and how absurd it is for seekers to wonder about different figures or to become fascinated as some do with their imaginary secrecy. When St. John calls his stairway secret, he means only that it is within, invisible, private.

In our culture we most easily understand the chakras as the terms of a spiritual psychology, as spheres of awareness, states of consciousness, from low to high, common to exalted. The first represents the life of instinct and survival; the second, the life of the senses; the third, the life of power. Most of us live most of the time in these ordinary states.

For the seeker, the inner way is first revealed when the flower of the fourth sphere opens inside him, an inch or two to the right of the physical heart. Here is the first flowering of love, and he awakens to an ever-enlarging awareness of his true nature.

St. Teresa is certain, and I am sure she is right, that we may enter the fourth mansion, as she calls it, only at God's invitation. By prayer and meditation, by selfless service and acts of devotion the serpent is encouraged to uncoil, and by our own efforts we may be able to rise for moments above the worlds of instinct, sense, and power.

But the heart opens fully only when God chooses. It is all His doing.

Swami Nityananda often used down-to-earth figures for describing the secret stairway. He liked to compare the chakras to railway stations, and the rising upwards to the train steaming through on its way to its final destination, the station at Kashi, at the crown of the head. Or he would describe the inner ascent as climbing up to the roof, throwing up a long rope, rolling a rock up hill, pumping up a bicycle tire, striking a match, or boiling milk. Saint Teresa, by her own confession, had more trouble finding the right language. "Some say that the soul enters into itself; others, that it rises above itself," she told her novices. "I can say nothing about these terms, but had better speak of the subject as I understand it."

It is especially hard when the seeker first encounters someone, usually a friend or relative, who cannot believe him. Such people are like virgins disputing the pleasures of sex, with a rigid conviction. St. Teresa insists, with disarming simplicity, that those who have not had this experience must realize that it does indeed happen. But if they will not, then the best course is silence, and the company of others in whom the heart has also opened, of whom there are many, in every walk of life; for the experience is universal and happens to everyone in time, wherever there is sufficient silence, and intense longing, and God chooses. The way is open to all, without any exception. Christ said, "Knock, and it shall be opened unto you," and that is the whole truth, and all that is needed. No one is ever left out, or behind, or alone.

Because Christ's victory was complete, sooner or later everyone, without exception, climbs the secret stairway and falls into the arms of the Beloved.

* * *

Ganga, who is five, has hidden behind the weeping bottlebrush, and when all the other children have been hauled hand over hand indoors she emerges, carelessly bold in case she is discovered. Ducking under the steps, she renews her attack on the pickerel weeds growing wild above the green shafts of tuckahoe on the bank of the pond. She shucks off the blue violet flowers, and as soon as she has a fistful of spikes, she sets them on the steps and with great attention treads them under her feet.

Watching her from behind the fountain, I see how fully she gives herself to this play of destruction. Her eye is single, her will unbending, her concentration spontaneous and compelling, a gift of absolute involvement.

All children have it, this terrible capacity to live without distraction. They are all tyrants of the moment. Ganga's moment is so full, and so empty; there is no longing in it, no waiting. She never steps outside its natural circle as she treads under her feet the blue violet pulp of smashed flowers.

She is not aware that I am watching her through the shifts of the fountain, nor is she watching herself. She cannot, she is a child. She has the innocence of the pure undivided self, which for all its self-absorption has no reflection. She is still a little too young to be aware of herself, except in small immediate matters, natural matters of childish necessity. Nor is she yet aware of awareness itself.

Sitting by the pond on the second or third evening of summer, awaiting its tidal heat, I long to be released from my longing into her world, where nothing is awaited—to fall through the surface of the water into a world without sound or surface, without reflection, where the eye is innocent and single, where the appetite of a child fills and empties with each breath, where the breath is never drawn or spilled, but always full, always empty—where love and awareness are one.

> *Dip him in the river who loves water.*
> —William Blake, *The Marriage of Heaven and Hell*

The fountain drenches me in its silence. Ganga's feet are dancing on the blue flowers, treading the world under, fearless, brutally happy, and wild.

* * *

> *How hard it is to meet my lord!*
> *The rain bird wails in thirst for the rain;*
> *she almost dies of her longing,*
> *yet she would have no other water but the rain.*
> —Kabir

After my year in Vermont I returned to Oxford to take up a fellowship which Tolkien, the creator of *The Hobbit,* had once held. I taught Old English and modern poetry. It was all I had ever dreamed of doing, and I loved it. I loved the deep quietness of the libraries, the curiosity of my pupils, and the whole business of learning. But I carried with me from that moment by the open door another and far deeper quietness, a thirst no amount of learning could quench, and a love beyond the life of the mind.

What exactly I was to make of this wonderful, perilous burden, I had no idea. My first act on settling into my rooms was to pin a photograph of an Indian master above my mantelpiece; it was a goodbye present from one of my students in Vermont. The master's name was Neem Karoli Baba, and I knew very little about him, only that he taught in the foothills of the Himalayas. But I was drawn to something in his face, something that answered the longing that I had brought with me, something inexpressibly simple, an abandonment, a shining emptiness. The picture was a kind of deep company in a world where I knew I would not be understood. From now on I knew I had to live a double life, and Neem Karoli Baba became my silent companion, observing everyone who came and went in my rooms, a constant, mostly unnoticed presence. Every morning and night I sat under his picture for about twenty minutes in meditation. In these first clumsy attempts to sit and compose my mind, my long academic training was only a hindrance. My head was conditioned to excite itself, and my thoughts were hopelessly eager and pressing. But I kept my seat beneath Neem Karoli Baba's gaze, and I found that while nothing spectacular happened inside, at least I began to feel emptier. It was as if a quiet wind was blowing in my heart, hollowing it out, and the sense of recollection, of impatient composure which had overtaken me in Vermont now filled most of my day. I enjoyed teaching, but I could not wait till my tutorials were over and I could walk down Broad Street to St. Mary Magdalene and light a shilling candle before Our Lady of Joy and, sitting there in the dark, watch the flame dip in the wind of the damp nave.

Old friends started falling away. I was neither surprised nor hurt. I had become a stranger in a restless, sleepy world. I was rubbing my eyes and stretching and trying to wake up. A few of my students understood, and so did my cleaning lady, to whom all this had happened years ago. But most of my fellow dons found me odd and inattentive, and they imagined I was rebellious or unhappy. I was indeed distracted—by an extraordinary happiness. I sat morning and night under the picture of Neem Karoli Baba and I waited, and in my waiting there gathered an ever fiercer longing. Then in the middle of the winter the friends to whom I sent the telegram from Pittsfield wrote saying they had found a teacher, an English woman in her seventies called Hilda, who had spent eighteen years in India and Ceylon, and who now taught meditation at St. Luke's Episcopal on Hudson Street in New York. They told me she had once studied with Swami Nityananda and other great masters, and she told stories about Neem Karoli Baba.

When the spring vacation came, I took down the photograph from above the mantelpiece, packed it carefully, and flew over to New York.

Hilda Charlton looked like everybody's fairy godmother. She had pale dewlaps and little caves behind her gray eyes, and a kind and courtly manner. In her youth she had been a dancer in a theatrical troupe—that was how she had got around the East. She looked frail, but she was a lot stronger than she seemed. She always held herself well, though she was stout, and her presence was graceful and commanding, her manner easy and unassuming. She wore a sari but otherwise observed no particular custom or belief.

Her classes, held in the rectory hall, were simple. We sang a few devotional songs, Western and Eastern, then Hilda told a couple of anecdotes about her adventures with various holy men and women, and sometimes she delivered a kind of informal homily to illustrate the practical uses of humility or forbearance or some other virtue; and at the end she gave a guided meditation.

What attracted me to these teachings was their lack of pretense, and the company of so many people who seemed to share my impatience, and above all Hilda's love, which was as practical as it was uncritical. There was an emptiness in her giving, an absence of pride or self-regard which I found deeply attractive. She neither proscribed nor prescribed; for her the inner life was open to everyone who sought it, and she took a deep and inspiring delight in the infinite varieties of seeking by which God draws us home. I suppose there were forty or fifty of us at first, and we all loved God with the same unreasonable expectation. We all suffered the same simple intensity. None of us were content with Church on Sundays, a merely sabbatical faith. That was not enough. We had to *know*, and we all knew that we *could* know, as long as we never gave up.

I sat in the back and listened, happy that my longing was no longer without company. But I was still waiting…

We were all waiting. Back in Oxford for the summer term, I saved every moment that I could spare for myself. I was thirsty for meditation and solitude, and in the long, light evenings I would go on aimless walks for hours in the back streets of Jericho or down to the river meadows along the Thames. And from above the mantelpiece Neem Karoli Baba observed everyone who came and went in my rooms.

As soon as my students were finished with their finals, I flew back to Hilda's classes and resumed my place in the back, listening and waiting.

It was not until toward the end of the summer that I found enough courage to introduce myself to her. She nodded and smiled absently. But a few days later I received an invitation to come on a weekend trip upstate with her and some of her close students.

An early fall was in the air. We set up camp in a clearing on a hillside above a stream, deep in the woods. It was cool and dark, and I remember there was a strong wind running up the hill under our feet.

At midday on Saturday, Hilda led me some way apart from the others in among the birches and maples. I carried a small chair for her, and when we were out of sight and hearing, I unfolded the chair and she sat down.

She had me lie on my back in front of her, on a patch of newly-fallen leaves.

I remember the sharpness of the stones under the leaves, and the wind running over me as it passed uphill.

Hilda gave me a simple breathing exercise, and when I had followed this for a few minutes, she leaned forward, and placing her hand in the middle of my chest, she repeated a short phrase in an odd, brisk, unmusical monotone.

"Pay no attention, dear," she said. "It's only a bit of Tibetan."

She repeated it several times in a matter-of-fact way, as if it was of little importance.

Nothing happened. I still felt the sharpness of the stones and the warmth of the wind running up from the stream. I got up, folded Hilda's chair, and we walked back. We repeated this casual ceremony in the same place and at the same time on Sunday, and again nothing happened. On the way back Hilda chatted happily as if nothing in particular was meant to, and she offered no explanation of what she was doing, beyond "Well, it's always worth a try, isn't it, dear?" Of course I had no idea what she was talking about.

But I imagined I caught her a little later that afternoon fixing me with a sharp, puzzled look, as if I had somehow defeated her expectations. She asked me to stay on Monday, which was a holiday, for a third attempt. But I had slept badly in the cold woods, and I was still shy of her students, and skeptical, so I accepted the offer of a ride back to the city that evening.

On Monday morning I woke up calm and happy, and sat for a while in meditation. I remember it was a very still meditation.

Just before midday I decided to listen to a record of Indian devotional songs, and suddenly, as the music filled me, I was back at the open door of my house in Vermont. I felt at first a slow uprushing of joy and then, to my astonishment, *a soft but violent explosion* in the middle of my chest, to the right of my heart, and I was carried swiftly on the waves of the singing into an extraordinary ecstasy. The sound of the name *Krishna* released in me a stream of nearly intolerable joy. I felt a hose of bliss streaming through me from my back to my front, and though I knew at once that this was the fruit of the slow seasonal change which had befallen me in Vermont, and which had been working in me ever since, still it took me so much by surprise that I fell to the floor, gasping and laughing and crying out.

I had never felt anything remotely like it in my entire life—it was far more powerful than orgasm, deeper, softer, inexpressibly more joyful, a continuous and unabating happiness that I had first felt in Vermont a year and a half before, when all that silence and pointless humor and clumsy passion had gathered me inwards—*yet held now in a single physical focus,* concentrated a thousandfold in the heart, a simple incandescence, a single blaze of immense, unsupportable happiness.

I went out onto the balcony and watched the gulls climbing, falling, and gliding along the walls of the Palisades, above the bright expanse of the river. The wind carried them wherever they inclined over the shining water, and in their movement I felt an amazing freedom, awareness, evenness, oneness, love. Was it love exactly? Yes, and yet it seemed so impersonal. Somehow it proceeded from the *sound* of the words Krishna and Christ, physically, as if I was crushing candy between my teeth, but also from an inner sound in which I felt, though their names represented different faiths, the very same uprushing of joy. And yet, as I say, this love was completely impersonal. It was not *for* anyone or anything. It just was. I heard a baby crying in a nearby apartment. Its tears and howling were entirely composed of a pure, uncompromised joy. They were without pain or complaint. They were a pure rejoicing.

I went for a walk in the streets of Riverdale. Everyone I passed had the same love in their eyes, shining and ineffable. Everyone had it, in exactly the same measure. Behind all the masks, thick or thin, of anger or pride, sorrow or weariness, everyone was undistractedly rejoicing. And with every breath I breathed a fresh draught of this cool fire of bliss. My whole being felt charged and brightened with a soft, passionate, chaste, singing bliss, and everywhere I looked I saw dancing before my eyes the same flame of happiness which was blazing in the middle of my body.

By some unintelligible grace my heart had opened to the wonder and beauty of the world, and there was nothing left for me to do, for the rest of my life, but to burn with gratitude from the depth of whatever thankfulness God gave me. And with all this I felt very *ordinary*, and safe, and above all grateful.

After my walk I called up Hilda. "Do you know what's going on? What have you done to me?" By now, for all the ecstasy, I was absurdly worried about my *civil rights*—no one had told me that this was *real*, that I might without my consent be suddenly transported out of the commonplace world.

I was like a man furious at having been woken before the alarm went off.

"I haven't done a thing, dear. It's just your heart opening. Relax and enjoy it. And ignore yourself." And she laughed and hung up.

Nowadays hardly a month goes by without Ma warning us—"Be careful what you ask for, you just might get it." When I put the phone down, I realized I had simply got what I had asked for, no less, and that I had only my own hesitation and disbelief to blame if I felt overwhelmed by the abundance with which my faint-hearted seeking had been answered.

As St. Teresa warned her novices and skeptics in general, it happens. Indeed it does. I have never encountered a more absolute understatement. I sat on the balcony all afternoon and evening, and watched the seagulls, flying free.

***

> *I marvelled more than I can say when I first felt my heart grow warm and burn, truly, not in imagination but as it were with sensible fire. I was indeed amazed at that flame which burst forth within me; and at this unwonted comfort because of my in experience of this abundance.*
> —Richard Rolle, The Fire of Love

I supposed that this torrent would soon slacken, such was its intensity. I felt that my body could not bear it much longer. But God was not fooling around. This was not just a free introductory gift offer. With such an immense infusion there came the responsibility to understand and to change, and for the next three weeks I had to learn how to carry this precious burden. On Tuesday the energy fell from the middle of my chest to the second chakra, the center of sex and the senses, and I found the pressure almost unbearable. I was consumed by a sensual fire, at first blissful, but as it grew in intensity, full of a scorching pain. I spent the day burning with sensations of lust and guilt, shame and self-recrimination, and finally fear, since I imagined that I was trapped in a hell world, my senses insatiably ablaze. I wish I had known then of St. Teresa's advice about the confusion that often follows the opening of the heart: "The mind... wanders hither and thither in bewilderment, finding no place for rest." There is only one solution, she says: "Let the spirit ignore these distractions and abandon itself in the arms of divine love."

If only I had known then how absolutely right she is, I would simply have reminded myself of God's love, and relaxed, and let the love rise back to its proper seat, the heart. As it happened, it was only when I was thoroughly exhausted in the evening that this occurred naturally, and only then that I understood how futile my struggle had been.

On the following day the pressure fell again, this time into my belly, where it turned into a kind of remorseless power, and I was assaulted by feelings of pride and intense unworthiness. One moment I would be puffed up with self-importance—what an extraordinary person I must be that this should happen to me! The next, I would feel the crushing weight of a pretentious humility—how could I possibly deserve such gifts! I was tossed between these two poles until by the evening, again bruised and beaten, I at last relaxed, and became a little simpler, and remembering God I regained my composure.

Abandon yourself to the arms of love!

Each day brought with it a fresh lesson, which I first had to fail in order to pass, until I perceived, slowly and imperfectly, the nature of my responsibilities, now that my seeking had been answered. St. Teresa sums them up better than I can: gratitude, detachment, humility, service. These were matters to which I had never given much thought. Now they became real and pressing, and I understood that I had been dawdling, making nothing of my life, content with its triviality, yet utterly discontent. Now I was on the threshold of a new education, a real education, and I knew I should not linger at the schoolhouse door. The Sufis have a saying: "He who sits on the threshold keeps the whole house in darkness."

The following weekend Hilda took us upstate again, this time to a Marist monastery. By then the intensity inside me had ebbed a little, but as we drove through the gates, it returned with redoubled force, and I understood for the first time how devotion, gathered intensely in a single place, can soak into the ground and make it holy. I understood the meaning of pilgrimage.

We stopped to pray at statues of Mary and Jesus. They were pulsing with joy and light, a physical radiance.

Later, in the refectory, I passed a monk and when our eyes met he held my gaze, and I saw that he *knew*, and that he knew I knew. He smiled like a child who has been found out. But I also saw that to most of his brothers this knowing—this unknowing—this extraordinary, unremarkable, intangible, completely physical sweetness was as yet unknown. They were knocking on the door, but it had not yet been opened.

For the heart to open, three things are needed.

The first is intense longing, and the second is silence, the spontaneous cultivation of silence. I suppose that is why St. Teresa called the doorway of her fourth mansion the Prayer of Quiet. By prayer she means the fervent concentration of longing. By quiet she means the cessation not only of self-willed action in the world, but also of "all discursive reasoning," of thought itself. She understands the radical premise of meditation, that thinking constrains awareness.

But she also knows from her own experience that trying to stop thoughts only provokes them. Therefore, she says firmly, whoever wishes to pray the Prayer of Quiet must leave himself "in the hands of God, leaving Him to do as He chooses with us...and resigning ourselves entirely to His will." For the heart opens only when God chooses, and to this final necessity the seeker must, however intense his longing or deep his silence, at length submit.

Looking back, I see that the silence, the longing, and the laughter which gathered me inwards during my last years at Harvard, and led me to the open door of my house in Vermont, and finally exploded one morning in the middle of my body as I sat and watched the gulls falling and gliding below the Palisades—I see that all these experiences arose from a single feeling of *gratitude*. When I was at last quiet enough for the heart to open a little, then I came to understand that the laughter, which had seemed almost idle, even irreverent, was a kind of gratitude, and that the longing was also out of gratitude, and the silence.

In everyone's heart there is a constant singing—"thank you, thank you, thank you," but we are all so loud and distracted we hear it only when God touches us, and we fall silent, and hopelessly in love.

THOMAS "BILLY" BYROM

Near the breastbone is an open flower.
Drink the honey that is all around that flower.

Kabir says: Friend, listen, this is what I have to say:
The Guest I love is inside me!

—Kabir

* * *

Swami Nityananda taught Ma every night for nearly a year.

He was a harsh and unbending teacher. There were days when she was in so much fear of him that she prayed the night would never come. He seemed to have no more compassion than a child tearing the wings off a fly. But she never failed to take her place at his feet and submit to his instruction. And after a while she understood that it was not his implacability which frightened her so much as her own fear of surrendering to his teaching, and of taking responsibility for the knowledge he awakened in her. She came to see in his austerity, as in his silence, both the provocation and the resolution of her fears.

Besides, the fire of his instruction, however scorching, was nothing next to the fire of her longing.

Every word Christ said had burned into her. His inflections, his gestures, his laughter, his silences, his black eyes, all these had branded her, and burned everything in her life—of little or great consequence—to ash, and left her in the undivided company of her own inconsolable longing.

It was a kind of grief.

What scripture she could remember from her childhood was of no use or comfort—in the *shul* on Coney Island Avenue that had scarcely been a woman's part. And what did she know of the Gospels? She ransacked Luke like an abandoned lover tearing at bundles of old love letters, and although at times she found a phrase or two in which she sensed him, his presence there was at best an echo of an echo, so faint it mocked her thirst. Every night she begged the old man to bring Christ back. And every night he promised she would find him again. But first she must listen. "If I speak to you, you must heed my words." That had been their bargain.

But *listening* was not in Ma's lexicon, let alone *heeding*. She had always had her own conversation with God, and it was she who had always done the talking. I doubt that God ever got a word in edgewise. All her life she had talked to him—"Mac" she had called him, "Hey Mac!"—but it was always on her own terms entirely. Perhaps, very rarely, by some special sufferance, she had allowed him a word or two, but that was all. It was fully as much as she could bear to have anyone else intrude upon this lifelong harangue—especially a strange dark man in a loincloth who shouldn't even have been there in the first place, occupying her bathroom while the family and the dogs slept, eating up her nights with his terrific silence and his implacable instruction.

Still she kept her place at his feet.

But in those first months, for all her longing and despite their bargain, she often rebelled. "What is this *teaching* shit anyway?"

"Who is the teacher?" he asked her, without pity.

"*You* are," Ma said, furious.

"No, Jaya, never. There is never any teacher. Only yourself. The moment you depend on a teacher, you live in hell. The only true learning is your own. I can only show you what you already know, and you know that you are his. I can only demand of you your own freedom."

So she learned at length to be attentive and to love him, as he told her about the responsibility of freedom and the folly of power, the rising of the Mother, the true passion of chastity and the true chastity of passion. And as soon as she had taken it all in, and had recognized that the source of her understanding was entirely her own, he dismissed everything he had said.

"There is only the sky in the heart," he told her. "There is only the single flight of love."

With these words all semblance of instruction dissolved, and all at once, to her astonishment Ma was drawn—beyond the distraction of words or the arduous passage of those long hours, night after night, of obedient attention—drawn into a world which has its being only in a single shining moment of the present. And instantly she found herself back in her first-grade classroom with old Mr. Lipschitz, large and swarthy and stern. Then as now she had rebelled against schooling of any kind, but she loved Mr. Lipschitz. He was like the stern old man in her bathroom—so much more than a teacher. Because he lived more deeply and more presently than other men, he had the gift of gathering the children he taught into a world of his own moment and making, beyond the petty labors of instruction or the dull measure of the school bell.

And Ma always carried with her—not his memory, since he did not live in memory—but his presence, because the world he had fashioned for his children had its being only in that shining moment of the present.

She carried with her his presence—and his vanishing too. For he had suddenly vanished.

One day the playground had been littered with leaflets. In big black letters, "Lipschitz is a ..." and in big red letters, "COMMIE." Bewildered, Ma brought one home to her mother. Anna, who had no politics besides a fervent patriotism, seized the leaflet and with fury and contempt tore it to shreds. "Joycie Mamala, this is *shit! Shit!*"

Ma had rarely seen her so angry. The next day she went back to school and tore up as many leaflets as she could find. But it was no good. Within a week, Mr. Lipschitz was gone from school. At first no one said a word. Later there were stories and gossip. He had hanged himself in his apartment in Coney Island, he had taken a Pullman to Tampa, he had defected. No one knew for sure what had happened to him. He simply vanished.

> *If the world hateth you, ye know that it hath hated me before [it hated] you.*
>
> —John 15:18

Ma found no tears to shed, but she never neglected or mislaid his gift to her, and now it all flooded back, the world Mr. Lipschitz had first shown her.

And in this same bright moment it came to her, then and there, as here and now it comes to her, beyond all schooling, and not in words but in some other, deeper, more physical mode of awareness, how the stern old man had brought her to a hut by the river, a long time ago when she was still a little girl, a long time ago in a past more present than the present, how he brought her to his hut not far from the foothills of the mountains and gave her into the keeping of an old woman, and how he prepared her there by the river. He brought her to the river. Even now he is bringing her to the river. And it all flooded back to her how he devoted himself there and then, as he devotes himself here and now, to her upbringing, preparing her for the one thing that is missing. For something, some one thing, is certainly missing—something already accomplished yet unfulfilled, something in her blood, in the roots of her hair, in the movements of her hands, in her breath. Day after day by the river, where it turns swiftly after falling from the high mountains, feeling the sharp coldness of the water, yesterday's snow, she understands that he is preparing her.

Night after night in the dark hollow of the city, while her family sleeps, she understands that he is preparing her still.

And in her longing, sitting by the river, where everything resolves itself into a single shining moment, she is happy and afraid.

* * *

Sitting by the pond in the last light of the longest day of the year, waiting for her to call me, I watch the light on the surface of the water and where it brightens the smoky blisters of blue daze along the banks and in the bright air above them.

The climbing fox grape has begun to throw its soft summer canopy everywhere over the wild bayberry and scrub oak.

Perhaps there will be no end to our longing.

The fountain catches all that is left of the light. It rises, a shaft of white, into the dark sky out of the dark water. A white scrim of matted innocence and sticky tarflower runs at my feet under the bench and down to the water, and vanishes. And I am vanishing too, drawn up into the white silence of the fountain, which has consumed all the summer noises of the dusk.

St. Teresa imagines the opening of the heart as a fountain that, "like divine consolations, receives the water from the source itself...we experience the greatest peace, calm, and sweetness in the inmost depths of our being; I know neither where nor how."

The summer rain will not come. It hangs just over the horizon, held back by the stubborn constancy of the north wind. The light will not go. It seems to brighten, not fade, in the single plume of the fountain as I sit and wait to be called.

Ganga, O my Ganga!

Perhaps there will be no end to our longing. Perhaps that is all that God is, our longing for him, the constancy of our desire. Now there is only the stubborn constancy of the north wind, holding everything back—the light and rain, breath and appetite, and the fountain showering me with its silence. And if there were no end to our longing, I would sit here still, waiting with Ma for the return of her Beloved, waiting for everything, waiting for nothing.

4

The Old Man in the Blanket

It wasn't easy getting to the water. We had to duck under the barbed wire, then follow the marshy horse trail among the wild willows down to the spit where the river turns. Tony, who is seven, sits at my side, trying to make out the alligator nests on the opposite bank.

We sit and watch the river turn. The sunlight blazes from the river grasses when the wind shifts them. I am still ahead of myself, restless, waiting. The river tells me to sit and simply to be.

But who is not restless? Looking around me in the middle of my life, I find that the single bond, the one certainty we all share is this: we are all waiting. Wherever I turn, whosoever eyes I meet, I see someone waiting—for something better or different or other, for something that is never there.

Most of us spend our lives pretending that this is not so. With shows of competence or in honest panic we stuff into the empty hollow of expectation all our worldly goods—spouse, children, job, house, car, money, class, status, friends. We work hard, we play hard. But our busy load cannot fill the vacancy, and we have no real holidays, only vacations, days of unfillable, unattended emptiness. After all our indolent, frantic striving we are still waiting, without will or object, aim or end, always waiting for something better or different or other, for something that is never there.

And most of us wait with such clumsiness and fatuous pain. Fearful of life, fearful of death, our waiting resolves itself into a general resistance.

> *We are all condemned to death but with a sort of indefinite reprieve.*
>
> —Victor Hugo

We attend ourselves in fear, flinching against the instant of our death, rarely embracing the occasions of our life, against which we continually recoil.

Yet there are moments for all of us when we find ourselves waiting graciously, even gratefully. Then we discover a natural gratitude, and this transforms our waiting into longing, and we start out at last on the path which God sets before us.

In this attending is true attention, and the beginning of meditation.

The sun blazes in the river grasses where the wind lifts them.

Tony is sure he has uncovered the nest of the alligator we call, with proper respect, "Big Sir." He is tugging at my arm, and he looks up urgently with a toothless grin that could swallow the river.

The river tells me that when we are at last still enough to discover that we are truly grateful, naturally grateful, and grateful for nothing, then all our fretful, clumsy waiting comes to an end, and out of our longing true meditation arises.

> *His disciples said to him, "When will the kingdom come?"*
> *"It will not come by watching for it. It will not be said, 'Look, here it is,' or 'Look, there it is.' Rather, the Father's kingdom is spread out upon the earth, and people do not see it."*
>
> —Gospel of Thomas, 113

* * *

She felt him in her eyes, in the roots of her hair. She felt him in the movements of her hands and in her breath. She sat by the river, the seasons passed, and the years. At night when the old woman slept and the old man sat still as a rock, she slipped outside and sat by the river. Looking up at the mountains, she felt the snow in her eyes, and whenever the wind blew off the high peaks and there was a storm in the stars, she was happy and afraid.

Before Christ came to her, Ma never waited. She was already full, living in the moment, without anticipation. But after he left her, promising to return, she found herself in a state of such ardent longing that her love for her family and her daily life, though it lost nothing of its depth and caring, suddenly felt unfulfilled and unfulfilling. She found herself burning with a terrible patience, knowing she could do nothing but wait, with an unquenchable thirst.

He had promised, he would come back.

She sat at the old man's feet all night, submitting to his instruction but keeping an inner vigil, her whole attention given over to the return of her Beloved.

The morning came. He was not there. In her journal she wrote, "Every day I live, I live in a deeper love."

> *Console thyself: thou wouldst not seek me if hadst thou not found me.*
> —Blaise Pascal, *Pensées*

* * *

One day in July her daughter Denise went to a school retreat at a Jesuit seminary, Mount Manresa, on Staten Island. When she told her mother about it, Ma felt a strong impulse to drive over the Verazzano Bridge and take a look for herself.

"Where is he? Where's Christ?" she asked the startled gatekeeper, and storming the office, "*Where's Christ?*" she asked the first Father who fell in her way. "*Christ!*" she demanded. "I want my Christ!"

"Yes, Christ, of course. Down there—" He pointed to a path leading among the gardens, around a small rise, and down.

Ma hurried down the path fully expecting in her simplicity to meet him coming the other way. Instead she came upon a small stony hollow and, looking up, saw a statue of Christ twice as large as life—but only a statue. Tears in her eyes, she started to turn away.

But then she noticed his right hand.

The thumb was missing.

"Why is your thumb missing?" she had asked him.

"You'll find out," he had told her.

Now she understood: it was not yet time, but he was with her still.

She sat at the foot of the statue for many hours, forgetting that Sal would soon be home from his Coca Cola delivery route, expecting lunch on the table.

One of the priests found her, lost to the world, and brought her up to the retreat house. His name was Father Atherton, and they became close friends. She told him what had happened to her, the whole story, and he believed her without hesitation. He was old, near retiring, not an important man at the seminary, but he introduced some of the younger priests to Ma, and before long, she began to share her experience with those who would listen.

They were her first students, and she struck a bargain with them, the bargain she strikes sooner or later with everyone who asks for her help: "Show me how to live and I'll show you how to die."

For the rest of that summer, through fall and winter, Nityananda sat with her at night; and by day, when she could get away, with Sal on his route and the kids at school, she would drive over to the retreat to sit at the foot of the statue with the missing thumb—and to juice up her Jesuits.

By all accounts they needed it. They were dry and scared of their calling and in their asceticism recoiled from the world before they had learned how to embrace it. She tickled them, cursed them, mocked their vows and scolded them for neglecting them. Obedience was not so important, she said, but celibacy was essential, and so was poverty.

Most of all, they must love life passionately.

I have often wondered, since I heard of her first, alarming ministry among these unsuspecting Jesuits, who were mostly in training for missionary work, how many confessionals Ma filled and how many hearts she lifted with the remorseless purity of her laughter and her terrible profanities and her baffling modesty. I know that at least a few of the priests must have survived the generous scourging of her curses and her ribald songs and her tireless boasting, and found themselves on the other side of her show, in a spacious and profound silence, where everything is resolved into a single, intolerable longing.

For this was all she had to teach them—her longing for Christ, her fiery patience.

"Every day I live, I live in a deeper love."

A year she waited, sitting at the old man's feet in a small room in the darkness of the city, sitting by the river and smelling the snow on the wind, and whenever the wind blew off the high peaks and there was a storm in the stars, she was happy and afraid.

*　*　*

As for me, I flew back to Oxford when the summer ended, and on the plane my heart closed up as suddenly as it had opened, and I was relieved. I knew I was not yet ready to bear the burdens of an open heart. First I had to serve a long apprenticeship, longer than life itself, as long as many lives. But at least I now understood the nature of my longing and the force of the silence which had gathered me inwards and why from now on I must try to find my place in a world in which all ordinary pursuits, all common appetites and satisfactions, were suspended. Now, looking back, I was able to comprehend in larger measure the moment on the balcony, watching the gulls climbing and falling along the Palisades; and the moment by the glass door of my living room in Vermont, when the blackbirds arose one by one from the stubble of the black field; and that first moment by the rock pool, tipped between the southern sea and the sky, when I first saw the wind in the water, and heard its voice in my heart.

I understood, but what I understood I could not share, and while I felt grateful beyond words, and glad to be back at my desk, I also felt useless, broken off, adrift—and oddly disconsolate, as if something wonderful had gone out of my world the moment I had entered it, right at the end of that summer of my awakening. Not that I was conscious of this loss. I lived it without knowing it, lived the feeling of it without knowing the cause, though I knew that in September Neem Karoli Baba had suddenly collapsed in a railway station near Brindavan in India and had died.

His picture above my mantelpiece welcomed me back to Oxford, but I did not then understand that in his radiant smile was the crucial meaning of both my awakening and my inconsolable emptiness, and the single end of all my longing, which was itself a secret kind of grief.

I understood, yet I did not understand, and I could share neither my understanding nor my bafflement.

All winter I lived in my own company, tongue-tied, ashamed, stumbling, on fire; and everything I said sounded self-serving or inflamed, and my family and friends were unalterably angry or distressed on my account and certain that I was making it all up, or compensating for personal or professional failures, or giving myself absurd airs.

Yet it really did happen!

I fell in love. I fell in love with the love which had been buried in my heart, unacknowledged, all my life, since that moment by the rock pool on the rim of the South Pacific, when I first felt myself enfolded in your breathless silence, one with the water and the blazing wind. And every day my love grew more foolish and complete, exceeding its own folly, exhausting its own fulfillment.

And no one would listen to me, and I did not know how to talk, or where to put myself, or whom to embrace.

Until I found You.

* * *

And suddenly there You were, sitting next to Hilda on the couch in her bedroom—long black hair, olive skin, a mask of green eyeshade and black mascara, false eyelashes an inch long and extravagantly curled, *there you were*, exotic beyond my experience, daring everyone with every lustrous dipping of your eyelashes to suppose even for a moment that you were not as slender and lovely and noble as you knew yourself to be. And so you were, behind the painted surface and the high, outrageous laughter, radiantly lovely and noble and even by some sleight of God's hand, slender.

After a fretful winter I had flown over from Oxford to be with Hilda during my Easter vacation, a change of clothes in my briefcase and some notes for a course of lectures on Whitman which I was due to deliver in the summer term.

Earlier that week I had gone uptown to visit Hilda in her apartment a block off Broadway, near Columbia. When I arrived there was an enormous excitement in the air. Leela and Mirabai, the two young women who lived with Hilda and looked after her, told me that I had just missed an astonishing visitor called Joyce who had turned up with only a brief phone call announcing herself, saying that

Swami Nityananda had sent her. I knew that Hilda had studied with Nityananda many years earlier in India. A little skeptically I pressed them for more, but Mirabai only smiled broadly as if in possession of an inexpressible secret, while Leela burst unaccountably into tears, and Hilda said, "See for yourself on Friday, dear," and invited me to meet her mysterious visitor the next time she came.

And there she was on Friday, sitting in full lotus next to Hilda, her huge eyes of a shining transparency and depth and softness, dipping her lustrous eyelashes, her astonishing beauty shining through the gorgeous, painted surface.

I had no idea what to make of her. I was by habit, if not by nature, too cautious even to feel my own astonishment. While Leela and Mirabai sat there spellbound, I felt nothing in particular—my heart did not stop, my pulse did not skip, I did not lose my breath, there was no sudden revelation, no trumpet call. I heard only the mid-morning traffic rushing by five stories below on West End Avenue. And yet, as she told us the story of the hidden loaves and Trim Away, and her mastery of breath and appetite, and how Christ first came to her, I felt myself drawn, unconsciously but undistractedly, into an apprenticeship that was to turn my life inside out and undo nearly everything I had done. And it is certain—perhaps the only certain thing I know—that from that day on I was never the same, never again sensible or prudent, never composed or safely contained or steady, never dependable....

Hilda, who from that day always sat next to Ma on the couch holding her hand, was no less exotic, but in another way entirely. She was nearly seventy, she always wore a sari, and her extraordinary pale eyes, deeply recessed below the bone of her brow, betrayed no feeling of any kind, not even when she and Ma were kidding around, which was most of the time.

They could hardly have been more different. Hilda was discreet, with impeccable manners, and a strong liberal moral sense. She chose her words carefully and gave an impression of grandmotherly kindness. She had studied with scores of teachers and had a deep knowledge of esoteric yoga.

Ma knew nothing of books or India or hidden teachings. She knew Brighton Beach, Coney Island, Flatbush, Brooklyn street life. She knew her family and her dogs and her closeouts and seconds. She knew her Christ and her stern Swami. She was brash and outrageous, no respecter of persons, in the church or on the streets, and she continually undercut moral pretensions. She sounded fiercely patriotic and puritanical, wearing on her sleeve the narrow, shrill aggressions of Italian Brooklyn culture. But at heart she was quite the opposite—utterly without prejudice, a natural feminist, a recklessly generous lover of people, a woman who lived without judgment and loved life passionately, and whose life was now absorbed in a single burning passion for her God, her Christ.

This is what Ma and Hilda had in common, dissolving all their differences. They loved God with undistracted fierceness, and without any proscription.

So Hilda, the seasoned wanderer who had spent a quarter of a century in the East, with her vast experience of exploring higher states of consciousness, took the hand of Ma, the novice of Christ, and patiently explained what was happening to her, as Nityananda cut the umbilical cord and sent her out into the world.

What Ma must have made at first of Hilda's world, I can hardly guess. In her bedroom Hilda had an entire wall covered with the pictures of her teachers. With some of these—Swami Nityananda, Paramhansa Yogananda, Satya Sai Baba, Mahadevananda—she had studied in India or America, but she knew all of them also "on the inner planes:" Babaji and his lineage, Lahiri and Yukteswar, St. Thérèse of Lisieux, St. Teresa of Ávila, the entire pantheon of Theosophy, Kathumi, Maurya, St. Germaine, Ramakrishna, Vivekananda and the Vedantists, Shirdi Sai Baba, Vajrayana and tantric adepts, Hinayana meditation masters—they were all there, a jostling crowd of smooth and ragged holy men and women, all devoted in Hilda's view to "the perennial philosophy" as Huxley and Isherwood called it, all travelers along the same inner path to God.

From the start, Ma did not seem greatly taken with this gallery of saints and charlatans. When Hilda left the room for a moment around midday, Ma uncrossed her legs and, hopping across the carpet, raised the curtain which had been placed over a portrait of Master Maurya, a Theosophical luminary of ferocious aspect. Hilda had warned us that he was too powerful to look at unless you were especially pure.

"I could eat him for breakfast!" Ma announced, and when Hilda returned she at once told her that she had raised the forbidden curtain. Ma could never keep a secret for more than the briefest moment.

Hilda had her own strong, dry sense of humor, and she was no more to be messed with than Ma herself. "I expect you could eat him for breakfast, darling," she assured Ma, laughing at her rebellion.

Yet Hilda took her holy wall seriously, and she believed sincerely in the sanctity of the whole crowd. Soon after she accepted me into her inner circle, she gave me a Theosophical primer, *The Masters and the Path*. I found it preposterous and said so. "Hilda, I simply can't believe the world is being run by a gang of spooks sitting up in hidden valleys in Tibet."

I fully expected her to reply, with sound British common sense, for after all we were compatriots, "Of course not, dear, rubbish, isn't it! Just testing you!" Instead, she shrugged with an amused and infinite kindness and said, "Well, dear, you may not believe it, but it's true."

I felt bad because I saw that "gang of spooks" had hurt her. But she never raised the subject with me again, and since I loved and admired her, I never bothered my head about it after that. Besides, Hilda strongly respected the teachings of Krishnamurti, who had exposed and rejected the whole muddle fifty years earlier, and who spoke with uncompromising sharpness against the psychic business of inner plane teachers and every kind of showy spiritualist sham.

And anyway, with Ma at her side Hilda was obliged to take everything and everyone, even the most august master, with a pinch of salt. Ma rejected the least breath of piety or reverence. She would chatter impudently and rather childishly about Ramana Maharshi, "Ronnie" as she called him since she could not pronounce his name, just as she would tease Nityananda for wearing a "diaper," or pretend to scold Shirdi Sai Baba for showing off his talent for removing various parts of his body at will. She found their yogic accomplishments (*siddhis*) occasions for unbridled mockery, and like a Jewish mother she often reproved Ramakrishna for being sickly. She would have fed him chicken soup if he had not been a vegetarian.

I think that for Ma it all seemed like a huge meal. The only book she got her teeth into was Swami Rudrananda's *Spiritual Cannibalism*, and her own approach was basically cannibalistic: consume everything in your path, good and bad alike! She was especially fond of a poem by the poet-saint Ramprasad, who was a devotee of the Mother, and who vowed in marvelous Bengali verse that he would eat the black goddess Kali and her husband Shiva and all their retinue—as the ultimate act of devotion. Ma frequently recited the song as it appears in *The Gospel of Sri Ramakrishna*:

> *This time I shall devour thee utterly, Mother Kali,*
> *For I was born under an evil star,*
> *And one so born becomes, they say, the eater of his mother.*

Ma's appetite was just as huge. And here she was, invited by Hilda to an enormous banquet of saints and spiritual riffraff. With great gusto she set about gobbling them all up.

I was part of the riffraff, and soon there was a growing band of us, a flotsam of spiritual exotica washed up in Manhattan after ten or fifteen years of spiritual adventuring all over the world—a Mafia gun moll from Hawaii, heroin addicts who had taken vows of *sannyas* in Indian hermitages, accountants and drifters, professors and fortune-tellers, psychiatrists and gunrunners, pacifists and Vietnam vets, table-rappers and carpenters, Russian royalists and Puerto Rican socialists, newspaper owners and chain store heiresses, poets and truckers, nuns and gamblers, dons and derelicts.

Tom Wolfe, Ken Kesey, Hunter Thompson, and all the chroniclers of our crazy generation could not have done justice to us. Within a year of Ma finding Hilda there must have been a thousand seekers clamoring at their feet.

But I am getting ahead of myself.

That first Easter things were pretty quiet. Ma could not leave her house often or easily. She had a husband and three children to look after, and she was very devoted to them. But she kept in touch with us by phone several times a day, and began to give a couple of classes a week for about a dozen of us at Hilda's—simple classes in which she talked of her love for Christ and of the yoga which Nityananda had taught her and, mostly, of how people could straighten themselves out.

Her work was, from the start and always, down-to-earth and completely practical.

"Shit or get off the bowl," was the way she put it, and she meant it.

This ultimatum broke down even my reserve, at least a little. Yet I continued to keep myself on the outside. I could not feel Ma's energy or *shakti*, which others said was intense, and I persisted in assuring myself, out of timidity and a self-serving rationality, that I experienced no particular alteration of consciousness in her presence. Nor, I told myself, could I feel her love, though the others were falling in love with her day by day with an openness which I could not help but envy even as I firmly resisted it.

But I could not deny that she made sense—rude, blasphemous, life-loving sense. Even when she spoke nonsense, it felt as though it came from a deep purity. Her words cut through our mental and emotional knots, reproving credulity, melting skepticism, loosening the mind and the heart. She lied like a bandit, with truly shameless conviction, and cursed like a trooper, and sang shrilly and way out of tune. I could not decide which was the worst offense. She was offensive in the extreme, yet from that first day I knew, if I knew nothing else, that hers were the offenses of purity.

As I say, it was all fiercely personal. Her way of teaching, as it unfolded, was a profane, scorching Socratic dialogue, all Brooklyn on her part, in which she blasted out of us some pocket of anger, fear, shame, greed, or whatever, and then turned all the power and understanding generated by these exposures into love—and this love would relax and straighten and fill us all.

She made it plain that it was not going to be quick or easy, and we would have to set aside our books and our comfortable spiritual ambitions. We had to get clearer with the outside world before we could hope to sit inside. The real work, for which we would need patience and courage, was in the chastening, the scourging and the flaying, and for this Ma appeared to us as Kali, the black Mother whose ferocity (scorn, sarcasm, corrosive teasing, goading to anger, biting petulance) consumes the dark aspects of our nature; and of Durga who rides a lion, brandishing two scimitars and a trident, and who cuts us down in our pride and our wrath and our pettiness.

Ma rode out of Brooklyn twice a week in her tantric red and black Cadillac, an avenging deity and a Jewish-Italian housewife, and with a soft fury she sliced us to ribbons.

She was too much for me.

When Easter was over, I went back to Oxford to teach the summer term, and to reflect. In Ma I knew I had encountered the rough, miraculous profanity of an authentic holiness. But I was afraid of the consequences of her truth, and too closed to understand or acknowledge my fear. In my reflections I relied on my growing trust in Hilda to keep myself at a safe distance from Ma. Hilda was formidable enough, but safe. Ma was from the start direct, all or nothing. To learn from her you had to put yourself at risk, and I was not yet ready to do that.

But swift and dangerous as she was, she was also deeply patient. She knew, more than I did, the persistence of my curiosity and of the love hidden in my fear.

Considering the insufficiency of our thirst and our understanding, her patience now seems to me all the more remarkable. We were a particularly ill-disciplined lot, clamorous and inattentive, easily dazzled, stupidly proud, astonishingly lazy, superstitious and hopelessly rational, fickle and quarrelsome. If she was too much for me, I saw that I could never hope to be enough for her, nor could any of the rest of us—not the mob of saints on Hilda's holy wall, not the ragbag of seekers gathering from all over the world at her feet, not even Hilda herself, for all that she was able to lend Ma some of her own hard-earned ground.

We were not nearly enough for her.

Little as I understood, little as I allowed myself to feel, I was at least aware that she was casting about herself at every turn in some mysterious anticipation, and it frightened me—I was quite consciously frightened—to see the intensity of her longing.

Was it love?

Was it longing?

I could not tell, I had no name for it. But I could not deny it. It was there in everything she did and said, in every practical revelation, in every act of service, every expression of personal help, in all her giving and sharing. As she unfolded, she seemed already finished, and yet even as she consumed everything in her path, she seemed strangely unattended. With considerable tolerance she let Hilda involve her in the diversions of inner plane business. But from that first day it was plain to all but the most psychically starstruck among us that these distractions, these astral fascinations, had nothing to do with Ma's being or instruction. She was only truly attentive, only truly *there* when these psychic circus novelties were set aside and our understanding was sufficiently open and large to allow her to express, in some special word or act of generosity, the stark simplicity of her longing.

I was not so dull that I could not feel the terrible impatience at the heart of her patience, and I fled before it, back to Oxford and the safety of academic life.

※ ※ ※

> *Ever since I have been separated from you ..., everything to me has become its very reverse. The young and tender leaves on the trees rage as tongues of fire; nights are as dark and dire as the night of final dissolution; and the moon is as scorching as the sun. Where lotuses bloom they appear as spears, and breezes once fragrant and soothing are become the breath of serpents.*
>
> *To whom may I speak of my agony? There is no one who will understand.*
>
> *My heart alone knows of the cord of love that binds me to you ... my heart that ever abides with you.*
>
> —Rama to Sita, from the *Sundarakanda* (The Ramayana, Book 5)

Every night, all night long, she waited at the feet of the old man as he sat still as a rock in the darkness of the city. The wind was blowing off the high peaks, as spring passed into summer. The child felt the snow in her eyes. And she knew from the quickening of the wind that he was coming.

Before I flew back to Oxford, Ma received one last sign from Christ.

As Easter approached we knew we would see less of Ma because she would have to be at home during the holidays to serve her family. But she promised to keep in touch by phone. There was no question of any of us going down to Georgetown and dropping in on her. Brooklyn Sicilians barely tolerate Neapolitans or Genoese. They would have received a visit from a group as vividly diverse as we were as infectious at best, and at worst as a declaration of war. It dismayed me to learn that Ma's Jewishness was only grudgingly accepted by her children, and that her in-laws called her "La Judatz."

"Don't even think of it!" Ma warned us. "My Sal would kill youse all."

Only Carlos, a Puerto Rican Arab with some Chinese blood, himself a native of Brooklyn, dared venture over there, and Ma hid him at once in the garage behind the racks of consignment clothes, doubtful TVs, and watches of questionable provenance.

But there was the phone, and if Ma was too busy, her older sister Shirley, who was by then an unwilling but loyal conspirator, would call us in her place.

I was up at Hilda's on Friday morning when she got the first call from Ma.

"I'm bleeding!" she protested. "My hands are bleeding, and I don't know what to fucking do!"

"It's nothing, darling, don't get upset." Hilda was cool as ice. "Now, where exactly are they bleeding?"

"It's my palms. Here, Shirley can tell you." And Shirley got on the phone and described how Ma's palms were slowly oozing blood.

Hilda laughed. "Don't worry, darling. It happens to lots of people. It happened to that Theresa in Austria, and Padre Pio, and lots of ordinary people, only the Church doesn't like it, and to St. Francis and—oh, to lots of people really."

And she explained the stigmata to Ma.

"But I'm *Jewish*, for Christ's sake."

In spite of Hilda's reassurance, the blood continued until 3 o'clock, traditionally the end of the Crucifixion.

On Saturday things quieted down. The bleeding stopped, and Ma busied herself preparing for the big meal on Easter Sunday when the whole family was coming over. They always had spare ribs.

Just before midday on Sunday, Hilda got another call. Ma had sneaked to the phone in the upstairs bedroom.

"Hilda, I started bleeding again! My hands and this time my forehead. And they're all coming over. Sal's mother's coming over.

What am I supposed to fucking do?"

"Do you have any gloves, dear?"

"Laundry gloves. I'll put on my laundry gloves."

"Put Denise on," Hilda said firmly, and she instructed Denise to wrap Ma's hands in bandages and put gloves on them and to make a turban for her head. She was very businesslike about the whole thing and not in the least impressed.

"Happens to lots of people," she reminded us with some briskness. And those pale, deeply-recessed eyes gave nothing away.

Ma was back on the phone. "It's like the broken thumb, isn't it? He thinks he can do this to me just because I'm Jewish. Well, I have something to tell him, Buster Brown."

Hilda listened patiently. "Yes, dear. Yes, that's right, dear," until Ma calmed down a little, and then Hilda said, "Well, what are you waiting for, darling. You've got a family to feed. Go serve the spare ribs." And she hung up.

Denise called her back at once. "Hilda, she's bleeding, you can't just hang up on her. I'm going to get a doctor."

"Denise, don't be silly. A doctor can do no good. If God wants her to bleed, she'll just have to bleed. But she has no business spoiling everyone's lunch." Hilda always believed strongly in rendering unto Caesar. So Ma greeted Sal's mother in the rubber gloves she used for mangling the wash.

Sal's mother was very devout, and as Ma came out of the laundry room the old lady screamed suddenly and fell to her knees. "*St. Thérèse!*" she shouted, banging her breast. "It's the Little Flower! It's St. Thérèse! The Judatz has turned into St. Thérèse! *Madre!* The Little Flower!" And she crossed herself frantically.

"Mama, for Christ's sake, get up!" Sal shouted, and all hell broke loose. "Mama, are you crazy, for Christ's sake...."

We could hear some of the pandemonium from the other end because Shirley had put the receiver down on the couch in the den, and Hilda passed the phone around. Somehow the dogs had got loose and were barking furiously at everyone, and you could hear the children yelling at each other, and Ma protesting that she was just sorting the wash.

So Ma served the ribs, and when Sal saw blood trickling from under her turban, she said she had cut herself with the can opener or the skillet, and the moment passed. The ribs were declared delicious, and the bread and the salad.

Sal's mother sat quietly at the far end of the table, every now and then stealing a furtive look at Joycie, La Judatz, her Jewish daughter-in-law who against all decency had turned into her *Santa Patrona*—a furtive look of awe and outrage and confusion.

And Shirley watched everyone out of the corner of her eye, always solicitous of her kid sister, but they were all too busy feasting to notice the wounds of Christ in their midst.

It was, as it was in the beginning, for the Jews to attend his Passion.

After all, as Ma said later with a bright inversion of the ancient distinction, isn't that what God chose us for?

* * *

The snow was blowing in the blackness of her hair.

On the last day of July, in the fullness of the summer, he kept his promise. He came back to her, not as she knew him, and yet as she had always known him.

It was a day like any other—Sal was up and out of the house early to finish his Coca Cola route before lunch. Ma's friend and confidante Fran came over from Staten Island to help clean. By mid-morning the house was shining, and Ma set frozen steaks out in the backyard to thaw. Then she and Fran lay down by the small raised pool to soak up the hot sun.

The snow was blowing off the high peaks.
There was a storm in the stars, a summer storm.

Around eleven a neighbor, a young woman from down the block, dropped by. Ma did not especially like her—she was too straight and a little strange. But she was in some sort of trouble, so Ma called her up the steps to the deck of the pool and sat her down by her side.

"I need your help desperately," she began, and Ma thought, "Oh Christ, here we go again, how am I going to get Sal's steak on the table in time for lunch?"

"I need your help."

MA & ME

Ma leaned forward to catch her words.

"I need…."

And then suddenly the woman's hands flew up in front of her face, pushing up her rouged cheeks with the heel of her palms. Her fingers stiff, her eyes wild, a slow rattle in her throat, she rasps out: "Joyce, *you got no teeth!* You got no teeth! You're an old man! *An old man!* You got no teeth!"

And then she's on her feet, scrabbling for the rail of the deck, backing toward the steps.

"Get me outta here! You got no teeth!" She is wailing and flogging her plump arms against her sides and backing away.

Ma jumps up too, astonished.

"*Outta here!*" the woman gasps halfway down the steps.

"Hey lady!" Ma tells her. "Who the hell are you talking to? Who bit *your* ass, lady?"

"I don't need no help," the woman shouts over her shoulder as she takes off across the yard. "You're the one who needs help! *You're an old man in a rug!*"

Ma lets her go, and standing there at the top of the steps, the snow blowing in the blackness of her hair, feeling him in her eyes, in her blood, she turns.

But here it is in her own words.

* * *

Right where the woman had been sitting came this old man.

All of a sudden I felt something coming out of me—like I was giving birth, and not a hard birth. It was easy.

THOMAS "BILLY" BYROM

And right there in front of me was the old man.

He had no hair and only three teeth, and he was wearing a big blanket.

"Who the fuck are you?" I said. "There's no more room in my bathroom."

But what bothered me most was this big itchy blanket in ninety-five degree heat. It bothered me in the worst way. All the other guys were walking around in diapers. I was sweating just looking at him.

And I looked in his eyes.

He just smiled and showed me his three teeth. And he said, "I am your guru."

I should have laughed, but you know what happened? I don't know how to explain it. I had the other old man upstairs in the bathroom for over a year. But I had never felt anything like this! Never anything.

There the old man was, cool as ice in his blanket, and I was drenched in sweat and shaking all over with chills. He was beautiful. He was ugly. He was everything, he was nothing.

I felt as if a web had been spun from my last life to this life, from my heart to his heart.

He was an old, old man. But he had stolen my heart, perhaps a thousand years ago, and never gave it back.

And I hated him. My first feeling was pure hate.

Why did I hate him? Because I loved. I loved, to the very depth of my soul I loved.

Then I heard Fran screaming "You motherfucking whores!" and she was running after Brutus and Isabel, the Neapolitan mastiffs, who had chased the neighbor woman over the fence and then grabbed the steaks, just as the Italian was about to come home!

I was so crazed, I didn't know where to turn.

But I couldn't leave the old man, no way.

He came for me at last, and I knew I would follow him anywhere. And I knew he would never leave me again. And the love I have for him is the same love I have for my Christ, and I know his love for Christ is no different than mine. So I had someone to share my love with, and then I understood how my Christ kept his promise, you see.

* * *

The snow was falling in the blackness of her hair.

It was a warm night, there was a storm in the stars, and the wind was blowing off the high peaks.

He came down the mountain to claim her.

She sat in the warm hut, not yet a woman, no longer a girl, and he sat outside by the river, waiting for her.

She wept. She begged Janaki, her old nurse, to come with her. She begged her friend, the hard old man who had raised her, to let her stay with him.

"Take her quickly," said the old man.

They walked up the mountain, in silence. The snow was wet and deep, the stars were bright.

She was a child, twelve years old, no more, and she was a woman, crying with pride.

They walked up the mountain, Janaki watched them go.

She climbed behind her husband. His robe was snow, and the stars and the moon lit the way. Where was the old man? Where was Janaki? She heard voices in the snow, "Ma, Ma, Ma…."

THOMAS "BILLY" BYROM

She kicked up the snow lightly at his heels, unafraid. She was drunk without wine, cold without cold, hot in the storm.

The snow fell in the blackness of her hair, and in the branches of the trees. Then there were no trees. They climbed higher and higher.

The snow was falling fast. The years were falling fast. There was no yesterday, no tomorrow.

And he brought her at last to his place in the mountains, and many came up, bringing supplies and wood, or just coming to be with her, the child bride of Lakshman[2].

* * *

And Ma turned to see the old man walk down the pool steps and into the house, his blanket clutched to his breast. She followed him into the living room and then downstairs into the basement, and she took out a blanket which her daughter Denise had knitted, and she spread it in a corner, and the old man sat on it, saying nothing, smiling his toothless smile. And while Ma rounded up the dogs, Fran ran out to the butcher and got some more steaks on credit.

Here at the heart of my story, a silence. His silence. He is the heart of my story, the heart of Ma's life, of all our lives, but how can I write about him?

The simplest word is not simple enough, the freest not free enough to hold him. Who is there to hold him? Who would break his silence? If I shouted out his name or whispered it, the wind would carry it off.

He had no name for himself, but he was known by many—Lakshman, Lingam Baba, Chamatkari Baba, Handi Walla Baba, Tikonia Walla

---

2 The name Lakshman appears three times: The brother of King Rama in *The Ramayana*, the man who came down the snowy mountain to find his bride, and Neem Karoli Baba. Ma felt a strong connection between all three.

Baba, Kainchi Baba, Neem Karoli Baba, Maharaji. He held none of them for very long, and none of them held him.

No words hold him, even years after he left us, years after he melted back into us and became again our pulse and our breath.

He was the wind itself, and Hanuman, son of the wind, a wanderer, blowing across the villages and towns of India for a hundred years and more, claiming all as his own, all as one, holding us in his crazy love, cursing and laughing, a child one moment, a king the next, a beggar and a warrior, a mother and a lover, holding us in his abandoned embrace, releasing us into his unbroken silence.

His silence, here at the heart of my story.

In his last years he mostly sat by the roadside or on a tucket, a low broad bench, wrapped even in the heat of the day in a plaid blanket, enfolding all who sat around him in an invisible blanket of love, woven with such perfect compassion that everyone was changed, changed completely and forever. There he sat, laughing and cursing, or simply in silence, and everyone was changed.

Then he would spring up and run away, saying that whoever seeks God should be like a river always moving, always free like the wind. He would run away where no one could find him, hiding from the immense longing he inspired wherever he went.

He was not a saint or a wise man. He was too profane to be saintly, too simple to be wise. He called himself a simple sadhu, a wandering renunciate, yet saints and masters would fall on their faces at the whisper of his name, and by the fires of holy men all across India his name was held in awe.

There are ten thousand stories about him, and at the heart of every story there is the same unbroken silence.

Whenever he heard Christ's name—*Issa* in India—he wept and fell silent.

THOMAS "BILLY" BYROM

He (Christ) never died. He never died.
He is Atman (the soul) living in the hearts of all.

—Neem Karoli Baba

* * *

I had been in India several times when he was still alive. But it had never been my fortune to hear of him. Yet Ma tells me I met him once without knowing it. It was in the summer of 1961. During my first year of studies at Oxford I had become fascinated with Indian temple sculpture. I really don't know why, but it became a kind of compulsion with me, and when the long vacation came around, I took a boat from Marseilles, steerage for thirty pounds, with fifteen pounds in my pocket and a bottle of sulphur pills, and sailed off to look at the temples at Ellora, Ajanta, Badami, Bagalkot, and so on. I had just turned twenty.

At the end of June I found myself squeezed into a crowded third class compartment on a slow train running an old narrow gauge between the ruined city of Hampi and the junction town of Guntakal, where we were to change onto broader tracks, miles away, somewhere the other side of dusk.

Opposite me were three sadhus, wandering seekers, one dressed all in green, one older and darker and nearly toothless. I don't quite remember the third, except that his skin was shiny and that he was playing a Jew's harp and took too friendly an interest in my small folding umbrella. They were full of mischief and joy, and they fed me Indian sweets and made more room for me, till they were nearly sitting in each other's laps, like children.

But I was not much interested in holy men, and though they poked me with their fingers and their questions, my attention soon wandered out the window to the silver fields and the battered yellow hills and the sun settling down the afternoon sky toward evening.

A few days earlier, walking along the river bank at Hampi, where some of Gandhi's ashes had been strewn, I had disturbed a camp of yogis. They were squatting on their haunches around a gray, crumbling Shiva temple in the large shade of a dilapidated banyan. One among them, a nearly naked Naga Baba, had risen suddenly and fixed me with fierce eyes, a deep, startled, searching look; and I had backed away, annoyed and frightened.

Around midnight our train erupted into the gentle pandemonium of an Indian country station, and I said goodbye to the sadhus. The one with the shiny skin tried again to take my umbrella from me, but I wouldn't give it up. The one in green laughed and gave me a photograph. When they were gone I studied it in the gold light of the platform: it was of an old man with white hair and a tender, very peaceful look, and under the picture was written, "Ramana Maharshi, the Sage of Arunachala."

I put the photo away in the leaves of my journal and forgot about it.

A year or two after meeting Ma, when I told her of this encounter, she said that one of the sadhus had been Baba.

"The one in green? Or the one who wanted my umbrella?"

"You figure it out. Anyway, why didn't you give it to him?"

"It was my Great Aunt Dorothy's. She bought it in Caracas. It was very expensive, and it folded up, and I needed it to keep the sun off."

"So you kept the sun off. What a fool! You could have saved yourself an awful lot of trouble, but it's too late for that." And so she shrugged off my folly.

What can I say about him now? He brushed my sleeve like the wind, and was gone before I knew him. All I can say at first hand is that he was a shining gold color, and rough, and full of tricks, and that he wanted my umbrella.

THOMAS "BILLY" BYROM

What can I say about him?

Everywhere in India there are ten thousand stories about him, everywhere saints and masters fall on their faces at the whisper of his name. In every bazaar, at every fire side his name is held in awe. His humility was so deep, he was the God he served. His love was so boundless, he was the God he loved.

In the fall of 1973, when Nityananda was still teaching Ma, and Ma was teaching her Jesuits, and I was first with Hilda, Baba suddenly died. For some days he had hinted that it was time to go. He called the body "Central Jail," and longed to be free of its confinement.

Early on the morning of September 9th he had a heart attack at Mathura railway station, on his way to his ashram in Brindavan. He asked to be taken to his Hanuman temple, but instead his traveling companion rushed him to the hospital. There he suffered the attentions of the doctors for a while, but at last he pulled the tubes from his arm, and saying "Jaya Jagadeesh Hare!" or "God wins! Glory to God!" he left his body.

And if I say he fulfilled Christ's promise to Ma and came back to her, to claim her again and take her up into the mountains, who will understand? If I say he wept for Christ, and tore open his own heart, who will understand? If I say he was Hanuman, son of the wind, and Lakshman, the brother of God, who will understand?

Only those who already know him, and already understand, only those who have been ravished by his Passion, and are folded in his unbroken silence, here at the heart of my story.

* * *

I will tell you a secret.
The essence of Hanuman is the essence of Christ.
They are the same.
Not many know this, now you know it.

I have put it on your tongue.
I have placed it in your heart.

—Ma

In the West the word *guru* has become debased, threadbare, partly because of spiritual fraudulence, partly because of the vulgarity of common prejudice or provincial fears of the unknown.

As a Sanskrit adjective it is the antonym of *laghu*, which means "light," "easy," or pejoratively, "insignificant." So *guru* means "hard" or "heavy," both in a physical sense and in the slang sense of not to be taken lightly, of real account. Of poetry it denotes a long measure, the sustaining of a phrase, holding the breath of the verse. Of people it signifies "revered" or "venerable," and in the home it is a title of respect reserved for a father, a mother, or an elderly relative.

Outside the house it means, commonly and simply, "teacher."

In spiritual life, however, it has an entirely special significance. To the seeker guru is much more than teacher. He or she is the Beloved, the guide of a thousand lifetimes who leads the disciple, the *chela*, safely over the ocean of *samsara*, of worldly illusion. He is the undisturbed image of your true self, and the untroubled reflection in the rough waters of life of the seeker's true face, of his divine essence, of his own heart. In the end there is no separation between guru and chela. They are one and the same, guru is self.

Christ was the perfect guru, first sacrificing his divinity to take form, and then, by giving his body up to be crucified, sacrificing his humanity—all to make us one and whole, so that no one is ever left out or behind or alone. As the old man in the blanket said, Christ is everyone's guru, living in every heart.

In a profound and inescapable sense, the guru is Christ. To fundamentalists, Hindu or Christian, this is blasphemous, as it is to anyone who seeks to limit the nature of Christ by exalting the letter over the spirit. There is an Indian saying, also profane to the literalist, that guru is greater than God. To explain the deep humor and devotion of this adage is to explain it away as the miraculous joke that it is. Only when the seeker has been overwhelmed by the mystery of the Incarnation and the Passion can he begin to understand in what way Christ is greater than his Father.

But, as always, Ma outdoes the worst profanity. If guru is greater than God, she says, then chela is greater than guru.

This was the first lesson Baba taught her, and here it is in her own words.

* * *

I was sitting in my basement, in my little temple in Brooklyn, minding my own business, the first day he came to me. I was trying to pretend as if nothing had happened when Baba said to me, "What is your life?"

"Ruined!" I said.

He laughed and showed me his three teeth. "What do you mean, ruined?"

"You don't know?" I said. "I'm crazy, you ruined my life. I lost a business, forty-five girls working for me selling on consignment out of the garage. I'm losing a husband, I'm losing my children, I'm losing my mind. And you ask me how my life is? You've got some balls!"

He laughed again and said, "But have you ever been happier than this moment?"

I looked at this old toothless man in my basement, wrapped up in a heavy blanket, who is not even meant to be alive for Christ's sake. I'm sweating, he's cool as a cucumber. I looked at him and I said, "No, never for one second. It's just you and me, I was never happier."

You know what he said to me? He said, "Ma, that's not real."

And I didn't know where to turn.

"Not real! Then what's real?"

"When you can share this with others, then you will know."

"Share what?" I said.

"Just this," he said, "Only in the sharing is it all real. I am the sharing. Share me."

* * *

Christ is the population of the world and every object as well.
—*Rumi*

It is all in the sharing, and from that first conversation Ma's own teaching, which she has called a sharing and not a teaching, had its true beginning.

Little by little, over the summer, the seekers who were drawn to her grew in number, and though she still ran the house, and her husband and children still came first, she succeeded in freeing herself from some of her household chores.

As I have related, we were a wild and ill-disciplined crowd, but from the start Ma's work was very simple. Sharing requires a simple stillness, the kind of loving and quiet attention which arises only from an inner silence. Ma sat simply on a couch or a chair or a cushion on the floor, and we mostly sat on the floor around her, while she would work with each of us in turn. But nothing was truly accomplished unless there arose between her and us a simple stillness.

There is a Sanskrit word, *svasthya*, which perhaps best expresses the nature of this simple station. It means literally "standing on your own," "staying still," or figuratively, "resting in your own true nature." It brings together the ideas of stillness, independence, and fidelity to truth. The poet of *Ashtavakra Gita*, an ancient scripture of Vedanta, uses *svasthya* to indicate the essential state of loving awareness to which all seekers aspire. "Staying still in your heart" is perhaps the fullest, best translation. And that is what we felt in common in those first days as we gathered around Ma. We found ourselves electing to stay still, to sit inside our own hearts, and to receive in this composure the silence, his silence, which Ma drew from sitting at his feet.

This simple physical station, sitting down next to the teacher, is a religious tradition of the greatest antiquity. It is also called *darshan*, which means roughly "sharing the inner sight of God" or "seeing God in the heart." It is the selfless sharing of the teacher and our own inner quietness which makes possible this common and miraculous insight. The earliest distillations of Vedic belief, the Upanishads, which mean "sitting down next to," take their name from this simple act of quiet sharing. And in the jungles of the Himalayan foothills, for four or five millennia seekers have gathered to sit at the feet of their master, and from these ancient apprenticeships there have descended lineages of communion which are alive today.

That summer, back in Manhattan from Oxford, I found myself driving with Hilda and a few friends over to Ma's house in Brooklyn a few mornings a week. I would help clean the house, polishing the dining room floor or cleaning the windows, while Ma and Hilda sat downstairs in the den and helped one or a number of the many people who were now seeking their help. When my chores were done, I was often invited to join them, and they would always be laughing and playing, and talking about spiritual matters which were completely beyond me. And then, just before one, we would all scuttle out of the house and run back to Manhattan before Sal came home for lunch.

After a few weeks these moments down in the den turned into formal meetings. Ma would sit on the couch, Hilda at her side, and gather us into her stillness, and the sharing would begin, and the silence would deepen—though to all outward appearances it was a rowdy, boisterous affair, full of laughter and profanity, or as I have described, a corrosive scouring of the pride and anger and fear which keep us from loving ourselves and accepting responsibility for our lives and our seeking.

But for me and for most of us, however loud and flamboyant the show, it was all in the stillness, all in the sharing of a common and passionate and deepening silence.

Not that it was easy or painless. I often rebelled against the stillness and resisted Ma's advice, however gently offered, and often with an ungracious and querulous roughness. But as I slowly submitted to the influence of her stillness and permitted it to spread inside me, I was offered a wonderful and utterly unexpected consolation, a mark of grace which gave me courage and hope to persist in my apprenticeship.

From time to time, whenever I was especially composed and relaxed, and only when I was somehow sitting there *without expectation*, I saw Ma change into a huge monkey!

Sometimes the monkey was black, sometimes golden, and a few times pure white.

This may seem peculiar and even absurd to the reader, but it was never so to me, for all my resistance and my skepticism, because it always felt altogether natural and *familiar*. More than that, it happened only when I was caught up in a calm and full feeling of love. If I blinked or rubbed my eyes, the monkey was still there, and if I tried to close my heart and wish him away, he would not go, and my heart only felt fuller, full to overflowing.

So I would just sit there and watch the monkey take Ma's place, and with every word I would feel myself falling deeper and deeper into the quietness of my heart.

And I knew with the same natural and easy familiarity that I was blessed with the darshan of Hanuman.

But what had I to do with Hanuman, the hero of the *Ramayana*, one of the principal scriptures of Hinduism, Hanuman the perfect servant of God, Hanuman the incarnation of Shiva, the destroyer of the vanities of the separate self? I hadn't even read his story, and I knew next to nothing about him.

Well, clearly that was for me to find out for myself, and with Ma's help.

And so began my first real steps on the path which God had set before me, and they were taken clumsily but confidently in the transfiguring knowledge that the old man in the blanket, who had brushed my sleeve a dozen years before, and in whose unbreakable silence we were all now summoned to sit, was revered by his Indian devotees as an incarnation of Hanuman.

When I told Ma what I had felt and seen, she said, "Of course, what do you expect?" And I realized that though I had expected nothing, it was strangely enough exactly what I had expected. It was the most natural thing in the world, by which I mean that I soon came to recognize these miraculous moments as an expression of my own deepest nature, though I still had only the dimmest notion of what that might truly be.

But whenever I saw Hanuman and felt his love and fell into his astonishing silence, I felt that my daily self was shallow and fictitious, and that I was myself at last, that I had finally come to my senses. I felt quiet, at rest, empty, fulfilled, whole, simple, one.

I felt in love.

And it was the intimacy of my moments with Ma and Hanuman that made them so reassuring. He was more than a friend and a companion. Somehow he sat inside my own skin—that's how close he was! And I could feel him eating my books, blowing the dust out of my head, and throwing open the windows of my heart, from within.

* * *

Once upon a time, long ago in the forests of India, there lived the most handsome of monkeys, born from the tears of Shiva, shed when he looked down upon the suffering of the human family, his own family, and his heart broke.

The monkey was son of the wind, Vayu, and he was named Hanuman, which means "great chomper" or "crushing chops," because he was the strongest of all God's creatures. Indeed, it was not a well-kept secret that he was really God himself, Shiva, and that he had taken the form of a monkey to show humankind that only humility may vanquish suffering. Of all virtues, humility is the mightiest. Anyway, he pretended to be just a monkey, and there was no creature in all the worlds with a heart as pure.

He loved Rama, the king whom he served, only a wisp of wind less than he loved Sita, Rama's queen, whom the evil demon Ravana had seized one day from the Forest of Dandaka and held prisoner in the palace of his island kingdom, Lanka.

Two great poets have told Hanuman's story. The first was Valmiki, who composed it in Sanskrit, and the second, fifteen hundred years later, was Tulsi Das, who conveyed it in Hindi.

They both sing of how Hanuman leaped across from the mainland and landed on Lanka, bearing a ring from Rama to Sita as a promise that she would be rescued. When he returned, Rama, together with his brother the archer Lakshman, assembled a great army of bears and monkeys.

They rushed over to Lanka, burned down the city, and rescuing Sita, put the great demon to rout.

And what the story means is this: when evil separates the soul from her Beloved, he takes form to rescue and restore her. Like Christ, Hanuman tore open his heart in a great and wonderful sacrifice, showing all the worlds the true faces of God as father, mother, and brother.

As recorded in the Ramayana, Rama once inquired of Hanuman, "How do you think of me?" And Hanuman answered, "When I regard myself as an embodied being, I feel that you are the master and I am your servant. When I think of myself as a separate soul, I see that you are the whole and I am a part. But when I perceive reality in its fullness, I know that you are I and I am you."

* * *

Lakshman (Baba's name in Ma's last lifetime) took her up into the mountains. The snow was blowing off the high peaks and in the branches of the trees.

Then there were no trees.

They climbed higher. The snow was falling fast. The years were falling fast. There was no yesterday, no tomorrow.

And he brought her at last to his place in the mountains, and many came up bringing wood and supplies, or just coming to be with her, the child bride of Lakshman.

* * *

And what had I to do with Lakshman, the brother of God, or Hanuman, his perfect servant? What had I to do with Neem Karoli Baba or Christ or Ma? What was my place in all this?

What did I know of the mountains?

Again it was all too much for me, and again I ran away, this time in the middle of the summer to an ashram in South India. I lived there for a month or so and busied myself by translating the *Dhammapada*, the principal scripture of Hinayana Buddhism. It was a safe and orderly undertaking, half a world away from the primal chaos of Brooklyn. I submitted myself to the strict daily regimen of monastic life, and for a little while I half succeeded in putting a safe distance between myself and Ma.

But it was not to be.

Towards the end of my stay, remembering the three sadhus and my train ride to Guntakal a dozen years earlier, I decided to take a long bus ride down to Tiruvannamalai to visit the ashram of Ramana Maharshi.

It was a lovely place, small and swept clean, with monkeys and peacocks, and I spent a peaceful afternoon with Swami Satyananda, who had attended the master in his last years, above us the huge tawny hill called Arunachala, sacred to Shiva.

In the evening I sat in the brass bazaar with Ram Surat Kumar, a simple and majestic sadhu who had given up a university post for the beggar's bowl and staff, and who had wandered for thirty years or more, apprenticing himself at one time or another to Nityananda, Ramana, and his own guru, Papa Ramdas.

I spoke to him about the various holy men I had visited, and he roared with laughter and slapped his sides at the busy futility of my seeking. Then he made me read a paragraph from Isherwood's translation of the *Yoga Sutras* of Patanjali, which he had found going through my pockets. It was a solemn enough passage, about discrimination and aspiration, but as I read it he kept bursting into laughter, and he made me read it again, many times over, as if it were a splendid comic turn, until he was holding his sides with the pain of his laughter, rocking from side to side at the hopeless folly of my seeking.

"How important!" he cried, poking me in the ribs. "This is such a serious matter!" And taking the book out of my hands, he was about to strike me on the head with it when a photo of Neem Karoli Baba fell out of it.

His laughter was gone in an instant.

He held the picture to his forehead for a long moment and then fell silent.

Then he said quietly, "O he is the sun! He is the sun! I am just a poor beggar. But he is the sun!" And with tears in his eyes he grabbed my arm and held onto it tightly for long moments, pressing hard, and his body seemed to shine with an astonishing radiance.

And after a while he sent me away without a word.

I knew then that however far I ran, I could never put a safe distance between myself and Ma.

It was simply not to be.

Without really knowing it, I too had been drawn up into the mountains, following her, as she had followed him.

I had no choice in the matter. There was no turning back. My head was full of snow. I felt the call of the mountains. His silence had taken hold of me, and I was lost.

Not that I really knew or understood any of this. All I knew, as the summer ended and I returned to teach the autumn term at Oxford, was that nearly every waking moment was spent thinking of Hilda and Ma and all my friends whose longing, like mine, was so—so unreasonable, so unquenchable, so crazy. And even as I was hearing my pupils' Anglo-Saxon declensions and conjugations or resolving for them some textual crux or another in *The Dream of the Rood* or *The Wanderer*, my attention would drift out the mullioned windows and fly up into the mountains, following her where she had followed him—until his face above the mantelpiece, laughing and scolding, brought me back to the puzzled stares of my pupils.

I did not understand, but as soon as the term ended, I flew back to New York, hungry for the silence of early summer, smelling the snow, distracted from all my worldly responsibilities in my thirst to understand what drew me up after her into the mountains.

* * *

In the crook of the river, Tony is skipping shells across the surface of the water. Where the wind shifts the tall sheaves of arrowhead, flowering white and yellow, or folds back the gray-green leaves of the sawgrass, the afternoon sun blazes with a cold fire. The river turns slowly, on its smooth brown breast the debris of the summer monsoon, rafts of dogwood and myrtle oak, rigged with the sharp green filigree of resurrection fern, serpent fern, cinnamon fern, their decks manned by the silver stalks and scarlet caps of lovely, rough lichen.

The wind burns in the grass, and for a while all I hear is its cold fire whispering in my ear, until suddenly I find myself in a hollow at the heart of the wind, wrapped around by its whispering fire.

Inside the wind there is a silent clearing.

I sit there watching the river turn, no longer waiting. Tony is skipping shells across the swollen surface of the water, every fling of the wrist clumsy and perfect, every shell sinking into a deeper silence.

The river tells me that everything that lives is holy.

The river burns in my heart.

I sit inside the wind, still and free in the fullness of the summer, and in its silence I hear his voice.

"It is all in the sharing. Share me!"

5

Summer Snow

Again it is cowdust time, a long late evening in August. One of the children has plundered the maypop vine for its dingy blue and violet flowers where they have spilled over the corral fence and the pumphouse.

I am sitting under the rosewood tree by the pond, watching the light go.

Over the water, under an immense umbrella of bamboo, there are a few milky shrubs banked against the tawny flagstone of the chimney stack. We call them summer snow—I don't have the botanical Latin for them. Not even the musky crimson and magenta of the water lilies is lovelier than their parchment white, dipped in red when they first unfold. They have no flower, yet each leaf is a petal, white as chalk, soft as spurge, the freshest leaves flecked with this morning's sunrise.

There is fulfillment.

There is longing.

There is the understanding that longing is only fulfilled in a fulfillment that is always longing.

Sitting by the pond between the rains, in the close wet heat of high summer, I can smell the snow.

* * *

For two years, from the day Baba came to her to the day she turned the van over on the Long Island Expressway, Ma tried by some magical sleight of hand and heart to make it all one—the mountains and the snows, the river of her teaching already bursting its banks, and above all, her household of twenty years, her family.

Christ had warned her from the beginning that the time would come when she would have to leave them. He had reassured her, too, that eventually, in their own time, they would come back to her. But she loved them too much to let them go without a fight, a fierce fight against Sal's absolute refusal to share her, against his fears for her sanity, his bewilderment, against in the end his broken heart raging at her calling. She wanted nothing so much as for Sal and the children to follow her up into the mountains, and she hung back for them until her reluctance and her patience nearly destroyed her.

But for two years, and more, she gathered it all together by some miracle of reckless will and love, caring nothing for herself so long as she served as fully as she could the seeking of her family, and of those who now scrambled about her from all across the country.

I arrived back in New York eager for the silence of early summer, smelling the snow, hoping to follow her up into the mountains.

But of course it was not to be.

In my absence a huge crowd had gathered, and though I had not lost my place, I saw at once that the intimacy of those first classes at Hilda's apartment and in Ma's basement had now to be shared with hundreds of others, most of whom were just as thirsty as I was, just as impatient, and often a great deal more abandoned. For a day or two I told myself that if there had still been just a few of us I might have found a quiet, necessary isolation, a real independence, and followed her up into the mountains. But in truth I would have felt too exposed, and I held back. As it was, losing my courage, I hid in the crowd and soon turned to the security of Hilda's instruction to keep myself from smelling the snows.

We were many and diverse, but we had two singular things in common—our longing and our wandering. Though some of us—nuns, monks or priests, or some of those who came from Alcoholics Anonymous—had not strayed beyond the bounds of traditional faiths, we had all been wandering inside, and most of us outside as well, for years. We were all exotic. We were all strays—the intensity of our longing had made us so, and we were gathered from all over the world, from many different paths—reforming junkies, show business folk, college professors, street people—drawn by our thirst from the strangest, most far-flung corners, gathered and stitched together in a crazy quilt of seeking.

Hilda's group was, as I have described, already very diverse. She taught in an Episcopal Church on Hudson Street, and many ordinary Episcopalians, Catholics, Jews, and Protestants attended her classes. But she also looked after the followers of a number of Indian masters, among them Sathya Sai Baba, Bhagwan Nityananda, Paramahansa Yogananda, and Sri Ramakrishna, and she had a small swarm of Theosophists and Vedantists, as well as Sufis and Native Americans, dabblers in ancient mysteries, Buddhists of every lineage, devotees of Krishnamurti, unfrocked Scientologists, including some very muddy *clears*, disaffected Transcendental Meditators, Hare Krishnas, and many others. Most of us, I suppose, had tried a number of these paths, and having embraced none of them, were at a point of unraveling. When Ma was being charitable she called us "guru hoppers" or, putting us in our places, "guru whores."

Foolish and exotic, credulous and fiercely skeptical—but above all completely dedicated to our seeking....

And to these Ma soon attracted many of the followers of Nityananda's disciple Rudi, Swami Rudrananda, who had been killed in a plane crash a couple of years back; as well as Jesuits like Father E., who taught at a Catholic High School on the upper East Side and spent his summers painting in Paris; and Larry, a famous game show host, soon to die in a car crash in Morocco on a holiday Ma warned him not to take; and Beirut Bob, whose brother was mixed up in something bad in Lebanon; and Ron and Randy, a gay Vedantist couple devoted to the teachings of a very desiccated disciple of Ramakrishna; and George, a gay hairdresser who sang plainsong like an archangel and possessed alarming psychic powers; and a randy Franciscan, Brother F., who wore his robes even when philandering; and Captain J., the master of a Greek cruise ship, who came, always in his uniform, more as a suitor than a seeker; and Doc, a professor of oceanography, who was involved with something shady in Haiti and later washed up dead on a remote cay in the Bahamas; and Ilan, an Israeli fighter ace, hero of the Six Days War, dashing and badly deranged; and Sufi Lady, a Parisian or Viennese lady who had been with Gurdjieff, with the air of a retired adventuress, very close about her past, and a heart of gold; and Mad Jack, a drifter, gravely paranoid, who once tried to sever my larynx with a blunt table knife at a dinner party because he found the way I said grace threatening. These and hundreds more were now seated at Ma's table, breathless and hungry to learn from her the mysteries of breath and appetite, to devour and to be devoured.

When I arrived a few months before Christmas, Ma and Hilda sent me to live with Rebecca, a generous heiress, quite comfortably off, who lived in a duplex penthouse overlooking the Park on West End Avenue. Rebecca's sons had just grown up and moved out, so we had the place to ourselves except for Roger the Lodger, who had some profession on the perilous edge of the film business.

Rebecca was approaching fifty, though she looked fifteen years younger. She had a quiet, austere beauty and a simplicity untainted by years of the shallow, expensive company of her barbarous class of corporate robber barons. She had come to a life of seeking after winning a long struggle with alcoholism. She was always going off in the middle of the night to rescue someone, friend or stranger, and her closer friends were mostly from AA—brave and rather battered people in various stages of repair, all of them humbled and in some measure opened by their suffering, all of them holding on to a peculiar hollowness. Without exception I liked them. But I was shaken too by their exhaustion and their dereliction, seeing in their precarious vacancy a fate I had only narrowly escaped. In their company I saw how much suffering it may take before a man or a woman at last assumes the responsibility to turn inwards.

Rebecca took me in with a natural openheartedness and the practiced forbearance of a gracious hostess, offering to burn my shabby black overcoat (to my shame I refused), and installed me for a generous pittance in the maid's room. She was turning deeply inward, and for all her steep, swift flights into exalted states of awareness, where I could never hope to follow, she turned out to be the ground of much of my seeking. I should have been quite lost without her uncompromising practicality.

The rest of us Ma scattered over the city, mostly in Queens, Forest Hills, and Kew Gardens, where we lived twelve or fifteen to a house in whichever combinations seemed to excite the greatest distress. Of course, a great many of us were already established in Manhattan or the suburbs, and Ma often boarded newcomers in these apartments, usually, so it appeared, with the intention of provoking fun and trouble. All her arrangements were provocative and theatrical.

It was all a show, a wine bath in a storefront window. *Da-da-Boom.*

With every week the cast swelled and spilled into the wings, Queens, and Brooklyn, and as new characters arrived, Ma convinced them that they had all taken center stage. There were very few of us who even for a moment imagined we were there just to swell a progress or start a scene or two. Ma made such a fuss of each of us, we were all reading for the main parts, and puffed up, and playing to the gallery, full of spiritual bombast.

Occasionally some brave and callow soul, flubbing his lines, would complain to her in the middle of a class that it was all too melodramatic, all too shrill. But to expect of a magician that she explain her tricks, to demand social realism of an illusionist, or of a teller of tales that all her tales be true was to miss the point exactly; and those who wanted Ma to be literal and serene were simply rejecting the conditions of her teaching. They learned little and never lasted very long.

Those who stayed had the humor and the courage to be taken in, at least for the term of their apprenticeship, which lasted for as long as they could willingly suspend their disbelief, and find their place like Tirza in the storefront window, and go *Da-da-Boom, da-da-Boom*, as Ma directed.

She was teaching us all, as Tirza had taught her, to be funny and brave and shameless, and to consume the grand illusion by becoming ourselves the show. She was showing us that the only way to turn the show off is to become so shameless that we are forced to see that it is *all* show, that the petty self is itself the show of shows, and in this understanding to call our own bluffs.

And so, month after month she packed the house, and all our names were up there in lights.

Of course, if anyone was truly center stage it was Ma herself, and next to her on the couch in a spotless sari, Hilda. Hilda had her lines down pat, and her sense of timing was perfect. She played straight woman to Ma, and they were a terrific act, impossible to follow.

They would travel from house to house—from the basement of St. Luke's to Rebecca's spangled dining room, from Hilda's flat to apartments in Queens where the furniture was kept, perfect and unsweating, under plastic—and draw us all into a fresh performance, full of confession and declamation, laughter and tears, much verbal brawling and mewling, self-serving soliloquies, rash undirected recriminations, choruses of denunciation that would have made the Red Guards blush, declarations of regret, wild promises, and always the question "How, how, how?" clamoring in every heart.

And at the end Ma would light, with whatever small spark of truth or sincerity had been struck from the flint of her patience a small blaze of silence, a deep and real silence, in which we would all sit for a few moments before we got up off the floor with aching knees, and scattered.

But every drama needs a leading man, and he soon made his appearance in the person, the very considerable person in spiritual circles, of Ram Dass.

Ram Dass was Richard Alpert who had taught in the early sixties at Harvard, where he had experimented with LSD and had himself thrown out along with Timothy Leary, and then had discovered on a journey to India a spiritual calling at the feet of Neem Karoli Baba, who gave him his name, which means simply "servant of God." He returned to America transformed and wrote of his experiences in *Be Here Now*, which quickly became one of two or three classics of the spiritual underground in the early seventies, awakening tens of thousands to an inner calling.

In the summer of 1974, he experienced Baba telling him that his next teacher would be in America. He happened to call on Hilda soon after, and she took him to visit Ma in Brooklyn.

I was there, polishing the dining room floor, the day he arrived.

It was the day after Baba had come to Ma by the pool, the day of her fulfillment, and one of the first things Baba had told Ma was that she should expect his "son" to visit her.

I was very much in awe of Ram Dass; his book had helped me during the year I had spent in Vermont, when I first came to realize my calling. And the awe did not fade. As he came in the front door, I could feel in him an astonishing light and purity.

She confided in him matters which he had shared privately with Baba, and in this intimacy he recognized Baba's presence. There arose between them a real affection and respect. He was gracious and open, and even a little protective of her, which surprised me because it had not occurred to me that a holy person might need protection.

He went away, encouraged and already a little in love, promising to keep in touch and to return.

He spent the next four months giving retreats around the country, and then in December, a week or so after I had settled into Rebecca's, he moved in with us to apprentice himself to Ma, which he proceeded to do with an abandon and a yearning and a discipline which I had not encountered in anyone else. And because he was himself a teacher, he attracted to Ma's storefront a great many—fifty or a hundred—of those Westerners who had been with him at Baba's feet when Baba was still alive.

From the start I treated him very unfairly. I was still very green and confused, too swift both to believe and to doubt, and I was quickly disillusioned to find in Ram Dass not the pure and simple teacher whose words had so excited me in *Be Here Now*, but an ordinary human being, still ardently seeking, and as bruised and battered by the world as anyone else—bitter at times, at times very afraid.

I found him tight and he found me tight. We were both angry at being here at all, let alone "being here now." Late one night in the kitchen he showed me photographs of himself in college and as a young professor at Harvard, before his LSD days. They looked like pictures of myself—sad, vulnerable, stiff, lost.

But I never doubted he carried the love and grace of his master, and over the year and a half that I lived with him, I saw him bring Christ and Hanuman into the hearts of hundreds of people. He had the gift of speaking a spiritual language we all understood, and with a sharp, dispassionate intelligence, and he was a born storyteller.

I recall another night when he came downstairs to answer the doorbell in his Indian whites. He had been meditating. He looked like a lighthouse—a gentle radiance poured from him.

Ma had him sit on her left on the couch, Hilda on her right, and that is how they usually taught. She was happy, both out of love and mischief, to have him play leading man in her troupe, a role he accepted without ever fully understanding the script and its denouement, and with a mixture of willing pleasure, as his natural due, and reluctance, befitting a man who was still seeking and had not yet found. He spoke very little, but for both Hilda (about whom he felt very ambivalent) and for Ma, he played the part of protector and defender with all the shining fidelity and good humor of a leading man born to the part. He even at times dropped into the role of the fool, with his natural talent for comedy, just so long as he was not required to be truly foolish, truly open.

Meanwhile at home and in private he applied himself to Ma's instruction with a tireless dedication, and then he was always at his best, willing to risk everything, a seeker of courage and discipline, firm in his resolve, independent in his submission, and rarely mistaking a humbling for a humiliation, a student of real generosity, always seeking from moment to moment to love, serve, and remember his master.

But like the rest of us he was fatally sure he was center stage, and though as leading man he had the most reason to suppose so, he was still some way from being up to the part. He did not know any better than the rest of us how to take Tirza's place in the storefront window and how to go *Da-da-Boom, da-da-Boom!* He didn't know how to be really funny and brave and shameless.

Looking back, it is now perfectly obvious to me, as it should have been all along, that the true center of Ma's world for the last year or so of her New York life was her husband Sal and her children. For all the sound and fury of her show, for all the many hundreds whose lives she now touched and changed, her constant and deepest care was for her family. Every day she had to face the terrible practicality of Christ's warning, so sternly confirmed by her implacable tutor Nityananda, that she would have to turn her back and walk away from them. It was never any reassurance to her that he had also promised they would return to her. She could not bear the thought of letting them go even for a second. And those of us who clamored around her were too self-absorbed and rapacious to consider her anguish; nor did she allow most of us the least inkling of how deeply the prospect of losing them hurt her.

Instead she submitted her struggle to her own teaching and used it as just another part of the show, blowing it up into melodrama, driving Ram Dass and Rebecca frantic with concern, even as she kept them safely at bay. It was her battle, and hers alone, and she fought it alone, until that fateful July 4th weekend out at Montauk, when she had to choose at last between losing her family or her sharing, her household or her storefront. Turning the van over on the Long Island Expressway, she fled from the emergency room to the airport, one eye closed, her body black and blue, and there she took a flight, penniless and alone, to Florida.

> *I came to cast fire upon the earth; and what do I desire, if it is already kindled? But I have a baptism to be baptized with; and how am I straitened till it be accomplished! Think ye that I am come to give peace in the earth? I tell you, Nay; but rather division: for there shall be from henceforth five in one house divided, three against two, and two against three. They shall be divided, father against son, and son against father; mother against daughter, and daughter against her mother; mother in law against her daughter in law, and daughter in law against her mother in law.*
>
> —Luke 12:49-53

* * *

I have gotten ahead of myself again.

Who is happy? Who is afraid? Before she flew to Florida, Ma pressed upon each of us these questions, even as she scoured the dark corners. She laughed and swore and sang, and became for each of us the mirror of his quarrel with himself. Seeing our image in her, sometimes we laughed and sometimes wept, or raged or embraced or spurned, and whatever face we pulled, she pulled another—an angry or a jealous mother, a seductress or a rejected lover, a scolding wife, a petulant sister, a delinquent or penitential daughter, a shrew or a saint—all to lead us deeper and deeper into a drama of destruction, where she could dance on the corpse of our petty selves. And at every encounter she was challenging us to reflect on the nature of happiness and the root of fear.

As spring passed, it became apparent to many of us close to Hilda that Ma had undertaken to help her as well, even though Hilda thought of herself as in some sense *finished*, a seeker who had found, and was now dedicated to bringing others along. I firmly believed her and pinned all my hopes on her, but as I have indicated my motives were not clean. I was really hiding in her skirts, and I could only with difficulty look into her eyes because I realized that I was not treating her openly and honestly. Ram Dass and Rebecca tried to have me understand this, but I was too afraid to see the sense in their advice, and I continued to cling to Hilda from fear of letting myself go.

I was beginning to appreciate that Ma would from time to time take it upon herself to offer Hilda help, especially when she lost herself, as she sometimes did, in psychic business. It is the peculiar burden of people who are gifted in this way to become engaged by their powers and to lend them too much authority. Hilda was sometimes taken in by her own visions and would go through various odd involvements, little infatuations with what she considered to be spirits from the inner planes. One month it would be the ghosts of Mozart and Schubert, the next Black Elk or some other Native American shaman, or again it would be Artemis and Athena, or one or another of the Hindu or Buddhist pantheon. She had a special cushion in her living room set aside for an invisible mouse, the vehicle of the elephant god Ganesh. One sat on the cushion only at great peril.

I suppose it is cheap to make fun of all this. For me, I never believed a word of it, and yet for Hilda's sake, for the sake of all the love and common sense she tirelessly dispensed to every stray who turned up at her door, I put up with it, just as long as Hilda didn't try to enlist my belief in any of it, as she had tried to do at the beginning, and as long as she treated it, as she usually did, lightly and with good humor.

Ma put up with it too, and more than that, she threw it all into the giant stew of illusion she was busy brewing. There was even a part of her, the Brooklyn part, credulous and mischievous and tricky, which seemed at times really to believe it—it was a great deal of fun, and after all, it must have seemed no less fictitious than the daily posturings with which we tried her considerable patience. She was always looking for new dimensions for her show, new stage sets, new props, new attitudes to strike, and this vast invisible world of disincarnate spooks must have seemed to her a gift straight from central casting.

Gradually Ma began to make it plain that Hilda was a little stuck in these illusions, and that others around her were also and more seriously stuck. She made it her business to extricate them, but she was not confident, and with reason, that Hilda would accept her guidance or her reproof, so she worked at it slowly, drawing away from Hilda's influence the psychically afflicted, and closing down their psychic faculties, and at every gathering speaking out frankly against any kind of meditative experience that strayed from the straight and simple path of deepening love and stillness.

Not that she abandoned the storefront window. The show had to go on, because it was only by entangling us ever more inextricably, only by puffing us up to new heights of spiritual vanity, only by weaving around us ever more densely the webs of illusion that she could ever provoke us into seeing through the pretenses of the petty self. Nor do I mean, by playing with a theatrical metaphor, to make light of Ma's pranks. Her business was show business in appearance only. In truth, it was deadly serious, and required of her the sober taking on of heavy responsibilities and the proper discharging of them. No one who sat before her and who looked her in the eye with any degree of open attention could for an instant doubt how deeply she had committed herself to a radical moral work of sharing and encouragement, and always on free and equal terms with whoever came seeking.

In the poses Ma struck, she meant absolutely nothing and absolutely everything.

And in all of this Ram Dass was her most able partner and willing accomplice. As long as he considered himself free from her wiles, as a teacher already proof against self-deceit, as a comedian whose sense of irony was equal to every self-exposure, as a leading man who could never be gulled and never tricked into playing the fool for real, then he was happy and vigorous in his collaboration with her, in the tireless weaving of her web.

It happened that he had made a little cave for himself out of a broom closet next door to the maid's room in which I lived, and I was in a unique position to observe, as the months went by, with what tireless and unconditional love Ma set about gulling him. She loved him in a special way, for who he really was, for who he really is, and she was determined, with a truly ruthless generosity, to save him from himself.

He was at that time a man deeply at war with himself, a sort of saint in public, in private a soul in torment. At home he would be on the phone with Ma half the night, while Sal and the children slept, and she taught him with the kind of persecution of which only a very great love, a heroic love is capable. Anything was fair game for her, and Ma applied herself to digging up the roots of his suffering with an extraordinary lack of mercy and a complete compassion.

She loved him simply and sincerely, and her persecution was the unreflecting activity of her purity. She loved him simply and truly, and in that love there arose occasions for his deliverance from suffering, chances for the reclamation of his happiness, as he had once claimed it at the feet of his master.

Whether he knew it or not, she was taking him through his paces. For the rest of us, his radiance was never in doubt. He was the only one in the dark about his own brightness. Little by little, I saw him grow in confidence and self-love. He was beginning to fill and open and love himself.

But it could not last.

He could not find the humor or the courage or the abandon to follow Ma and Tirza up into the storefront window. Little by little, in the early months of 1976, he turned away from her.

I remember coming upon him sitting one evening in Rebecca's vast drawing room, the lights of the city burning all around. He sighed deeply and said, "Either she is the only pure woman I have ever known, or…she's just an exquisite psychotic system."

I sat there next to him, unable to help, and watching through the huge windows the burning city with its walls and walls of light, its incandescence, I reflected how brightly we burn as we die; and even as I saw his flame guttering and failing, my respect for him was renewed, seeing in his failure the measure of his surrender.

By spring he turned against Ma, at times bitterly.

But Ma was not willing to let him go without a fight. There was never any pretense about her. She knew she had to give him everything, and so she prepared for one last assault upon his defenses, even as she struggled to keep her family together.

By the early summer Ram Dass was holed up in the penthouse, trying to avoid her, in a state of self-imposed siege.

Ma, determined still to scale or undermine his fears, decided one day in the middle of June to attack the penthouse. It happened that I was flying back from Oxford that Friday, and of course I had several keys to Rebecca's. If Ma had wanted to get in, all she had to do was meet my plane.

But then where would have been the show?

Gathering to her side a small band of devotees who had been with Ram Dass in India and who understood something of what she was up to, she mounted a full-scale assault on Rebecca's. They took the service elevator and got up onto the roof, hoping to climb down onto Rebecca's balcony, enter through the bedroom windows, storm the broom closet, and confront the hapless Ram Dass.

Unfortunately it was a very large roof and they lost their way. The penthouse next door was occupied by a Wall Street lawyer and banker whom I had befriended years before at Oxford. He was a reserved man who had with considerable bemusement and good-hearted tolerance shared the elevator with the wildest bunch of people for over a year.

His wife was French, and while of good courage and bearing in the social circles in which the family moved, a little high strung and with halting English.

When she found Ma, wild, loaded with bangles and beads, jet black hair flying everywhere, cursing at the top of her voice, descending into her drawing room followed by four or five heavily bearded yogis and demanding the disclosure of her favorite, at first she screamed, and then remembering her breeding, as if her guests not uncommonly descended unannounced from above, she offered them all tea or coffee—until, seeing their business was really pressing and elsewhere, she invited them firmly to return back up to the roof.

Hearing the commotion, Rebecca and Ram Dass and Roger the Lodger hastily bolted all the windows and glass doors to the balconies.

They need not have bothered. The descent, at twenty stories up, was too steep and dangerous. So Ma and her little army gave up and settled themselves at Rebecca's front door on the eighteenth floor and began to bang at it.

Looking through the peephole they saw Ram Dass, in miniature, running from the library to the kitchen in his briefs. Ma could never abide the sight of underwear, such was her modesty, nor of an uncovered mattress, given her childhood poverty, and she spent the next quarter of an hour explaining this to Eddie, the Irish elevator attendant.

Then she collapsed in tears against the front door and sobbed shamelessly.

Meanwhile Ram Dass had summoned the police, and as they arrived, he and Rebecca had fled in the service elevator and out the back door of the basement.

The police were all Irish, and Eddie, who had by now taken Ma in his arms, sent them all away, explaining it all as a case of a broken heart. One or two of the cops, who were his drinking companions, offered to take care of the heartless son of a bitch who had done this to her.

At length Ma dried her tears and drove out to Mt. Manresa, the Jesuit retreat, where she had a large class waiting for her, and with whom she shared the day's adventure.

When I arrived at the apartment a little after two, Eddie told me the whole story, already richly embroidered and full of dark imprecations against the gentleman who had broken Ma's heart. Letting myself in with the latchkey, I started at once to pack, since on their return they were likely to ask me to move out to Queens.

I knew it was all over, as Ma had predicted five months earlier. She had called me up late one night and had laid it all out to me: Hilda was too drawn to spiritualism, and Ram Dass was unlikely to free himself, and I should "shit or get off the bowl"—her very words. It took me a few months of turmoil and reflection to acknowledge Hilda's limitations, or rather the dishonesty of my unswerving loyalty to her, but by January I had made my choice. Every time I went up to Hilda's, I came away feeling out of place, and though my love for her was undiminished, I knew that my time with her must come to an end, and that I needed to trust to myself, as Ma had always insisted, and to embrace my fears.

As for Ram Dass, I had lived intimately with his losing quarrel with himself, and I knew roughly the considerable measure of his courage and his unhappiness, and I had never expected him to get off the couch and take his place on the floor in front of Ma, which was the only way he could ever have hoped to devour her.

* * *

I am silence that is incomprehensible
and insight whose memory is great.

In my weakness do not disregard me,
and do not fear my power.

I am one you pursued,
and I am one you seized.
I am one you have scattered,
and you have gathered me together.

I am one you have professed,
and you have scorned me.
I am uneducated,
and people learn from me.

MA & ME

I am one you have despised,
and you profess me.
I am one from whom you have hidden,
and you appear to me.
Whenever you hide, I shall appear.

Hear me in gentleness,
and learn from me in roughness.
I am the woman crying out,
and I am cast upon the face of the earth.

I cry out and I listen.

—The Thunder, Perfect Mind

After the penthouse siege Ma let Ram Dass go his own way. I was asked with the greatest courtesy to give up the maid's room, so with Eddie's help I took my trunk out to Kew Gardens and settled happily in one of Ma's many households.

Ma let Hilda go too, though it all but broke her heart. She knew that without Hilda she would never have found the ground to share herself. She owed her everything, as each of us who were close to her owe her always far more than we can ever know. But Ma would not, she could not, compel her to see things freshly. Their love was so deep and full that she had to allow her the freedom to suppose she was finished, though she ached to convince her of what she felt to be the franker truth: that they were both seekers, and that the sacrifice each of them had made in freely taking flesh required them to acknowledge an ordinary fallibility, a true and real humanity. Much as she cared for Ram Dass and Hilda, and as devotedly as she had fed their need to be honored, she could no longer sustain their pretenses without hurting them. She had already given them as much time and love as they wished to take, and now she had to return to her first concern, which was for her family, and after them, without favor or discrimination, the rest of us—so many hundreds of hungry mouths to feed. Too many!

After a few months she had us rent a cottage out at Montauk, and at all times of the day and night she would pack us into cars and vans and head out for land's end, and there she would sit on the rocks by the sea, beneath the old lighthouse, and set us against ourselves in struggles of love and fear, breaking us down, giving each of us the chance to see that the quarrel is always solitary, within us, the ancient quarrel between the mind and the heart, between love and the fear of love, between pure and possessive love, at every turn encouraging us to make our own stand and stand on our own.

We would sit there at dawn, broken, in her silence, few of us guessing how much of her was still at home with Sal and the children, whom she had determined never to let go, whatever Christ had told her, however bad they thought her calling, however bitterly they fought to keep her to themselves.

Who is happy? Who is afraid?

Everything now rapidly unraveled. Too many characters were demanding center stage, too many Mad Jacks and hungry nuns and reforming addicts and gun molls on the run…

She would often disappear for hours, driving off by herself in a small blue van which a defrocked priest had given her in gratitude for saving him from some trouble he was in. She never let us know where she was going, but one Sunday, driving back to town, we spotted her van inside the gate of a small convent just outside Amagansett, and she admitted later that she had been hanging out with some nuns but would tell us no more. At weekends she would have a number of small groups, none of whom knew about each other, scattered around the end of the island in motel rooms or beach cabins, and she would shuttle among them.

At other times she would simply go off by herself and spend hours alone in the woods or by the beach, gathering shells or talking to strays, but always truly alone, in the company of her Baba, her only real and constant companion, her only true leading man.

For the last two weeks of June she kept us all going in a kind of traveling circus, running in a banged-up flotilla between our houses and the Jesuit retreat at Mount Manresa and the cottage at Montauk, and all the while she juggled her little groups of priests and strays and professional derelicts in motels, beach houses, roadhouses, and cottages up and down the Belt Parkway from Montauk to Quogue to Amagansett.

She kept running us out to land's end, to the lighthouse and bluffs and the ocean, at all times of the day and night.

What else could she do?

We were none of us—not even Hilda and Ram Dass—ready for the mountains and the snow, and that is all she cared for, the snow and the mountains and how to bring her family with her on her spiritual journey.

But Christ had said it was not to be. One day they would follow her, but in their own time, according to their own understanding.

As for us, with however much abandon she ran us out day and night to that most sacred place of transfiguration where the sea meets the sky in the Mother's eyes, not one of us was ready yet to enter fully into her moment, none of us truly breathed the life that gave breath to her life, not even those who had sat at Baba's feet in India. We had not yet come close to uncovering the roots of our fear, nor to understanding the nature of happiness. We were still so very far from any mastery of breath or desire.

So what could she do?

She had us diving at dawn into the icy waters of the Atlantic, her Ganga, and I remember coming up morning after morning with forty or fifty gasping friends all around and watching the sun rise over the ocean, feeling the ice turn to fire in my limbs—and I knew that none of us was ready for her, and that it would all soon come to an end.

And so it did, on the July 4th weekend.

Ma had set this aside for our first public retreat, out at the Montauk cottage, and a number of curious souls, perhaps thirty in all, had answered advertisements and began to appear on Friday evening, sleeping bags in hand.

But by some unlucky chance Sal also found out about the retreat.

The first I knew of it, Ma was walking across the main street in Amagansett just before dark on Friday, hand in hand with one of her shaggier students, when an enormous Sicilian with rippling muscles grabbed the hapless devotee from behind and with the lightest slap split his lip wide open, and reclaimed his wife.

"Sal!" Ma cried in unfeigned delight, and falling into his arms, she signaled us all to scatter.

Our courage and fidelity gone in an instant, we fled in every direction, back to the cottage and down to the beach, into nearby stores and motels and back alleys. Someone—Mad Jack, I think—flagged down a ride and sped off to the convent to warn the nuns, who were at their evening orisons.

The main street of Amagansett was suddenly deserted, and Sal put Ma in the Cadillac and drove off.

Somehow or other she managed to reconcile him to what she had undertaken, and they put up for the night in the Golden Sands

Motel. In the morning she brought him over to the cottage where to everyone's astonishment he apologized sheepishly but with good grace to all the people he had hollered at on his way to hunting Ma down the previous evening, and he even submitted to having his photo taken with his arm, that massively muscled arm, around some of the hairy yogis, as if they were long-lost friends. Then, making his excuses, he went back to the motel, leaving Ma to begin the retreat.

She taught for an hour or two, and everything was proceeding according to the rough custom of her instruction when the phone rang and a freshly enraged Salvatore was shouting on the other end, *"Get back over here!"*

It happened that in going through Ma's bags he had come across a photo album in which Ma was innocently pictured on a beach in Florida wearing a regular shirt but without a bra on. Sal's blood boiled.

Back at the motel, Ma taunted him. "You think that's bad! Wait till you see this!"

Throwing all caution to the wind, exhausted at last by his Sicilian strictures, Ma took out another album in which a number of us were photographed on a beach in the Gulf of Mexico skinny dipping, entirely in the buff, though Ma, who was excessively modest, was as always fully clothed.

Ma escaped downstairs with the keys to the van and took off. Sal was only a few seconds behind her, and as she turned the corner of the drive, he threw himself across the hood. She braked sharply, threw him off to the side, and made it out toward the highway.

But Sal, limping back to the motel, called the police, and before Ma had reached the highway, they flagged her down and took her and booked her for speeding.

And so she found herself hauled into traffic court.

But she was ready. She had used her phone call, not for a lawyer, but to summon her students from the retreat, and when the judge entered from his chambers, he was faced with a large gathering of the most ill-sorted characters, all happily drumming out a devotional chant in medieval Hindi, forty-two verses by the poet Tulsi Das in adoration of Hanuman, Son of the Wind, the perfect servant of God and man.

It was too much for him.

He took one look at Sal, bashful and fuming, and another at Ma, beaming with pride, proud of Sal for no particular reason, proud to stand at his side whatever the circumstance, and proud of her motley band of seekers, and when his gaveling could not end the singing, he dismissed the case out of hand, and returned to his Saturday morning golf game.

Ma and Sal made up at once and went out for breakfast at House of Pancakes while the yogis returned to the cottage to await further developments.

But this time it was all subterfuge on Ma's part. She knew it was all over. She knew she couldn't take him with her.

She slipped away to the restroom and out the back door, and soon she was on a ferry sailing over Long Island Sound to the mainland.

She needed to take for herself a moment, a few hours, to reflect on the general unraveling of her best hopes.

She stayed on the ferry when it docked and let it carry her back over the sound. Disembarking, she drove down a country road, and as evening approached, she lost herself in a nearby wood of oaks and larches.

She had struggled for more than three years against Christ's counsel. In the end she was compelled to surrender.

The International van was fitted with a second gas tank, both tanks were full, and Ma decided at once to head for Florida, where the land finally runs out into the sea, realizing now that Christ had been right all along, that it had all come unstuck, it was all flowing.

Halfway back into the city, she changed lanes behind a little red car festooned with newlywed ribbons and mountain bikes, which suddenly stopped, and to avoid hitting it Ma swerved onto the edge, skidded a hundred feet and turned the van over. She told me later she couldn't bear to ruin their honeymoon.

She blacked out for a moment or two, nothing was broken, but she was very badly bruised and shaken.

The medics called up the Montauk cottage, and a couple of her closest students ran to the emergency room and got her out of there and took her, at her insistence, to one of the houses in Queens, where she patched herself up, changed her clothes, and headed for the airport, where she took the first plane to Miami, alone.

And so here she is, a few hours after singing to the judge about the perfection of God's service to mankind, extracted upside down from a demolished van, black and blue, one eye closing, on a plane to Miami, alone, her teaching in suspense, her future on hold, her family having forsaken her, all the balls she had juggled for so long spilling from her hands, all the ground cut away from under her, thirty thousand feet up in the air, alone, entirely alone—*except for* the miraculous company of her invisible leading man, her Baba, in whom she found without the slightest hesitation all the courage and faith she needed to follow him high above the clouds, wherever he led her.

It did not seem so wonderful to the car rental agent at Hertz, who was shaken by her appearance.

"Lady, you ain't going nowhere looking like that."

And he called up his wife, who insisted Ma come home with him to Coconut Grove and she would look after her.

But the only help Ma would accept was a ride to the nearest hotel, where the house doctor attended to her free of charge, no questions asked. Eventually she slept and woke the next morning, her New York life behind her and a new world opening.

Once more she had followed her instinct and run out to land's end, as she has always been running out from the moment Christ first came to her and made all things new for her, as he is making them new for her even now, and if her heart was newly broken, leaving her family behind, she always had him with her to mend it, as he is always mending it, and lending her the courage and faith to follow wherever he leads her.

There is always fresh snow falling.

* * *

In the vermillion petals of the summer snow, a sense of sacrifice. Winter and summer gathered in a single moment, the passage of the seasons gathering us into a common moment.

It is the sacrifice of God taking flesh, the mystery of incarnation, of Christ's Passion. "(This is) My blood ....which is poured out for you." It is the mystery of Hanuman's sacrifice, when he tears open his heart to reveal God in the form of father, mother, and brother.

I'm sitting by the pond at cowdust time. The September heat drenches my senses, the scent of night-blooming jasmine enfolds me in its blanket. Here is my Ganga.

Sitting by the pond at cowdust time, I remember her eyes and how they have nothing around them, nothing guarded or flinching, nothing dissembled, only a complete openness—and her tears.

But who understands? Who understands the imperfection that attends her perfection? Who understands the fullness of her sacrifice, and how the petals of the summer snow are dipped in her blood?

There is always fresh snow falling.

Photos

pp. 134-137 Billy Byrom as student and professor, mostly at Oxford.

p. 136 The handwriting is Ma Jaya's, from scrapbooks she created after Billy's death in 1991. She called the series "Bones and Ash" and dedicated them to him. They are the source of most of these photos.

p. 138 Ma Jaya and Billy in front of the Himalayas, 1977.

p. 139 Waiting for Ma in India, near the banks of the Ganga, 1977.

p. 140 Top: 1976. Ma, Billy and others would gather often informally by the Ganga Pond at Kashi Ashram.

p. 140 Bottom: Ma greeting neighbors at Kashi, with Billy always there to assist.

p. 141 Top: Ma and Billy with Shiva Baba (Bruce Cummings) at a Kashi event. Shiva Baba was the head of a West Palm Beach AIDS organization.

p. 141 Bottom: Ma and Billy, undated.

p. 142 Top c. 1984. Billy with Ma and others would ride along the Sebastian River at dawn.

p. 142 Bottom c. 1988. Graduation day at the River School. Ma embraced each child, as Billy watched.

p. 143 Billy wrote often about the children at Kashi. Pictured is Ganga; this book is dedicated to her.

pp. 144-45 The handwriting is Ma Jaya's, in the Bones and Ash scrapbooks.

p.146 At the height of the AIDS pandemic, Ma kept another set of scrapbooks, "The Yama Books," memorializing those, she loved, who had died.

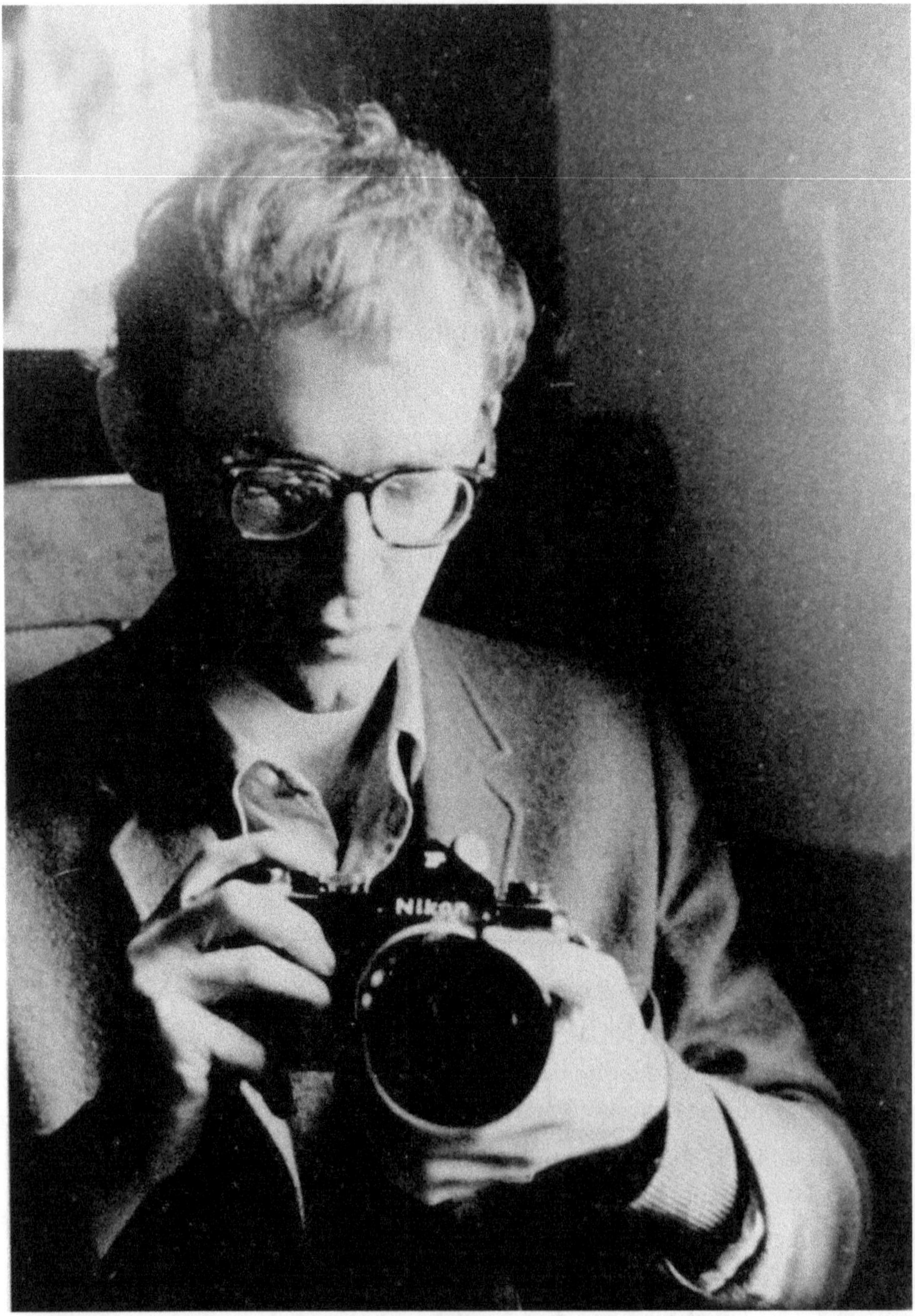
Nikon

THOMAS "BILLY" BYROM

MA AND ME

My Billy many years ago.

I made him laugh a lot and he gave me joy.

THOMAS "BILLY" BYROM

MA AND ME

THOMAS "BILLY" BYROM

MA AND ME

THOMAS "BILLY" BYROM

MA AND ME

THOMAS "BILLY" BYROM

MA AND ME

on my 51 birthday Billy making a speech for me.

Always with Kya, now I am always with my Billy.

Where have you been Billy Boy
   Billy Boy
Where have you been Charmin Billy

THOMAS "BILLY" BYROM

1977 Kashi ashram

We loved the River. Together we swam then the myriad the clear waters gave us comfort. Now I swim alone my sweet Billy. So alone in my River. So alone in my feet.

MA AND ME

I sit here at my computer with the ash of my dead on my hands. I am putting their bones and ash in my Yama book and when i am made of ash and bone those who read this book and see the pictures will keep us all in their hearts and never forget this time of Bones and Ash. Right My Billy Boy??

My Billy fought this battle with me even when he was dying of yukemia fight for them he used to tell Ma

Part 2
Unfolding

6

River Song

We spent the rest of that summer of '76 on the run in Florida.

After leaving the Hertz counter, Ma took a room in a motel near the airport, and on Tuesday night called me up and asked me to drive down with a couple of friends. She had already been joined that day by a wealthy and reluctantly passionate student who had flown in to help her.

She was convinced, with more theatricality than reason, that Sal had followed her to Miami, half-convinced that he had been cuckolded, swearing a Sicilian revenge. Nothing could have been farther from the truth: Ma's celibacy was beyond reproach, and Sal was at home in Georgetown nursing his savaged pride, and we were as free as birds.

Still, Ma persisted in the melodrama, and we drove down to Islamorada and the Keys as if the combined underworlds of Dade County and Brooklyn were marking our flight at every turn.

Once more Ma's instinct was to head for land's end.

The sunsets were lovelier in their dusky opals and dark purples and luminous greens than anything I might have imagined, but Key West turned out shabby and harsh, a competition of commerce and voodoo.

We turned north driving through the night.

The next day we checked in at The Breakers in Palm Beach just out of bravado, in order to declare ourselves outraged by the accommodations, then fled a couple of miles south to the Howard

Johnson's on the beach, which had a bed that jiggled when fed quarters. There under the full moon of July we celebrated our first Guru Purnima, the night sacred to the teacher in India for many thousands of years.

To sit with the guru on this night is to be freed forever, so it is said, from the wheel of birth and death.

We all crowded on the bed together and fed it quarters and shook until they ran out, and then with the full moon rising over the sea and flooding the balcony, Ma subjected a few of us to an hour or two of riddling questions, of which I could make not the least sense, though I think those who had been with Baba in India understood a little more of the mysteries she was patiently celebrating.

The next morning Ma went out to a pet shop on Worth Avenue and bought a black Belgian shepherd puppy and two very large fake marble drinking bowls for two hundred dollars apiece. Two students who had inherited money were invited, to their fury, to foot the bill, and since King Ram, for so she named him, was not housebroken, it fell to me—and to the rest of us by hourly turns, night and day—to clear up his excrement from the deep shag rugs of the motel.

It was my first real introduction to what in the Indian tradition is called *tapas*, that is, the practice of austerity designed to straighten the aspiring soul. It may sound trivial enough, but the discipline which arose from it turned out to be unexpected and remarkable: instead of exhausting me, this disruption struck at the root of habits of awareness which I had not realized were constraining me. It all had something to do with the fact that I had not been allowed a dog when I was young, and we all soon became very attached to the puppy and his trials of our patience.

It was something to do, too, with St. Thérèse of Lisieux's "little way," of which Ma talked now and then, with the mastery of small hourly things before the larger matters can be consumed.

It was no accident, of course, that Ma gave her new dog the name of God, and that her lesson to me that first celebration of Guru Purnima, under the full moon of the richest community in the world, was that only in austerity is there love. It was Christ's teaching, of course, about the camel and the eye of the needle, and the meaning of inner surrender to the true self.

Out of austerity, love—her crazy love, the love she first met at the foot of her stairs, the love that called her up the mountains after him.

Ma soon devised another form of *tapas* for us as we continued to drive north, sustaining all the while the pretense that Sal was still hot on our trail. Whenever we stopped in a motel, she would demand that the furniture in her room be moved around, however late the hour of our checking in. And however adroitly we moved it, she was never satisfied, and demanded we exchange this piece or that for pieces from our own room. When this was not enough, and it never was, she would have us call the management, even after midnight, and commandeer furniture from whatever rooms were empty. It was not that she ever *used* the furniture; she spent most of her time cross-legged on the floor. Her appropriations were entirely capricious, and to my bewilderment, far from angering the motel staff, she invariably delighted them. They always found her funny and charming and could not understand the exasperation we were often driven to express—against our better judgment, for at the least sign of impatience, everything had to be rearranged.

After a few days of this we reached Vero Beach, sixty miles down range from Cape Canaveral, and settled for a couple of weeks in the Ramada on the beach. This allowed Ma the opportunity of working seemingly endless permutations on the rearrangement of the furniture. The heaviest and most settled piece was always in a state of flux, at three in the morning if necessary. And hardly an hour went by without King Ram soiling the carpet, which was of the hairiest shag. Again, the staff found her demands diverting and original, but to us they were the source of a frustration so constant that we were forced, little by little, to undo our habits of awareness and to begin to suspect the fiction of choice which we allowed to rule us. In forcing upon us at all hours the pointless necessity of choosing a fresh arrangement of chairs, table, cupboards, and lamps, she was having us rehearse the confining drama of illusory choice which shapes our sense of reality. She was showing us that awareness, true awareness, is choiceless.

And sure enough, after a while I began to feel a certain marginal freedom in my role as scene shifter, just so long as I had the good heart to surrender to it when my cue was called. I began to realize, after all the puffery of New York, that I was not Prince Hamlet, but one that would do, well enough, to swell a progress, start a scene or two, or short of that, to change the flaps now and then.

I was a scene shifter in Tirza's show, of course her road show as it now was, and Ma was taking us all on a provincial tour of our petty selves.

Before long, having reworked every possible variation upon the Ramada's furniture, we moved into a small house a block from the beach in a village called Indian River Shores, three miles up the road, and there we spent a couple of months, always somehow with the feeling that we were still on the run, still at risk.

We soon filled the place with guests from the eight or nine households of Ma's chelas in New York which had held together when Ma had left town.

By the first week in August there must have been twenty or thirty of us, and every Wednesday we would set off an hour or two before dawn and drive right across Florida to Sanibel Island, spend the day together on a secluded beach miles from the nearest house, swim in the Gulf, and then drive back at dusk—a couple of hundred miles on the road, on the run, without burdens or expectations, running with the setting sun at our backs through sleeping miles of orange groves, into the warmth of the night, running into our hearts.

Back at the house, every morning Ma would take a different group of us on a walk up the beach, a thin thread of sand, till our legs ached, five miles up, five miles back. The sun folded itself deep in the water as the brightness of the white sand smarted in our eyes. The sea was light green, purple, or black, and dazzling. And our conversation, while we walked, was always casual. The emptiness of the sea, the brightness of the sky, the long walk. Then we would sit and meditate, and on the way home resume our casual conversation.

Sometimes toward the end of the walk Ma would encourage us to play free association games, saying whatever came into our minds without hesitation or flinching, gathering the morning's spontaneity to a single point. In this way inhibitions were quickly exposed, and we began to eat one another's fears and to talk freely of the troubles that arose from living so closely together; and then we might start quarreling, at which point Ma would intervene to bring the anger back to the fear that always underlies it, and force us to face what the emptiness of the sky and brightness of the sea had exposed.

Anger covering fear, fear always underlying anger; and fear, so I began to understand, always had to do with keeping or losing our sense of separateness. We were struggling constantly, within and without, not to become one; and at times it seemed to me that all of life may be reduced without simplification to our resistance to the single self.

It was a magical summer.

One morning, at the turning point of our walk, we went into the water and sat in the shallows talking for a while.

It was Ma who first saw the sharks.

"Everyone out of the water," she said so quietly none of us listened at first. Then someone else saw the fins circling us.

Back on the beach, my glasses on, I counted fifty fins or more cutting the water inside the reef close to the shore.

THOMAS "BILLY" BYROM

We had been sitting in a pool of spawning sharks.

At that moment a man happened to walk by us.

"Eating machines," he said, "that's all they are. Just eating machines."

Ma let him pass, but she was furious and deeply hurt.

"They're so beautiful," she said. "God made them," and then, *"Watch!"*

And walking down to the lip of the sea, she stood there for a moment and then started singing a strange, wordless song.

To our amazement, after a moment or two the fins farthest out near the reef turned toward us and swam *in a straight line* to the shore, toward Ma, and soon sixty or seventy sharks were suspended in the water directly at her feet, a few yards out from the sand, and they stayed there for as long as she sang.

This is the only occasion upon which I have ever seen her openly show her power—driven in a moment of private adoration to protest the terrible condemnation of God's creatures, and inspired to command them for the sake of their beauty.

A magical summer, and I was astonished most by the courage and abandon with which Ma had at last followed Christ's word and had turned away from Sal and the children. Turned away, yet somehow she had brought them with her, and placed them inside her, and nursed them there. She gave herself to each of us completely, as if she hadn't a sorrow in the world.

A magical summer—but it could not last.

One Sunday morning in early September there was a knock on the door, and there stood the mayor and the police chief. They were quiet-spoken and scrupulously courteous. "I guess," the chief suggested carefully, "I guess some folks around here aren't too happy with y'all. Course, I don't have nothing against you myself. But you know, folks might say there are a few too many of you, and well, no offense, but they don't take to long hair and beads and all. I'm sure y'all understand...."

At noon the realtor, a Swedish lady with psychic gifts and a very affluent business, came by and gave us our notice, and offered to help us find another place—one able to put up the twenty or thirty of us now crammed into her beach house.

For the next week we split up into teams and scoured the state, as far north as St. Augustine, Carrabelle, and Sopchoppy in the panhandle, Jupiter and Juno Beach to the south, Bagdad and Odessa, Arcadia and Paradise, Mango over near St. Petersburg, St. Cloud and Cinco Bayou, Kissimmee, Christmas, La Belle . . .

But nothing seemed to suit us.

Then at the end of the week the realtor from Malmo turned up in a brand-new white Cadillac and took me twenty miles north to look at a couple of houses a stone's throw from the Sebastian River.

There were some lovely myrtle and turkey oaks, pine flatwoods, a few rare sand live oaks where the old beach used to be, thousands of years ago, and a rather barren pond which a developer, a local dentist, had excavated.

I loved it at once, and especially for the two-minute walk to the river.

It was the river that won me, unspoiled, with a small spit where it turned, and a river meadow where a couple of Appaloosas, mother and foal, belonging to the pastor of the church which bordered the property on the north, were grazing.

We rented it the next day, four acres, the pond and two houses, one large with a high vaulted ceiling of Carolina cedar, the other more modest.

THOMAS "BILLY" BYROM

"We'll call it Kashi," Ma said. "This is our Kashi."

This is our Kashi.
This is the kiss pressed to his lips.

—Ma

* * *

Just before we were ready to move, I had to return to Oxford for the Michaelmas term. As luck would have it, I had been offered a new post at another college. I was engaged to write a study of belief and modern poetry, and I was required to be in residence, and to do a little teaching, only three months of the year. My new college was a much happier place, and I was blessed with the company of three English dons who were devoted to their pupils, good-humored, and prepared to put up with my odd inwardness.

I sat morning and night for a couple of hours and gave myself the hopeless task of winning over the Irish butler Murphy, who was without question the most enraged individual I have ever encountered, a man of a savagery so churlish and unpredictable, except in its constancy and intensity, that I could only comprehend his existence as a kind of affliction, a new Egyptian plague, visited upon me by a punishing God to try my deepest resources.

I was no match for him. He routed me at every encounter, and most of the dons in the college cowered at his approach. Even the bursar, a retired general, fled before him.

In my first term, missing Ma and my fellow seekers, I suffered another spiritual misadventure.

A number of undergraduates, hearing that I practiced yoga, asked me if I would set aside an hour before dinner every evening to instruct them. I saw no harm in this, so I invited them to join me, and for forty minutes or so we slowly deployed ourselves in sun worships and ploughs and fishes—a gentle routine of standard asanas.

Then, as was customary, I suggested we all sit still for a few moments, legs crossed, backs straight, in meditation. Since I had been sitting for nearly five years without experiencing anything more than aching legs and a wandering mind, and at times an uncertain peacefulness, I imagined that there could be no harm in their sitting either.

But to my dismay most of my charges began to rocket upward into exalted and alarming states, in which they experienced blue and white lights, all kinds of fireworks in their foreheads and at the crown of their heads. Not surprisingly a few of them were considerably disturbed. I remember one boy who found himself stuck above his body and rapidly dissolving; he returned to earth and solid form only when I struck him sharply in the middle of his chest.

I stopped the classes at once. Having had no experience of my own which corresponded with theirs, though I knew well enough from Taoist, Tibetan, mystical Christian, and Indian scriptures something of what they had undergone, I considered it folly to presume to lead or guide them in any fashion, and I was mindful of Ma's fierce prescriptions against fooling with the "astral."

One of the boys, looking at me very sharply, demanded to know if I had been moving the trees outside my windows.

"Have you been smoking hash?" I asked him, to deflate his suspicions. I knew they were all very straight, and there was no doubt that their experiences were genuine, and that they had risen above their ordinary senses in a way I was not able to follow, let alone guide.

So, a little ashamed and resolving never again to assume the place of a spiritual teacher, I sent them off to dinner, and for the rest of the term we exchanged yoga for beer in the buttery.

THOMAS "BILLY" BYROM

Before you can straighten another,
You must first do a harder thing,
Straighten yourself.

—The Buddha, Dhammapada

* * *

This book, if I could resolve all its words into a few pages, would be simply and completely a song—a single song of love.

As soon as we settled at Kashi, on our few acres of flatwoods with a derelict orchard by the Sebastian River, Ma began to sing this song, the same, single song with its many and simple variations. In describing how Baba returned to Ma, I have already set down a few snatches from it: how Lakshman came down the mountains to take his child bride Bhagavati from her old nurse Janaki and her teacher Nityananda; how she followed him in joy and trepidation up into the mountains, alone; how people came up after her bringing wood and supplies, or just to sit with her in the snows; how Lakshman loved and indulged her and took her as his bride; and how she ran away and danced under the full moon with the Naga Mas, under the watchful eye of an old Naga Baba.

I have set it down directly in a few snatches, a refrain or two, because my own words could never do justice to it, and if I wrote it all out at once and at length, with its many and simple variations, my story would all be told, there would be nothing more to say; and besides, the reader might take it as figurative—lyrical figures—when it is my book and my words that are figurative; these unsteady, grasping chapters, and the truth, the reality, are all in the song.

If I have learned nothing else, I have learned that the reality of the mind and language is itself a complete fiction, one we choose to believe and inhabit from the instant we separate ourselves from our true selves; and that the only constant moment of truth I know is the moment into which we are gathered every Sunday night as we sit on the planks of the little wooden amphitheater in front of the Hanuman Temple and Ma takes up her double gourd and, plucking its single string, sings her song of the mountains and the river, of Kashi and her Ganga, in whose waters she sacrificed herself a lifetime ago so that we would sit with her every Sunday night in a newly-fashioned life and hear her singing at cowdust time on the night wind.

But who will understand? Who will understand her love or her sacrifice?

For now I can set down only a few lines, taken from the night wind and our single, constant moment.

Here is Lakshman singing as Ma wrote it:

Let me teach you
Of the harsh world beyond the mountains

You must learn of Kashi.
Many times we will take the road to Kashi.
Come child,
Let's go down to the plains,
Following the Ganga.
And yet one day
In days to come
I will have to leave my child to her children.
One day
I will not be there
As she goes down to Kashi,
For I must alone roam the world
Without flesh.

But they will take care of her…
They will see my eyes in her smile,
And they will know their Baba lives…
Look, the snow is falling fast.
The years are falling fast.
And her own words:
In her sixty-first year
Down the mountain they walked,
Hand in hand,
The old woman and the older man.
He was taking her to Kashi to die.
She didn't even have to ask him why.

There they sit by the river, the old woman and the older man, their River Ganga, their daughter. And the river is the song, the song is the river.

Children play by my river
Sadhus stay by my river
Cities old by my river
Temples gold by my river
Cows stray by my river
Night into day by my river
Sadhus yearn by my river
Wise men learn by my river
Ghats burn by my river
How I yearn to return to my river
Hand in hand, the old woman
And the older man

MA & ME

Old man, why cry by my river?
Did I not die by my river?
Was I not born by my river?

* * *

December 1976. Maruti is waiting for me in the dark. The frost shines off the scrub oaks by the tack shed. I give him a little sweet feed, brush and saddle him, dip his bit in the steaming bucket of warm water and get it in his mouth. He is a young quarter horse, ginger or sorrel with gray in the mane. Ma has named him for the Wind, the father of Hanuman, and when I let him out on our practice mile run it is like treading on the wind. I talk to him as I fix the tack. His breath smokes in the cold.

We set off, eight of us, just before dawn.

The moon is so bright in the western sky that we cast long shadows on the grass, and the first light, which stretches from north to south along the entire eastern rim in opal reds and smoky amber, stands still in the long ditches by the run, glazing the black water by the pine woods.

Run into your heart.

Ma tests our anger and our fear on the way down to the gate, but we are too clear for her this morning. We have learned a little—just a little—how to consume her provocations, how to devour Kali the Black Mother and Durga with her tiger. She gives up in sweetness and softness, a mother who does not need to discipline her children, or a young girl whose father holds her safely.

How cold it is! The cold cuts through my gloves and aches in my bones. We tie up by the river and build a fire out of frosted palm fans. We are very quiet, we have ridden into this silence. And there is no quietness like the quietness of accepting the earth. None of us, in this moment, want anything other than its sufficient, simple loveliness.

I reflect how astonishing it is that we take the forms we do, and give breath to the world, and create all that we create. We are born out of our mother's womb into this womb of the mother, the earth. We stand, we look around in wonder, till our sight grows dull and our mind loud with habit and fear and grasping.

But whenever we stay still, how complete and gentle we find the world.

The fire spills its ashes on the sand. We wait for its heat.

An otter slips along the far bank, and in the wild orchard over there a fish crow sits in an oak. Softly, fiercely, the fire burns into a pine log.

As the fire and the sun, boiling up through the treetops, palm and banyan, pine and oak, warm us, we turn to the simplest scripture of all, the *Ramayana*, and read the message Rama sends Sita in her captivity: "Ever since I have been separated from you ..., everything to me has become its very reverse. The young and tender leaves on the trees rage as tongues of fire."

I watch the sun ascend and fall on the water. The reflection runs across the river to our feet. We are so still, the sun climbs and falls, and the water holds it. Where the light and the river meet, which is the reflection?

Ma says nothing. Lately there has been less and less to say, now there is nothing to say. We are all held in the moment, like brightness on the quiet water, like the sun running across the river into our hearts.

* * *

I have observed that with the opening of the heart there comes a responsibility so absolute that if you had the choice you might prefer to remain closed. That responsibility is to undertake your personal death, to die to your little self. This is just the point at which so much fashionable spirituality ducks, takes fright, and either slides off sideways into a fascination with small powers and astral distractions or retreats to the firmer ground of healing therapies.

But for anyone who seeks to die, these are both dodges. The seeker cannot squander a moment of his resources on communion with spirits or out-of-the-body flirtations, nor can he expect a necessary continuity between spiritual and mental health. Restoring the mind to health is a happy and fruitful activity, but it has nothing in itself to do with seeking, where the mind must be excoriated, deracinated, stripped. One of the most sacred objects in Vajrayana Buddhism is the flaying knife. It's there for the flaying of the petty self, with all its righteousness, mental vigor, seductive harmonies, and terrible sanity.

When I returned to Florida, as soon as the Michaelmas term for 1976 was over, I indulged the expectation that I was returning to the company of good and reasonable people. I had allowed myself to forget some of the sharper lessons of the previous two years, in my old and ordinary instinct to find order and sense in everything. I was, of course, quickly set right, and quickly recovered the truth: that spiritual seekers, those who have a real and consuming vocation, are peculiarly mad, bad, and sad. And looking back, I can still say without the least hesitation that if I were able to choose my friends on the grounds of their gentleness or temperance or generosity, I would desert my fellow seekers at once and take up again with my older companions. They were mostly kind and sensible.

And yet I hear the words of the poet Rumi in my ear, urging that he not be given back to his old companions, for in God alone, his true friend, can he rest from wanting.

Anyway, I have no choice. God has so arranged things that I cannot stay long in the company of people who are settled in the world, and when I bump into them, I sense that so many of my old acquaintances are not just settled but stuck—in the summer of 1969, or the fall of 1964—in some earlier season of their lives, stuck like fixed stars in an old and superstitious cosmology, bright, but forever treading the waters of an old heaven.

No, I found myself in those first days at Kashi, on my return from Oxford in December, once more in the company of people as desperate and as muddled as myself—fools and misfits, not principled, not civil, never temperate. But none of us was stuck, or at least never for very long. We were captious, sly, inconstant, stubborn, talkative, taciturn, quick to blame, slow to forgive, grasping, lazy, morose, pushy, and frequently insincere. But we were always changing, always shedding our skins, and as the months went by, we began to feel freer.

My new friends, whose company was both exhilarating and tiresome, did nearly everything badly except for one thing—dying.

We submitted ourselves again and again, not with grace but with persistence, to the flaying knife. We all undertook the difficult business of being skinned alive, and if we led our lives not with dignity and the patience of those who serve God and are content, but with the flinching, the crying out, the insolent curiosity, and the desperate lack of reserve of madmen or gossips or thieves, it was because we were always under the knife, always raw and freshly flayed.

Abrupt—yes. Nosey, bearing grudges—yes. Passive, reckless, imperious—yes.

But we were all in love, and dying, and since that was what mattered, we were happy for the most part to leave the decent codes and agreeable manners of the world to others.

> *Let the lover be disgraceful, crazy,*
> *Absentminded. Someone sober*
> *Will worry about things going badly,*
> *Let the lover be.*
>
> —*Rumi*

Nevertheless, Ma has always said the trick is to die gracefully, an accomplishment which has escaped every one of us without exception.

As I have said, this dying is not a matter of personal growth. That is another business altogether and can safely be left to transpersonal psychologists, counselors, therapists, healers, the Aquarian legions of the New Age, and all the survivors of self-help seminars.

The excoriation of the self requires a quite different kind of attention, and in our particularly hopeless situation, it demanded from the start the fatal ministrations of the Mother, who as Durga in the Indian tradition rides a lion, brandishing in her many arms the fearful weapons, daggers and bludgeons and scimitars, with which she murders our anger, pride, fear, ignorance, sloth; or as Kali, blacker than the night, wearing a garland of skulls around her neck, her fangs drooling blood; as Bhairavi, breasts smeared with blood, roaming the cemeteries covered with the ashes of the dead; as lustful Chinnamasta, who holds her own severed head in her hands and drinks her own blood; as gap-toothed Dhumavati, the smoky one, whose body trembles with insatiable thirst, instigator of quarrels, restless and disheveled; as Bagala, with the head of a crane, the power of cruelty, whose talents are for secret murder and black magic; as Matangi, the night of delusion, who carries a noose and an elephant hook; as ravenous Tara, the night of anger, whose matted hair is alive with poisonous snakes and who wears above her three red eyes a diadem of bleached bones; or as Chamunda, withered, hideous, her breasts slack, her voice hoarse from shouting, her eyes bloodshot; or as a hundred other ghastly forms of herself.

Yet, for all the flaying and the fury, Ma's most urgent business has always been our happiness. What gave confidence to the fresh start we made that autumn and winter was the understanding most of us shared that her endings are nearly always happy, and if our obduracy at times prevented her haste, she drew upon a crafty, but still impetuous, patience. Often she would slay and revive us within a single moment, but sometimes she killed with a kind of desperate slow motion, over a month or even years, restoring us finally and with elaborate care not to goodness or sanity but to happiness, self-respect, and love.

I cannot pretend that we have all ended up morally sound or clear-headed. We are still mostly fantastic and muddled. But she has compelled us all along to aspire to happiness, and to live more and more deeply in love.

How has she accomplished this? As a teacher, yet not as a teacher but more simply as one who shares, as one whose sharing will not be put off, as one who invades your heart and claims it as her own in spite of every protest. And when you have recovered from this outrage, she may whisper the secret of the crossing in your ear, the secret of the river.

Her river, Ganga.

Her crossing, Kashi.

Her secret.

Until then we are all sitting by the river, smelling the snows, waiting.

> *Any man who has the spirit of philosophy, will be willing to die....*
> *The true philosophers, Simmias, are always occupied in the practice of dying.*
>
> —Socrates

* * *

There is the madness of the world and the madness of the spirit. The second often passes for the first. But the derangement which sometimes afflicts a seeker is altogether peculiar, and the world can neither comprehend it nor make it better. Some people are simply in love with God, and like all lovers too open, unreasonable, reckless. The English idiom is *touched,* and it says a great deal. One in love with God has been touched so deeply in every part of her being that she cannot bear a world which recoils from every contact or embrace.

But how do we get out of our depth?

In spiritual people—in anyone, that is, who turns her face toward God and demands His attention—there is a rising of awareness, an uprushing of power and love. Using the Indian figure, I have already described the uncoiling of this kundalini shakti, the serpent power, and the way it brings the inverted flowers of the chakras to open as it ascends—those flower-wheels in which different states of awareness are gathered. It's just one of many figures, of course. The word *chakra* also means a potter's wheel, an oil press, a squadron of soldiers, a flock, and it sometimes is used to describe the circling of birds in the air. Any of these would do just as well as the notion of a wheel of flowers. Or I could draw on the alchemical figures and the colored landscapes of Taoism, the pastoral and courtly metaphors from Sufism, or the vivid figurative language of Vajrayana Buddhism, contemplative Christianity, and Native American faiths, with their profound and sophisticated imagery for states of awakening. But the Vedic model will serve, and besides it is probably the oldest literary account we have of the ancient, common, and universal experience of unfolding awareness.

This power, having uncoiled, must rise straight. If for any reason it shoots off to the side, fails or flutters or sprays, then all kinds of illusory perceptions are precipitated in the seeker: disorientation, hallucinations, delusions. He enters the psychic or astral worlds, which are merely the projections of his mind, and to which he ascribes a specious autonomy and authenticity. And if he loiters there, he may find himself unable to get his feet back on firm ground, and before long he begins to imagine that he can read or predict or even control the thoughts of others; or that his own feelings are entirely unique, or on the contrary shared by whomever he meets; or again, projecting his own internal conversation and imagery, he supposes he hears spirit guides imparting a special wisdom or demons berating him, and so on.

If she is spiritually gifted, these voices may call her with some of the purity and force of her own deeper self, and this seduction is perhaps the most compelling and dangerous of all.

In these ways the seeker is betrayed by his own image in the glass and falls victim to a sedulous narcissism.

Before there can be a straight rising, there must be a firm grounding. If you live crookedly, you will rise crookedly. The seeker must be simple and love himself sufficiently. He must already have surrendered a little to his own nature. He must love and honor "the Mother," by whom I mean the natural world, his own form, the earth under his feet, and the wind on his face. He must first feed himself and feel his own power to nourish others. He must open to the simple, sufficient loveliness of the created world.

"There are hundreds of ways to kneel and kiss the ground," says Rumi. The seeker who wishes to run without stumbling into the arms of his Beloved must first kneel in gratitude and praise.

*　*　*

Mad is my Father, mad is my Mother,
And mad too am I, their son!
Shyama is my mother's name ...
Shyama, whose tresses fall in disarray;
Shyama, about whose lotus feet, crimson in hue,
Swarm bees beyond number.
As She dances, hear how her anklets ring!

—*Ramprasad*

I have recounted how, in the first two years or so of Ma's teaching before we arrived in Florida, she had to work with a great many students who in one way or another had risen crookedly and were caught in all kinds of dim and dusty crevices. They lingered in twilight zones, fascinated by the shadows of their lower selves, thoroughly spooked. Some of them had even acquired siddhis, psychic powers which evolved from too pressing a familiarity with these sideshows of the spirit.

When we came to settle on our land by the river in the fall of 1976, Ma was obliged to continue some of her work with those still swept around in the *chakravata*, the psychic whirlwind, as the scriptures call it. This required a certain indulgence on her part: they would not have listened to her at all if she had simply swept their corners clean. They would have taken it all back. But one by one she now set about straightening them, stripping them of their petty powers, and generally dusting them down.

I remember in particular how she helped some of the former students of Rudrananda, a man who had studied with her own teacher, Swami Nityananda. Rudi had been killed in a plane crash about the time Nityananda was teaching Ma. He had inspired many of his students with a deep love of God and had imparted generous draughts of his own shakti and understanding.

Many of his students shook uncontrollably when they meditated, and prided themselves on this, as if it were an accomplishment. Ma made it very plain that this shaking was invariably a sign of being unable to hold the power with which Rudi had invested them. These undisciplined *kriyas* are characteristic of beginners. With particular care and strictness Ma brought Rudi's students back to earth by disabusing them of their fascination with such experiences, and by having them work on their ordinary daylight problems, on their pride or fear or anger.

Some, suddenly exposed and robbed of the pleasures of power, left her teaching. Others stayed, kissed the ground, and prospered. And of these, not a few might have ended up on the mental wards if Ma had not set them straight.

If there is a single reason for the rising to go awry, it is the seeker's resistance to living. The pilgrim who wishes to die only because he doesn't want to live will never find Kashi, never hear the secret of the crossing. He must first consume his life, and with love embrace it, live it to the full, accept it unconditionally as the unconditional gift it is, devour it utterly as only crazy love can.

To die, the seeker must first learn to live. Living fully is second only to sharing in Ma's list of commandments—and really they are the same thing. And until it is got by heart, the rising and the circling of the birds are best left alone.

We make ready to live, we make ready to die.

But it's all in the readiness.

> *I have lived on the lip*
> *of insanity, wanting to know reasons,*
> *knocking on a door. It opens.*
> *I've been knocking from the inside!*
>
> —*Rumi*

* * *

Last night, two days before the New Year, there was a slight frost, and with it a hint of snow in the morning air. Sitting by the pond in the first light and seeing the fat hoop of bayberry around the Hanuman Temple and the holly banked at the feet of Christ beneath the bamboo towering thirty feet in an arc of simple loveliness, I find it hard to remember how barren the land was, for all its untouched beauty, that first Christmas when we gathered to ride our horses before dawn every morning, and in the evening to listen to Ma's song, or her simple riddling poem, a light phrase of pure poetry, with which she would sometimes leave us at the end of the day:

Who will leave this place?

What place?

No place.

And always she would answer the first question with an even simpler assurance:

I will.

A bride breaking her lifelong vow, to make another, as a mother.

Who will leave this place? What place? No place. I will.

It was many years before I understood these simple questions and their simpler answer as a poem of sacrifice, and her greatest gift to us.

Looking across the water, I see that the summer snow, protected by the stone shaft of the chimney, has been only a little burned by the frost.

Perhaps it will last the winter.

> *This is our Kashi.*
> *This is the kiss pressed upon his lips.*
>
> —Ma

* * *

The reason Ma is so good with crazy people is her own crazy wisdom. I have been with her nearly every day for fifteen years, and I cannot recall an hour with her when she has not broken the bounds of sense, offended decorum, or subverted the rules in some way. She is always wild, so wild that it has required an enormous sacrifice on her part to establish an ashram, with its settled and orderly life.

Her mother Anna left her with a rule by which she has faithfully measured her every action: "Never leave well enough alone." Even as she flays you alive, she calls on you never to say die—offering no quarter, breaking her promises, betraying confidences. Her attentions feel offensively excessive. In all things she exceeds whatever is proper, normal, considerate. She is certain, with Mae West (quoting Oscar Wilde), that *"nothing succeeds like excess,"* and with Blake, that *"the road of excess leads to the palace of wisdom."* She is mad and completely maddening, and not by design but with an unnerving spontaneity, because she is herself madly in love.

When I was teaching at Oxford and still preferred the quieter scriptures—Thérèse of Lisieux rather that Teresa of Ávila, or a little *abidhamma*—Ma's unrelenting craziness upset me a great deal. But seeing her at work, lunging and plundering and swaggering, swinging Kali's sword, boasting and talking too much and telling impossibly tall tales and cursing in public places, dancing shamelessly, and driving at terrible speeds, I gradually came to perceive in all her wildness a secret, constant stillness. I felt at the heart of all her theatrical chaos an unassailable quietness, and when I came to read at her direction the exotic hagiographies of the Tibetan masters, especially Tilopa, Naropa, Marpa, and Milarepa, I recognized in their intemperance and composure the same furious tranquility that I was given to taste every day in Ma's dangerous company.

A few years after we settled, hurricane David hit the ashram. We filled the tubs with water and boarded up the windows and sat huddled together with the dogs in the steaming darkness, listening to the pine trees being uprooted and hurled around.

The eye passed right over, and in the space of a few moments an extraordinary stillness descended. We were at once drawn outside the house into an immense, humid quietness.

Water had been sucked out of the pool by the storm's thirsty vortex, and the grounds were littered with broken-backed turkey oaks and splintered lattices of yellow allamanda, smashed boxwood and trampled ginger; and the candy-pink blossoms of the coralberry vine were strewn in thick trails between the drowned marrow beds and the tack shed, which leaned to one side with its roof half off like a drunk tipping his hat.

But it was the stillness that startled us, so complete that our pulse stopped with it, stalled in a magical hiatus—nor could we talk much or hardly dare to breathe. We did not stray far from the house because we knew that the hurricane would return in a matter of minutes, circling in the opposite direction with redoubled savagery. Yet we felt no danger walking across its eye; the silence was too deep for that. It must have been the most intimate, the closest silence any of us had ever encountered, and the narrowest, barely a mile or so in breadth; but in depth, infinite—a silence so boundless that when I cupped my hand to my ear, I imagined that for once I could not hear the sea.

And there in the unshaken eye of the storm Ma walked. In her blue jeans, hair loose, she walked at ease as if both the fury and the quiet were unremarkable; and it seemed to me then, as it does now even more strongly in the recollection of it, that this was her true element, this is where she lives all the time, in a hollow of perfect stillness, in the storm's unblinking eye. And trailing behind her, I knew she had gathered the storm around her with all its chaotic madness, its primal destruction, and enfolded herself in the hollow of its terrible heart.

At least that was my fancy then, and I have spelled it out because I have no better way of describing or accounting for the paradox—how she rides the storm, yet sits in its eye. At least, I cannot submit her wildness to psychology or make it rational or spiritually sensible. It cannot be subsumed in the narrow, fumbling life of the mind. It is too much a fact of nature.

> *It may be that in all her phrases stirred*
> *The grinding water and the gasping wind;*
> *But it was she and not the sea we heard.*
> *For she was the maker of the song she sang.*
> *The ever-hooded, tragic-gestured sea*
> *Was merely a place by which she walked to sing.*
> *Whose spirit is this? we said, because we knew*
> *It was the spirit that we sought and knew*
> *That we should ask this often as she sang.*
>
> —Wallace Stevens, "The Idea of Order at Key West"

* * *

One of the ashram residents had a friend called Violet, a small affectionate woman who had been locked up in more than one mental hospital. Once when she was between hospitals, Violet accepted an invitation to visit us and meet Ma. She turned up one day, off the Greyhound bus with a cardboard suitcase and an orange hibiscus in her hair, a little distracted but with a fetching smile and a certain unchecked eagerness which at once won our confidence, at least until she looked up from the supper with which we had welcomed her and, pushing the bread around her plate, asked brightly, "Do all the patients have beds here?"

Violet was like one of those distant stars that burn with a great but unsteady radiance. One moment you would be basking in her warmth, the next you would be suddenly burned alive in the sizzling focus of her attention. I don't think she accepted our explanation that we were a monastery, not an asylum.

We were not very convincing.

She settled in, and for a while seemed comfortable enough. She shelled peas in the kitchen, talking all the time to the husks, which she could not bring herself to discard but laid in neat rows end to end around the table. She played with the kids, who loved her empty, undirected reproaches and her aimless intensity. Every hour she hatched a dozen schemes for reforming the ashram, but they all vaporized in the steam of her next enthusiasm. For a shy person, she was astonishingly bossy. For a bossy person, she was disarmingly without purpose, just like the rest of us, and indeed we recognized her as one of our own and loved her and hoped she would stay on.

But just as she seemed to be relaxing, she faltered and became abusive and started talking nonsense. She shrank from the children and spoke sharply at shadows and chewed her thumbs, and soon none of us could reach her. Violet shut up shop, and no matter how her friends tried to call her back to us, she remained adamantly mad.

At this point Ma stepped in. One afternoon when Violet was at her worst, babbling in her palms, Ma sat her down on the rug in the boys' room and demanded a conversation. I recall the look in Violet's eye—furious, trapped, but determined to outrun her pursuer.

Ma sat down in front of her, cross-legged, arms akimbo, no makeup, no jewelry, just jeans and a shirt, Ma unveiled, Ma without all the drama, the Ma you never mess with, Ma terrible and unadorned, the Ma who cannot be denied. God help you, Violet!

Violet started talking, scrambling desperately for higher ground. But Ma took every broken phrase and mended it, every vacant sentence and filled it, every crumpled paragraph and smoothed it out. There was nothing Violet could say which Ma could not make sense of. She parsed her mangled verbs, restored her tangled syntax, corrected the grammar of her madness. Violet never had a chance to sustain her craziness. Ma absolutely refused her the indulgence.

But Violet still resisted, threw down her hands, and started gabbing again. Ma was on her tail in an instant, unraveling whatever Violet twisted, loosening the knots with which she tried to bind herself. To put it a little coldly, it was like watching one of those video games where you have to keep a racing car on the track at ever steeper curves and faster speeds. However fast Violet went, Ma kept her on the road, unswervingly sensible.

At last, her madness outstripped, Violet collapsed in Ma's arms and cried for a long time.

Ma held her, stroked her hair, told her over and over that she loved her, and demanded to know when she was going to stop the nonsense. She made it plain to Violet that it was all a matter of will, of free choice. If she wanted to be well, she would be well. The responsibility was all hers.

But even as she held her, like a rumpled rag doll with all the strenuous craziness tugged out of her, Ma looked across at me and pouted, and I knew that Violet was not going to choose to recover her wits, not yet at any rate. She still wanted to be crazy, and Ma had to let her go.

Last we heard, she was in a hospital outside Atlanta. The conditions are all right. She has her own bed, at least.

But when I think of her or of any of the crazy people who for one reason or another have turned away Ma's help over the years, I remember a few lines of Rumi, with their comforting but terrible hyperbole:

> *Don't run away from this dying.*
> *Whoever's not killed for love is dead meat.*
> *In the shambles of love, they kill only the best.*

When I remember to put Violet in my prayers, I ask that she be given the courage to die. She was one of the best.

Make ready to die, make ready to live.

* * *

It is the middle of January. Yesterday some of the children made kites at school, and just before noon I walked down to the river meadow, and there was Ganga, all by herself, having once more escaped from the pine grove by the old church where we have our kindergarten, Ganga drawn down past the grazing Appaloosa mares to the banks of the river where it turns in the winter sunlight, launching her kite hand over hand and not with much success until, as I came up from behind the wild primrose willows, the wind suddenly snatched it and snapped it taut in her tight grip, and she tugged it down, her eyes fierce with self-possession and sudden mastery.

We both held our breaths as the breath of the wind heaved in the thin breast of the red and black bird she had fashioned out of paper and sticks and string.

The river turning at our feet, the kite flying high above, no words.

Who will leave this place?

What place?

No place.

No words, no teaching, no place, only this place we have called our shining Kashi after the sacred city on the Ganges, this place which is no place, with its river meadow and spit of brambles, its pond and pine flatwoods and oak hammocks, its screen of bamboo running along the county road, the wooden temple to the Son of the Wind with its hoop of bayberry proof against the winter frost, and the garden of holly and blue daze and yellow thryallis consecrated to Christ.

No place, where Ma has sung her simple song of the river for twelve years.

> *Children play by my river,*
> *Sadhus stay by my river,*
> *Cities old by my river,*
> *Temples gold by my river,*
> *Cows stray by my river,*
> *Night into day by my river…*

What place? For three thousand years, Indians at the end of their lives have gone to Kashi to die, in the belief that dying by the Ganga frees them forever. *Kashyam maranam muktih:* to die in Kashi is to live forever. Here in the center of the ancient city are the great burning ghats, Manikarnika, where the dead are brought on bamboo litters to be burned, their ashes scattered on the river.

With her last breath the dying wanderer is held in the lap of the goddess Annapurna, she who gives life, while Shiva, who takes life in order to restore it, whispers in her ear the secret of the *taraka*, the crossing, which will carry her over to the shore of life. The whisper fills her with understanding and light, the life-giving, luminous awareness from which Kashi, which means "shining awareness," takes its name.

No place. A place to die, a place to live. Wherever one sits and makes ready to die, makes ready to live, is Kashi, so Kashi is any place and no place, and death in Kashi is not the death of the body but of the separate self, the death of ignorance and delusion; and Shiva's whisper forbids Death himself, Yama, who by a tradition as old as the river is not allowed within the bounds of Kashi, nor ever to bathe in the Ganga.

Everywhere and nowhere. Ma's teacher Nityananda says as much in his *The Sky of the Heart*: "But Kashi is the sky of the heart. The mind is Kashi, everything is Kashi, the eternal Self is Kashi."

Ganga, barely six years old, tugs at her kite as it dips and hurtles over the brown river, its red and black breast of paper and brittle ribs of sticks puffing on the wind.

And every time the kite climbs higher, Ganga lets out the string, mastering with fierce and joyful concentration the breath of her flying bird. And I see in the stillness and freedom of her wild eyes not just the mastery of the breath that gives breath to her young life, but also the purity of her appetite for living, and the fulfillment of all possible longing, the resolution of every fear that may ever arise to assail her, and the constancy of her happiness.

My Ganga, eyes of black pearl, river of dazzling white…

Mother, child, my river.

It is for our freedom that Ma has made her sacrifice and sings her song, a song of mother, child and river.

> *Children play, sadhus stay*
> *Cities old, temples gold*
> *Cows stray, sadhus yearn*
> *Wise men learn, ghats burn*
> *Men die, widows cry*
> *All come, saying Ram*
> *The sun falls, the sun rises*
> *The river holds no surprises*
> *Always the same, never the same*
> *The Ganga—that is her name*
> *The black pearl sheds such light*
> *Even in the darkest night*
> *The old woman, the older man*
> *They come down the mountain hand in hand*

THOMAS "BILLY" BYROM

He takes her to the Ganga to die
He does not ask why
The river
The giver.

7

Grandma Lulu Breaks Her Silence

Midwinter.

Last night it dropped just below freezing. The tow burners were set out in the orange groves at the north end of the lines to catch and carry the wind. The river and the woods gave us some shelter from the cold, but by morning when the frost had melted off the spike rush in the pond and the bracken fern in the flatwoods, they had been burned black. Even the hardy toestripper and the saltwort had been a little singed, and most of the rattlebox was gone, except in the low places, and the summer snow blossoms had blackened and melted with the frost.

A frost first whitens, then blackens, and we have lost most of our garden.

Yet this is just nature's pruning, the first of the winter, and there will surely be another, and then everything green will spring back in a few months, with hardly the touch of human hands.

For now there is a peculiar absolute beauty in this white and black visitation. It has nothing desolate about it, only the promise of reviving life.

We make ready to live, we make ready to die.

* * *

THOMAS "BILLY" BYROM

The inner life commonly requires three practices: devotion, contemplation, and service. The first is the ground of the second, the second of the third; yet they are of one essence, and they succeed only when they are not practiced, that is, when a white and black frost, a frost without the least desolation but only the assurance of resurrection, has burned back every intention, all striving.

"Striving is the root of sorrow," says the poet of *The Heart of Awareness*, "but who understands this?"

When we first settled that fall of 1976, most of us still perceived the inner life as purposeful, and coming as some of us did from the various forms of commitment to social action of the sixties and seventies, we supposed we would soon find a chance to serve the local community, even perhaps—such was our vanity—to reform it.

It was on the face of it grievously in need of help. The Old South was everywhere, deeply entrenched. Black people were confined to two towns of the deepest poverty. As for the New South, it served only what a British Conservative Prime Minister once called "the ugly face of capitalism." Everywhere we turned there was a deep apartheid, white and black, rich and poor, separate and unequal.

On the barrier island between the Indian River lagoon and the ocean, large enclaves of wealthy whites had settled, guard houses at their gates, mock Georgian mansions on the sea or inland waterway, no Blacks, a few Jews in deep disguise. Half a mile west as the brown pelicans fly lay Gifford, a classic of rural poverty, and a fifteen minutes ride north on U.S. 1 was Wabasso, where Blacks and a few migrant farm families lived in shacks along dirt roads without water or toilets.

Vero Beach itself in the late '70s was almost completely segregated. Civil rights laws were in place and enforced by a fair-minded city council and county commissioners. Blacks attended desegregated schools, and if there had been a bus system, they could have sat up front.

But there was little common life between White and Black, little shared, except in a few of the churches. Segregation was still the natural order, the town was the home of two societies. All that had truly changed was that it was no longer always respectable to express racist sentiments in public.

I was reminded by all this of Vaucluse, the affluent white suburb in Sydney where I had been brought up after the War, and of La Perouse, a few miles away, a ghetto for aborigines.

Within a few months of our settling in Sebastian, the Klan had burned crosses two or more times on our front yard, the local version at that time of the welcome wagon. The police showed up in the morning, a strictly unofficial visit, to kick over the ashes and express regret. It was just their way of letting us know that they recognized us all, by our dress, our manner, our odor, as Yankees—no matter that we were a very curious mixture of German, English, Irish, Australian, Spanish, Greek, Polish—to them, our nature and provenance was Yankee.

But for our changing their world they need not have worried.

Ma, who rarely had time for politics or social ideologies, soon made it plain what she thought of our fretful social schemes, our professions of altruism, and the vague intensity of our desire to serve.

"What have you got to give?" she wanted to know. "You're all so self-important, so dry. You're all too messed up."

We could talk all we wanted of Tolstoy's *Resurrection*, or St. Paul to the Galatians, or Lincoln's Second Inaugural, or Gandhi or King or Chavez, of our days in SDS and at the barricades in Paris and Berkeley and Harvard Square. The more conservative among us, the mortgage banker, the stockbroker, the businessman, the heirs to a few not immodest fortunes, could talk philanthropy till they were blue in the face.

"When you have something to give, then give," Ma said. "You want to help the poor? What about the rich? Have you thought of their poverty? Who's going to care for them when they're lonely and left out? Did you ever really think of their fear and unhappiness? You want to serve, serve down and dirty, inside not outside. And you have to be down and dirty yourself to serve from the inside. So put up, or shut up."

Actually her language was a good deal rougher than this, but that was the gist of it, and we understood that before we could pretend to feed, we first had to embrace an inner poverty. First, the mastery of appetite, and only then the true servitude of service, that most presumptuous of privileges.

If I had known then that with this scolding Ma was setting us up for an exacting and arduous apprenticeship in the art of service, I might have kept my tenure at Oxford and pursued an academic life. Yet the setup was purely spontaneous and inescapable. At first she never declared a program of service. She simply put us down in the country in a couple of houses and said, "Now live together."

We assumed that this would come naturally since we loved each other and shared an intense, inner calling.

What was it, after all, to clean the kitchen, empty the trash, feed the dogs, mow the lawn, weed the garden? I had to polish the silver, iron the handkerchiefs, and wax the floor at the age of seven. What was it to rise at six, sit for half an hour in meditation, sing for a little, and then start work? Nothing, to be sure, that most people could not accomplish without too much trouble every day. As I say, the routine of my childhood had been a great deal stricter, and never harsh. The only truly different circumstance was that we lived more closely together, and not always as family or chosen friends, but as fellow seekers whose common interest was spiritual, not social or biological.

Naturally we assumed that our high ideals would quickly master these merely material arrangements.

But something very strange and untoward happened.

Almost from the start, after perhaps a week or two of cleanliness and moderate domestic amity, we began to resist and resent our tasks. We fudged or skirted them altogether, or if we finished them, it was with a dry and angry perfectionism. I cannot say that everyone faltered or strained. There were some to whom service of this kind continued to be natural and easy.

But for most of us I began to perceive that our little tasks suddenly became huge, and the occasions of a great contest between our positive attitudes and a potent host of negative passions.

In the first six months, when I wasn't at Oxford, it was my job to feed the dogs and give them their medicine, a task I shared with a young woman whom I loved very much. As I've said, I was never allowed pets when I was young, so I was not used to looking after animals, though I liked them a lot. My friend on the other hand was a great and experienced dog lover, who enjoyed playing with them and teaching them tricks. She taught me how to administer their heartworm pills, how to hold the jaw shut and stroke the dog's throat so he can swallow easily and safely. I was clumsy at first, but I soon learned.

Then my friend and I fell out.

I observed that while she loved the dogs and always played with them, she often forgot to feed them or to give them their pills. When I confronted her with this, she became incensed and accused me of not really caring for the dogs—after all, did I ever play with them? I merely did my duty.

Of course, we were both wrong. I was too busy looking after them to love them, and she was too busy loving them to look after them.

She was slack, I was taut. Neither of us had found the proper tension between awareness and love, and beyond that tension their essential identity. And in judging each other we abandoned ourselves first to irritation, then to anger, and finally to fury. We all but came to blows over the poor animals.

Unable to resolve our quarrel, we took it at last to Ma.

Her only comment was, "See! You can't even feed the dogs! And you want to go out and save the migrant farm workers? You'd treat *them* like dogs, you're so *righteous*."

Righteous?

I had trouble with the word. At first I concluded that she meant self-righteous, and we were certainly that. But on reflection I realized that she meant simply that we were too attached to *any* idea of right or wrong, not merely an obviously self-serving view, and that any fixed or settled moral opinion is likely to be just another mental fiction, a strategy by which the little self secures its authenticity and its radical perspective of deceit—and is therefore always a false ground for service. And for the first time I was able to understand the very odd opening of the tenth chapter, "On Desire," of *The Heart of Awareness*, the essential scripture of Advaita Vedanta which we took with us on our morning rides:

> *Seeking or striving,*
> *For pleasure or prosperity,*
> *These are your enemies,*
> *Springing up to destroy you*
> *From the presumptions of virtue.*

Whenever there is the *fixed* presumption of viewpoint, both in the sense of morality and perspective, whenever opinion takes hold, there can be no identity of love and awareness. And we were both surely fixed, very stuck in our righteousness.

Of course the lesson did not end there.

It was also my duty to supply and turn the compost heap which we were tending for our garden, and in this work my partner was a gentle Bavarian whose theories were as firm as his actions were vague. He had a very confident, indeed a visionary, idea of how the heap should accumulate. But when it came to doing any of the work, he was at best irresolute. This he felt was properly my business, while his was to stand off at a distance and measure my progress, to determine the true *Gestalt* and biology of the pile with a detachment at once aesthetic and scientific. He devised a pleasing arrangement of rows, but he was not eager to hear how much extra work his particulars demanded, though he always received my protests with a great deal of patience and love.

From time to time he would lend a hand. But more often than not his back bothered him, and then he felt compelled to sacrifice the active life for the contemplative.

As the heap grew, so my fury mounted. I could not figure out how I had been eased into such an arduous subservience, and my temper was held in check only by two wholly selfish reflections: the first, that the hard work was good for me, body and soul, for after all I was every bit as lazy as my overseer; the second, that in the scheme of things his laziness would come back upon him like chaff blown against the wind, with biblical or karmic retribution. What God must have in store for him! I fumed, as my shovel flew under the steaming humus with avenging fury.

Before long we were nearly at each other's throats, he astonished at my rage and lovingly sure of his own sacrifice, and myself maddened beyond reason by his foolproof indolence.

I came very close to felling all six foot four of him with my hoe.

When we took our quarrel at last to Ma, all she would say was, "You see! You can't even shovel shit! And you want to go out and save the world."

THOMAS "BILLY" BYROM

The months passed, and the seasons, and neither our tempers nor our patience greatly improved. I came to see that Ma had engaged all of us, unsuspecting, in a long and epic struggle. Our few acres on the banks of the Sebastian River were the true battlefield, the Kurukshetra of the *Bhagavad Gita*, upon which all our inner warfare was waged. House chores and yard work became the focal points of intensely hostile feelings: not irritation but rage, not spite but savage malice, not passing envies but barbarous jealousy, not mild conceit but monstrous pride, not flirting attraction but incendiary lust, not little grudges but obdurate hatred.

We were burning in a bonfire of passions, and the fuel was the combustible powder of judgment which we flung at each other.

When at length, after warming her hands at the blaze for a few seasons, Ma spoke openly of our firestorms, she drew our attention again both to St. Thérèse of Lisieux and St. Teresa of Ávila.

"This is St. Thérèse's little way, but it's no different for the bands of sadhus who wander around India sharing their fires at night, and their rice and dhal. Do you think it's so different for nuns and monks in closed orders?" And she reminded us that St. Thérèse won her final battle when she was able to accept the splashing of the nun who washed clothes next to her as a blessing, not an insult. And for Teresa it was the same, only fiercer.

"You think these are little things? They are what you make them. And if you're ready to get really down and dirty, you can master them, and in mastering them you master yourself. But first you have to get down and dirty like Teresa."

It was a matter of abandoning the clean presumptions of virtue, which lie at the root of all seeking and striving. It was a matter of surrendering all judgment, all righteousness, so that by sticking my head in the dirt of my own downright sense of right and wrong I might discover within myself the love I lacked while feeding the dogs or shoveling the compost, so that my fellow seekers, embracing the earth, might discover for themselves an awareness without which their love, however full, was incomplete.

Service is possible, so I came to see, only in the measure that judgment, dissolving, no longer divides love and awareness.

In orthodox Hindu fashion Ma sometimes identified these engagements as the eternal struggle between Shiva and Shakti, a divine battle of the sexes which takes place not only between men and women but between the man and the woman in every human heart. Shiva represents essence, pure awareness, unconditioned emptiness and stillness. His consort Shakti represents the power of creation, manifest abundance, the fruition of love, fruitful form. When they merge everything is as it is. In each of us, in every moment, this warfare is freshly engaged, this militant making of love, until we discover the true and constant identity of Shiva in Shakti, and Shakti in Shiva: that is, until we resolve the illusory tension between awareness and love, emptiness and fullness, stillness and activity, tight and loose, inside and outside, essence and existence, and we affirm them as one.

True service can only be undertaken as this struggle becomes more aware and more wholehearted, as the wholeheartedness becomes more aware, and awareness more wholehearted. Of course the seeker does not simply sit around and wait for the illusion to resolve itself. He works to awaken awareness with love, and to arouse love with awareness. And in those rare, spontaneously-won moments when love and awareness are, as they already are, naturally one, then "they also serve who only stand and wait," as Milton says.

Ma's way, as I have sketched it here, is to accomplish this by first laboring at small things, the immediate, natural, and spontaneous occasions for service which present themselves to us every day.

"Who sweeps a room," George Herbert wrote, "as for thy laws, makes that and the action fine."

THOMAS "BILLY" BYROM

Only in the fierce patience which alone masters the little things may we hope to dissolve righteousness and all its spotless presumptions, and discover that identity of love and awareness which is the only ground of service.

> *Before kingdoms change, men must change.*
> —Attributed to John the Baptist

* * *

The call comes from Chicago. Mark, who has AIDS, is dying.

Mark is Ma's chela, but he has chosen to live in the world and perform *seva*, service. After Stanford he took a job as an investigative reporter on the *Chicago Tribune*. In his first year he worked with street gangs, and his report won him a place as a finalist in the public service competition for a Pulitzer. The following year he won the Robert F. Kennedy award for helping write a series, "The American Millstone," about the plight of the urban poor. And this year he won first place in the Education Writers Association for his work on immigrant children and bilingual education.

He has been a true servant of oppressed and destitute children. He has served them from a profound faith in Christ, and he has been encouraged along the way by his devotion to Ma. Now he is dying, and he needs help.

In a few hours Ma and Yashoda are on a plane to Chicago.

Every day for a year Mark's roommate Michael, who has also been Ma's student for many years, has helped bandage his feet and disguise the lesions on his face so that Mark can go out and work. He cannot give up his children, despite his terrible debility. He forces himself to eat: if he throws up, he forces himself to eat again. He has Kaposi's sarcoma and now lung cancer, but such is his determination that no one at work knows he is sick. No one knows he is dying.

Every day he goes out into the city to investigate abuses in the juvenile justice system.

In his moments of despair he has asked Ma, "What difference can it make?"

She has always said, fiercely, "Yes, it matters. *You* must fight death. You must fight for your kids."

Yet a week before the call from Chicago, a wealthy woman from the beachside, suffering from breast cancer, came to see Ma. She had just learned that the cancer had spread to her liver. Ma did not tell her to fight. Instead, she spoke quietly, firmly and for a long time about preparing for death, and she made her promise to keep coming back to her.

We make ready to die, we make ready to live.

I, too, have cancer.

Fifteen years ago I began to have drenching night sweats. After a while I had a blood test, then a bone marrow aspiration. I was told I had leukemia, and had four, perhaps five, years to live.

But Ma said, "Fight it. Beat it."

In the first five years I must have tried every therapy under the sun. Since no healing system had ever cured my form of cancer, I felt the only rational course was to try everything, without prejudice. So I went from conventional chemotherapy to macrobiotic diet to Bach flower remedies, imaging, metabolics, enzyme injections, Tibetan herbs, iridology, reflexology, acupressure, shiatsu, homeopathy, Ayurvedic potions. I even went down to one of those holistic hospitals in Mexico.

When I returned from Mexico and found I was still alive, riding a horse every day at dawn with a bloated spleen, a platelet count of two million and a white blood count of a quarter of a million, I decided to settle for ordinary chemotherapy—blessed as I was with a doctor of the deepest caring—and a diet free of meat, toxins, sugar, with plenty of grains, fresh vegetables, fruits and large daily doses of vitamin C and beta carotene, and a little homeopathy.

But I knew then, and am even more certain now, that what has mattered is not the therapy but my attitude, which I learned from Ma—*"Fight!"*

And I understood that fighting death means, above all, loving life.

Sick or well, this is the first lesson of our spiritual apprenticeship, our *guruvasa*. The first and last service the teacher renders her chela is teaching him how to embrace the earth. It is both her lesson and her sacrifice, the burden of the river song, how she sat on the banks for a year and a day and then gave herself back to the river, to herself, losing him, but winning us—Mark, myself, hundreds of others, all in order to show us how to love life, and live to the full.

So today she has flown to Chicago to tell Mark he is not yet ready to die. She dips him once more in the river. She holds him in her arms, and helps Michael change the dressings. The lesions on his feet are so bad he has to be carried to the bathroom.

"Next week," she tells him, "you will be up and about again. And out the door if you want, and helping those kids. Even if you touch only one more kid, it's worth it. I'll help you," she bargains, "if you help them, OK?"

"OK," he says, and falls asleep, a rosary in his hand and a small figure of Hanuman on the table by his bed.

Ma and Yashoda take the evening flight back to Orlando, where we pick them up. Coming out of the folding tunnel, Ma looks battered and happy.

MA & ME

"I never bet on a dead horse," she reminds us. "He's not dying on me yet, the little...." As usual her language was rougher than I care to represent it.

Mark struggled for another five months through the winter. Towards the end, though his lungs were riddled with cancer and he had open wounds on his face and his feet, he grew quiet and happy.

Then Ma said it was time, and she called to say goodbye, almost casually. She did not make much of it, and neither did Mark. He fell into a deep sleep the next morning.

At noon his father came by with a plaque—yet another award, this one for his investigation of the juvenile justice system in Chicago—but could not rouse him.

*　*　*

St. Vincent's Hospital, Sydney, Christmas Eve, 1947.

I remember her walking down the corridor toward us, a very small woman, barely a head higher than my sister or me. I was six, my sister five. She swept toward us with an air of deep conspiracy, her finger at her lips. I remember the white nurse's habit and the nun's white cowl, and her fresh cheeks and sharp blue eyes. I suppose she must have been in her thirties.

My father had forgotten some papers and had returned to his laboratory, leaving us with Quispel the Registrar, his desk looming over us in the dark lobby. And the corridor was darkly burnished with floor wax, heavy with the smell of ether and carbolic, and the sunlight through the glass doors was a long way off. I remember we were both sleepy with excitement because tomorrow was Christmas—rising at dawn to tear open our presents, a dozen of us sitting down at noon with the windows thrown open to the summer winds, and then excavating the plum pudding for threepenny bits of shining silver wrapped in greaseproof paper, and brandy butter balls. And on Boxing Day the prospect of two months on the empty beach, Whale Beach, beyond Avalon and Bilgolah, which we shared with a few other families just after the war.

"There you are my dears!" she said, sweeping us up as if we were the only people in the world. "I've been looking all over for you. *Here!*"

And she took from the folds of her robes a couple of presents, brightly wrapped and tied with gold thread, and with the same deep air of conspiracy, she pressed them into our hands.

"Now don't open them till tomorrow, mind!"

She stood there like a bright bird, only a little taller than us, a child herself, her eyes full of a strange happiness and gratitude, as if we had given *her* presents; and then, seeing my father coming, she vanished.

"I see Sister Clare has found you," my father said roughly, when he returned. He had a North Country suspicion of papists, and, besides, he was a professed atheist. "Cum dona ferentes!" he warned us darkly, and of course I had no idea what he meant. But I could see that he was also secretly pleased, and he let us keep the presents, and tipped his hat to the sister's back.

In this brief encounter there was nothing extraordinary, except that there were many poorer children to whom Sister Clare might have given the presents, and that my father's scruples had mysteriously melted a little. Yet I think there has never been a month in my life when I have not remembered it. I cannot recall what my present was, nor my sister's, but the feeling with which it was given is as fresh in my heart as if I had received it yesterday.

I realized, if not at once, still at an early age, that her gift had not been the toy or the sweets or whatever the wrapping held, but the feeling of gratitude with which she gave. I say *gratitude*, for that is what it was, yet it was something else as well, something I cannot properly describe or account for now, any better than I could then.

Somehow she gave me a measure of her own love. She simply reached out and put it in my heart. I never saw her again, though I was often at the hospital with my father. But I have never forgotten her, and that single moment of giving nearly half a century ago runs like a thread, unbroken, through all my years. Something mean and fearful in me was so discomposed in that instant of love that my life has always been, because of her gift, larger and more daring.

* * *

Day in and day out for more than a dozen years we have toiled in our small orchard, and it is clear that most of us have many more years of apprenticeship to our deeper natures before we can hope to serve freely. Of the fifty or so who are assigned yard or house work, only three or four are able to serve with a clear emptiness, and only nine or ten make themselves freely accountable to direction. If we had rules for work, of course, it would be quite different: so many prostrations for failing to polish the kitchen floor. But rules compel, and no service is free if it is in the least manner compelled. So we have no rules, except against drugs, which mean instant expulsion.

But for all our resistance, Ma began a few years ago tentatively to entrust and encourage a few of us to engage in outside service, and we set up a small group to which we gave the name *Annadana*, "the gift of food," "nourishment," and also, to honor Ma's mother, "the gift of Anna." And one of the first projects was to help open and run a soup kitchen in the Black township of Gifford.

The teachers take with them some of the teenagers from our school, which we had established years before in order to protect our children from the racism and drugs in the public system. One of our young kids came home from school one day and asked his father, who is Jewish, and his mother, who is Black, what a "n----r" was. Within two months we had built a small red schoolhouse in our front field, and later we added a day care center and a kindergarten. Soon we had eighty children, a third from the neighborhood.

We don't mind the teens missing school a couple of mornings a week to help out in the soup kitchen. I run them through their Latin declensions and conjugations after dinner, if necessary. Besides, we conceive of practical service as essential to their learning—more important than religious instruction, which we have so far left out of the curriculum in the belief that children should be free to make their own religious choices, and that God draws each of us to him in the way that most pleases him.

But curiously enough, our first work was not with the poor, but with the wealthy. It happens that many of us, even those with advanced college degrees, have chosen to work as housecleaners or caretakers in the affluent enclaves over on the barrier island, jobs which offer flexible schedules that allow us to spend time with Ma. And in many of these engagements in service, we have had the chance to relieve the terrible poverty of the rich—a cruel poverty indeed! I would hazard a guess that there are more broken and damaged hearts in John's Island, one of the richest developments, than in Gifford. The poverty of inner neglect and friendlessness and loneliness can be cruel beyond all imagining, especially when there's no inner faith.

We have not shaken the earth or changed the world. We have simply touched a few who needed help. But I am confident that because of our long and painstaking training we have not done much harm. Our help, though tentative, has been direct and uncomplicated. In very small ways we have started to give, if not unconditionally, at least with some wholeheartedness and some measure of awareness. Because we have been scrubbed a little cleaner ourselves, we have been able to give more cleanly, without taking too much in return. And in our beginning to serve we have learned to understand, with Mother Teresa of Calcutta, that what matters is not how much we give, but the love we put into giving.

She inspires us even more deeply, though it is difficult for those who are not in religious life to understand, when she says serving the poor is not her vocation; belonging to Jesus is her vocation. Ma says the same thing: "See everyone you serve as God, just as Hanuman did."

I have a few old friends who, in the spirit of our generation, have dedicated themselves to lives of service. Some now run large programs that literally help millions. Our ideals are mostly the same, and their work, in its reach, far outruns my own.

But I cannot pretend that our deepest motives are any longer the same. They have not heard the same call, nor can they understand its mystery, which they are often given to decry. For them Martha of the Gospels had the better part, and to persuade them otherwise, as I tried to do a long time ago when I was new to all this and eager to convince, is to quarrel uselessly.

Besides, I have come to understand that my own attribution of motives, especially to myself, is bound to be self-serving, however loudly I profess Christ and Hanuman, and that what matters is the purity of heart with which we give, and never our account of it.

But if we are still quarrelling, still unable to give even in small ways without withholding or wanting something in return, still grudging and mean-spirited, if we are still unwilling to see that to leave dirty dishes in the sink or a floor unswept is to lose the whole battle, entirely, then we will find ourselves still confined to our small orchard, as yet too clumsy and self-serving to assume the larger task that awaits us. If we offered our services without restraint now it would be a useless condescension, and we would change little or nothing.

For it is a hard-learned fact that suffering can never be relieved by merely material means. It will only return, because its roots have not been taken up. Real relief only occurs when the spiritual infuses the material. When Mother Teresa lifts a leprous beggar from the gutter, as I have seen Ma do in Rishikesh in the Himalayan foothills, it is only their love for Christ and Hanuman which truly raises him.

They bathe him in the juice of their devotion, and God loosens the bonds of their suffering a little, or once and for all. Or when Ma flies up to Chicago to encourage Mark to fight a little longer, she helps him not so much by dressing his lesions as by drenching him in the love of God, which washes away the roots of his suffering.

Service can never be dry. It must always be wet, sopping wet, always soaked in the love of Hanuman or the wounds of Christ.

True service raises the cup of God's love to the lips of the broken man who cries out, as God Himself cried out, broken on the cross, "I thirst!"

> *Service is from the heart, not the hands.*
> *It is from being, not doing.*
> *Not what you do, but who you are, changes the world.*
> *Only the heart serves.*
> —Ma

* * *

Lulu is from Gifford. Longer ago than anyone clearly recalls, Lulu fell into a deep depression and lost her tongue. Her husband deserted her, leaving her in the care of the county. They put her in the nursing home on the road to the new hospital, though she was barely forty. All she had was a cotton print dress, a yellow cardigan, and a pair of plastic pumps. No one had heard her speak a word since she was a young woman.

There she sat on the edge of her bed all day, or on the wooden chair beside it, not yet fifty going on seventy, staring at her hands or off into the distance, marooned far away on some reef of silence from which no one could rescue her; and no one knew by what terrible mishap or simple grief she was stranded there.

We have fifteen children in our kindergarten, six boys and nine girls. Last year Ma asked the teachers to take them once or twice a month to visit the nursing home. So they polished up some of their songs and every second Thursday rode into Vero Beach to entertain the old folks.

Ganga is five. She naturally took command when the children arrived, and from the start they were a big hit. When they sang, the old people crowded around and some joined in, and afterwards they played with the kids and put them on their laps and chattered happily.

All except Lulu, who held back, never saying a word or paying any attention, however keenly the nurses prompted her. She just sat in a chair, staring at her knees, and after a while, knowing her intractability, the nurses always gave up.

But on their second or third visit Ganga noticed Lulu, and when their songs were sung, she went over to her and sat on the bed beside her, and talked, and talked.

Ganga hardly cares if she has an audience or someone who will talk back. For her the important thing is the breathless unraveling of the endless narrative of astonishing events which constitute the personal histories of her and her friends and her family, and it would not occur to her that these tales might be less fascinating to a stranger than they are to herself. She is the sun in her own sky, and she does not mind whom she warms.

On the third or fourth visit, in the middle of this one-sided conversation, Ganga happened to take Lulu's hand, the better to fix her attention, or perhaps without any real thought or design; and after that, since Lulu did not resist, Ganga held onto her, and from time to time, she would shake or poke or pat her hand, though Lulu scarcely looked at her, and never smiled, and never said a word.

A few months went by. Ganga always sought Lulu out and made sure to fill her in on the latest amazements in her huge, singular life, always pressing the really breathtaking parts into Lulu's palm or milking her fingers for the right words whenever they would not come.

But Lulu said nothing.

Then one day, in the late fall, Ganga suddenly stopped in midstream, and fell silent herself, and letting go of Lulu's hand, and drawing her into the black depths of her eyes, she said, "Grandma Lulu, I love you. Why don't you talk to me? Don't you like me?"

A tear, held back half a lifetime, gathered in Lulu's eye, and fell down her cheek.

She took Ganga's hand in her own and she said, "I love you too, Ganga."

And now Lulu's sorrow often lifts, and then she talks to everyone.

She doesn't say much, but she talks to everyone.

* * *

By the pond, as I've said, we have a small temple dedicated to Hanuman. To the local fundamentalists we are lost souls because we worship a monkey. It is no use explaining to these strenuous literalists that Hanuman expresses the perfect humility of God, that he takes a form lower than human in order to serve humanity, before whom he kneels humbly, in the traditional figuration. And to the local liberals and sophisticates we are superstitious cultists. It is one thing to steep yourself in Joseph Campbell, and quite another to find your neighbors trying to live freely the universal truths he discovers in his comparison of religious and folk traditions. We have learned through painful trial that it is futile to reassure either the literalists or the symbolists that Hanuman is both the real and the ideal expression of compassion and social service, and that his tradition is of the greatest antiquity, and the deepest practical meaning, and the occasion for a hundred generations of lovely sculpture and exalted poetry and paintings.

Were I to tell them that I have known him as entirely real, a living presence and friend, they would want to lock me away.

Anyway, we offer both anathemas, secular and religious, to the eternal fire which we keep burning day and night in front of Hanuman's temple, and we ask for clarity and generosity, never to judge in return or to put another out of our hearts. Hanuman's teaching, like Christ's, is against all judgment, against opinion itself, which lies under a rotting leaf-drift of pride and ignorance at the root of judgment.

Hanuman would have us see everything as one, without distinction, as it truly is.

Hanuman is service. In Tulsi Das's *Ramayana* he is the ideal servant of God and man. When the demon Ravana steals Sita, the wife of King Rama, and carries her off to Lanka, Hanuman springs across the ocean, and setting fire to the demon's city with his tail, he rescues Sita and restores her to her husband. That is, when the Mind rapes the Soul and steals her away from God, the Heart slays the Mind, and restores the Soul to her Beloved.

This is the heart and the true form of all service. When every act of giving, however small, is dedicated to restoring the ravished soul to God, it becomes infinite. When the heart submits itself to this single and essential service, all its actions are consecrated and holy.

In their own way the fundamentalists are right in supposing us guilty of a terrible blasphemy, since in aspiring to live up to Hanuman's example and in hoping to imitate Christ's, we make no distinction of conscience, inspiration, or action between them. Hanuman is often represented as tearing open his breast to reveal God, Mother, and Brother in his heart; just as Christ is sometimes depicted with his heart exposed, crowned with thorns and a single flame, an image we owe to the inspiration of Saint John Eudes, a priest from Normandy who worked with prostitutes and the sick and who first encouraged devotion to the heart of Jesus.

For us these images are equally moving, indeed they are the same, and therein lies our blasphemy, I suppose.

For us Hanuman is Christ. Christ is Hanuman. The love of each assumes the other. Each exposes his heart to serve God. Each submits in perfect humility to the service of humanity. When the soul cries out, "For I was hungry and ye gave me to eat; I was thirsty, and ye gave me drink; I was a stranger and ye took me in; naked, and ye clothed me," so Sita cries out with the same sublime gratitude, "O my Beloved, who fulfills my every need, O my Master, remember your compassionate promise to the afflicted and relieve my grievous distress."

Then God sends Christ and Hanuman to help us.

The purpose of service is not just to relieve material suffering but to put an end to the soul's separation. Indeed, to the true servant of Love, they are one and the same. *Karma yoga*, of which Hanuman is the perfect emblem, means "one with God through service," both for the one who serves and for the one who is served. When Christ fed the five thousand on a few loaves and fishes, the miracle was not just that he made the food go so far: it was in feeding a more than material hunger. The fish and the bread, so wonderfully multiplied, were what devotees of Hanuman would call prasad, food for the hungry soul, to end its terrible isolation, to slake its burning thirst when it has wandered from the one well of all being.

So it is with all true service, which is never merely material. It must treat even the grossest form as pure spirit. True servitude always remembers that matter is an illusion, Ravana's cruelest trick, Satan's perfect temptation. But when they are outwitted by the simplicity of the naked heart surrendered to God, the hands that feed the poor feed Christ, and Christ himself is called to take his own communion.

What we give in the knowledge that everything that lives is holy, we give to God, and our giving becomes infinite, like Christ's.

This is the mystery of the body of Christ, my own body, as it is the mystery of the torn breast of Hanuman, my own breast.

When Christ on the cross cried out, "I thirst!" he cried out for all mankind, the cry of all those who suffer, the cry of the body broken by the world and the spirit torn from her Beloved—the same cry, one and the same, which we must all hurry to answer, until every broken body is mended and every hungry heart is fed.

> *Now pray the prayer of action,*
> *which is the fragrant flowering of the soul.*
>
> —St. Catherine of Siena, The Dialogue

* * *

Tonight Ma is talking to Eddie. He is West Indian, a psychiatric nurse in charge of a ward full of troubled teenagers in a hospital to which the local courts refer their more difficult cases—assault, drugs, attempted suicide. He has two or three children who have resisted his best efforts to help them. Like Lulu they have just given up, they won't be touched. Eddie has come seeking Ma's advice, knowing how many troubled teens she has taken off drugs and restored to sound livelihood, good schooling, and hope.

She listens closely, but when he has finished his account, she asks him about himself and not about the children.

Soon he is spilling his own troubles into her lap, and I can see that she has first undertaken to give him the strength and self-love he needs at home so that he will truly have something to give at work.

She talks to him about the need for detachment and humor, how one requires the other, and about the value of laughter in compassionate service. He is dry and tight. Ma tickles him, dunks him, teases him, cuffs him; and only then, when he has reclaimed something of his own independent strength, she gives him specific advice for some of his troubled charges.

Unreformably theatrical though she is, Ma has no time for tragedy or the posturings of sorrow and fear. She does not make light of Eddie's concerns, yet she makes everything light—light and deep that is—with the kind of humor that is both self-critical and all-embracing.

St. Catherine of Siena's nickname as a little girl was "Euphrosyne," the muse of comedy, because she was always laughing. It is recounted that even at the height of the plague, when she worked day and night in the hospital, she was always playing tricks and making fun of her *bella brigata*, her little band of helpers.

It is the same with Ma. Her classes, her conversation, her every exchange with the world are wrapped in laughter, and if tears come later, there is always more laughter to dry them.

If helping people depends upon the identity of love and awareness, and this in turn arises from the mastery of desire, and if judgment lies at the root of our appetites, as the ancient poet of *The Heart of Awareness* insists, then what more powerful solvent of judgment than laughter?

Who can laugh and judge at the same time?

This truth is not just poetic or scriptural. It is entirely practical. In the deep and spontaneous joy of our essential nature, and in the free and natural laughter with which we most deeply express our true selves, love and awareness lose all distinctions, and in the unfettered joy of giving we discover who we already and always are, infinitely happy and undivided and free.

MA & ME

That my joy may be in you,
and that your joy may be made full.

—*John 15:11*

* * *

In front of the Hanuman Temple overlooking the lake there is a small wooden amphitheater circling the *dhuni* fire. Sitting there after the evening darshan, I watch everyone walking home in the dark to their beds, some carrying sleeping children on their shoulders, others pausing to sit for a while in meditation by the water. A candle in a red glass jar flickers at the feet of Christ in the sheltered garden at the eastern end of the pond, and opposite over the water, with only the water lilies and the speargrass in between, Hanuman sits in a small hut of gold, with his bare hands tearing open his breast to expose his heart, the perfect servant of love.

The winter constellations turn slowly in the water: the burning studs of Orion's belt, the blazing hoop of the Dipper. A chuck-will's-widow, the southern whippoorwill, disturbed by prowling cats, calls from among the slash pines; and a few fireflies, skipping the water in the lea of the pontoon, copy the stars with spurts of lazy fire. A small wind lifts their bright flotilla for a moment above the pond's margin, brushes quietly the face of the stars, and then with hardly a ripple washes under the dock in the far shadows.

One thought fills immensity.

I warm my hands against the leaping fire.

Midwinter.

Out of love's silence, the strength to serve.

8

Wild Cotton

I am sitting halfway up a shell ridge overlooking the beach a little south of Wabasso. It is a bright winter morning in early March. The sea is unusually quiet, except where it stumbles over the sunken reef half a mile out, though still untroubled; and beyond, in deepening violet and hardly broken blues, it runs in a single sheet of silence to the horizon, where under a fine cover of low cloud it vanishes into a seamless sky.

Meditation is the elision of love and silence.

I am sitting in the bright sun above a patch of sea daisies, yellow and black like black-eyed Susans, only larger. There is a kind of slow attentiveness about them, if flowers can be slow, such bright flowers, or attentive. How carelessly we suppose that nature does not look back at us. At the very least, it sees itself. Anyone who sits in a patch of flowers and closes his eyes for a moment or two knows this for certain.

Perhaps the daisies only seem slow because the wind, like the water, does not run far up the shore. The shell ridge is a secret world, a world within. I could sit here all day in plain view, and no one could see me except the daisies. But it is not the ridge, it is the sitting that hides me. The world cannot see you when you sit. You are truly hidden, and that is one reason why it is so hard to say what meditation is.

A hollow inside the wind.

A few years ago I came here with a friend whom I loved very much, to this same spot. We swam, then sat above the daisies, though there were many more of them that year, and we had to make our way carefully. With no particular intention I straightened my back, set my hands on my lap, and finding the thin seam of green and blue where the water touched the sky, I closed my eyes. I heard the wind, a little stronger than today, but like today I could not feel it. I felt only my own breath, rising and falling in the hollow of the shell ridge. I watched this rising and this falling, at first almost negligently, but closely, and then from farther away, and farther, and farther, until after many long unbroken moments I felt my edges go.

I felt like the sea, a surface without an edge. And then one with the sea, where it meets the sky, without a surface, without an edge.

When after a long while I opened my eyes, I saw my friend looking across at me. "You disappeared," she said. "I saw right through you. You were not there. I saw the sea."

Where the water meets the sky in the mother's eyes....

I vanished because her love held me, and Ma's silence.

On the crest of the ridge a clump of sea oats rises high over my head, blown gently back toward a single pigeon plumtree, its dark red fruit fallen a month or so ago into the scrubby understory, now a startling solitary, tall and groomed by the wind, a deeply fallow green above the beach grasses. Neem Karoli Baba, whose name was taken from a tree, liked to say that all trees fulfill desire. And down the flank of the ridge, holding it together where the vigilant daisies give out, there is a low federation of marsh elder and gopher apple, or ground oak as it is often called. Yet if you did not pay attention and look closely, you would see none of this diversity, this extraordinary fecundity, especially in the late winter when so much of the coastal plain quietly saves itself, holding its breath in fruitful suspense.

If you sit in a patch of winter flowers and close your eyes for a moment, a few things make themselves certain: that every living thing is awake, that even flowers may be watchful, that our scrutiny, when it is sufficiently carefree, is certainly returned, that there are no surfaces and no edges in ourselves or in natural things, that in nature all our desires are fulfilled, that all around us there is a natural conspiracy of love and silence.

We sit by the water, and vanish.

> *All water is the Ganga.*
> *All land is Varanasi (Kashi.)*
> *Love everything.*
>
> —Neem Karoli Baba

* * *

Today, for the first time in the history of human awareness, the spirit and form of every religious tradition has become available to nearly everyone. In the West the work of Swami Vivekananda, Suzuki Roshi, Paramahansa Yogananda, Swami Muktananda, Shri Ramana Maharshi, Pir Vilayat Khan, Munindra and Goenka, Baba Ram Dass, Thomas Merton, and many other contemplatives has made itself familiar to our generation; and in an urgently practical way, the traditions of Vedanta, Shaivite monism, Vaishnavite bhakti yoga, Zen, Sufism, Tibetan and Hinayana Buddhism, Taoism, Gnosticism, Christian contemplation, Navaho and other Native American faiths, and a dozen other paths have become open to the serious seeker, open for business and practice.

But this sudden abundance has led inevitably to a flurry of religious consumerism. For a while everyone went shopping, and when we reached the checkout counter and found our carts full of more spiritual goods than we were ready to pay for, the flurry became a panic. Some returned their surplus to the shelves, others simply fled the store. There was confusion, stridency, gluttony, despair. Eventually most settled down to a single discipline, but many are still adrift in the bazaars and supermarkets, still babbling about Indians and vibrations, hearing voices in their heads, spirit guides or dead Egyptians, all the shuffling devotees of Madame Sosostris, famous clairvoyant, who lost their wits in the crowd, out of laziness and loneliness and impatience.

When we established the ashram in 1976, we were as strident and as confused in the face of this profusion of conventions as anyone else, though we were very cool about it. We knew how to dissemble our opinions as if we had none. But underneath we were full of a specious excitement, buzzing with a dozen ways to sit and a score of half-formed commitments. Or if we had committed ourselves, then we were guilty of an unspoken fundamentalism: if not "mine is the only way," at least "my way is the best." And we still suffer from this childish prescriptiveness, though in subtler forms. It is a very companionable delusion, and I suppose we need it for reassurance in order to convince ourselves that what we have chosen is worthwhile, and because we are naturally proud.

The truth is different, and Ma made it plain at once, long before we settled, and ever since. There is no such thing as the right way. Christ's first instruction to her as a teacher was to teach all ways, and he claimed them all as his own. That is what he means when he says in John 14:6, "I am the way, and the truth, and the life," not, as fundamentalists suppose, that the way of the Gospels is the only truth, but that all ways are his, whether they bear his name or not, because his nature is truly infinite.

More than any other scripture in the history of human seeking, these words are an absolute proscription of sectarian prescriptions.

All this is especially true of meditation. With Ma's continuous scolding, we came slowly to perceive that the true point of this abundance that had so stunned our sense of direction, was its marvelous poverty. St. John says that if you ever succeed in reaching a state of contemplation, if you ever find out how truly to sit, it will come about, because in your openness to all systems and methods you have given them all up.

This precaution, grounded in a saving and discriminating humility, is the first condition of all meditation. Ma has never encouraged any of us to sit before we understand it as best we can. Her instructions for beginners are simple—gazing at a candle flame, following the breath in and out, focusing the breath in the heart or at the crown.

For Ma meditation is most important in the beginning of seeking, and the whole trick lies in keeping it fresh, spontaneous, and original. The moment meditation accumulates its own experience, it fails. The true practice of meditation is to defeat practice, though it requires the most arduous constancy.

For this a second radical precondition, another poverty, must be taken to heart. Meditation begins and ends in failure. If you sit to succeed in sitting, you have already mistaken the way. You have already failed. The seeker can sit only to fail, and it is only by degrees of disappointment that he may make any progress; and this process may only be toward an even deeper failure, until when he has most failed, he at last recognizes, with Thomas Merton, that "this bafflement, this darkness and anguish of helpless desire is the true fulfillment of meditation." Only with this resounding defeat is there a faint chance in which lies the seeker's only real hope: that he may at last begin to sit.

> *Wanting nothing*
> *With all your heart*
> *Stop the stream.*
> *When the world dissolves*
> *Everything becomes clear.*
> *Go beyond*
> *This way or that way,*
> *To the farther shore*
> *Where the world dissolves*
> *And everything becomes clear.*
> *Without fear, go.*
>
> —*The Buddha*

* * *

Our first winter in Sebastian, as I have described, we used to get up before dawn, saddle the horses in the dark, and go out riding for a few hours in the pine flatwoods and palmetto thickets and the low hammocks of oak and primrose willow along the river. As the sun came up we would dismount, and gathering firewood in the dark scrub, make a fire on the river bank and warm ourselves. Sometimes Ma would have us read a few lines of scripture from the *Ramayana*, *Chidakash Gita*, or *Ashtavakra Gita*. Sometimes we would just sit in silence, watching the sun rising above the trees, falling on the river, running across the water to the fire at our feet. If we read, nothing stirred in the woods around us, and there was a deep silence. But if we did not open the book, after a while we could hear the birds and the animals getting back to their business, and then there was an even deeper stillness.

I remember one morning we got to talking about this stillness, and someone asked if you could meditate with your eyes open. Ma said of course, that is one of the goals of meditation. And then Nancy, who was once a nun, said, "You know, the one thing I really like about Billy is the clarity of his mind."

Ma kicked the fire, fixed me with a look that might have killed one of the large rat snakes which rule the scrub along the river, and said, "What I hate about Billy is his mind and its stupid clarity."

I was not so foolish as to say in my defense that by then I too was beginning to deeply suspect my mind and its intellectual acuity. After all, I was still teaching at Oxford, and still attached to my old disciplines and the livelihood they afforded me and the sense of vocation which had summoned me to teach. Yet with Ma's merciless instruction I was growing more and more exasperated by the vigor and orderliness of my mind, especially whenever I sat in meditation, which I had undertaken as a regular practice morning and night.

It was my understanding then that concentration precedes meditation, so I would patiently construct in my mind's eye geometric forms, piece by piece, hold them steadily in my attention, and then undo them, piece by piece. At weekends, when I had more time, I would do this for three hours at a stretch. I was very clear about it all, and I was soon able to design and undo the abstract pictures in my head with an impressive, athletic clarity.

But it was all futile. These mental gymnastics led only to a greater rigidity, a greater degree of that terrible mental muscularity with which academics constrict their awareness and hold their souls captive. Reluctantly I came to see that for the meditator there is no training more disabling than the academic. Everything has to be relearned.

But I was slow to understand, proud of my academic position, which I had worked so hard for, and glued to my ambitions. I see now that I need not have fretted, since my love for God, which was an absolute gift and happily had nothing to do with me and my self-important striving, was real and had its own confidence, so that every time I sat, I sat in love. And that is all that matters. Sooner or later, but usually later, through long trial and continuous error, the seeker realizes that meditation, like service, can only be undertaken when he is in love, and that without this no power of attention will ever bring him beyond the methods and techniques of his practice to that perfect failure in which his petty self and his quarrelsome, wayward mind at last subside into the heart.

When I was subdued at last in some measure by my own striving, Ma took pity on me, and directed me to the practice of "falling into the heart" which Ramana Maharshi had taught. Ramana, who died in 1950, was a Shaivite master of the greatest simplicity and purity, revered by his devotees as a reincarnation of Shankara, the reformer of ancient Shaivism, and as an incarnation of Dakshinamurti, that is, of Shiva in the form of a young ascetic of surpassing beauty who sits under a tree facing south and teaches in complete silence. The name Dakshinamurti means "the form on the right," and Ramana taught, in accordance with the Katha Upanishad and many other ancient scriptures, that freedom is to be found in the spiritual heart, which sits to the right of the natural heart, and into which, by the practice of self-enquiry, the mind will at last subside. The seeker must ask himself, "Who am I?" repeatedly, not as a mantra, but urgently and spontaneously, always demanding an answer until the mind is sapped of all its motive power and falls at length into the heart; and then he is free.

I had already received this instruction at first hand from Swami Satyananda, who was Ramana's attendant in his last years. But it was not until Ma reminded me of the three sadhus on the train and the picture which one of them, the one in green or the one with the umbrella, had given me, that I actually began at her urging to practice this way. "Your Baba told you what to do fifteen years ago," she said, "but you're so stupid you sat on your butt and wasted all that time getting nowhere." Then, "On second thought," she said, "why bother? You'll never make it anyway!"

With this encouragement I set out to follow Ramana's simple method, and before long I found my inner enquiry reduced to a single classical mantra, which like all real mantras is best not shared, because it is a lover's secret; and since then I have let this ancient phrase melt under my tongue, on the off-chance that my mind may dissolve a little with it.

> *The size of a thumb*
> *He lives forever*
> *In the heart of all things.*
> *As you would blow the pith from a reed*
> *Steadily blow him out.*
> *For see!*
> *He is everlasting and bright.*
> *He is everlasting and bright!*
>
> —*Katha Upanishad 4:13*

THOMAS "BILLY" BYROM

* * *

I have already described how hard Ma worked in the first years of her teaching, when she was still living in Brooklyn, to disabuse her students of psychic distractions. Most beginners develop with an easy application a little clairvoyance or clairaudience, and most, as the Dalai Lama says in his refreshing instructions for sitters, quickly become bored with these sideshows and press on. But we were an especially self-indulgent crowd, and some of us were inclined *to dope ourselves with light.* Ma's strategy with these was to stuff them with the very spectacles and pyrotechnics which so fascinated them until, surfeited and dazed, they sought their own relief.

It didn't work with everyone. Some remained stubbornly spellbound. They persisted in sliding sideways instead of going straight up. Some even supposed, to justify their excess, that Ma herself was stuck in these silly shows, though it was obvious to anyone with the least sense of humor that she was simply playing the part of Maya, the Mother of Illusion, wrapping her devotees ever more densely in their own projections and delusions until, sensible at last of the veils that bind them, they blow them away of their own accord. This is the marvelous paradox at the heart of Maya's treacherous instruction. Her whole purpose is to bind in order that her captive free herself. She blindfolds her only so that she may see with her own eyes.

But as I say, there were some who never understood this, and who clung to what Thomas Merton calls *"the miserable little consolations that are given to beginners in the contemplative way"* instead of discovering a *"close friendship with God."* Today some have turned to "channeling" or other modern versions of table-rapping—the pursuit of psychic fun and comfort wherever they may be had. And while there is a contingent reality to some of this psychic business, to the serious seeker it is all sadly sideways, and nonsense.

Yet it is not as if, once we settled in our ashram and applied ourselves to a steadier course of sitting and service, we were all at once delivered from our impatience and folly. Fresh troubles arose.

Most of us, in order to survive in the world, build a kind of crust around the heart. Each time we sit, as long as we sit in love, a little of this crust may crumble, and from time to time whole chunks of it suddenly fall off. Then all our feelings may flood out in a kind of intoxication. We weep what Christians call tears of compunction. We dissolve in what Hindus call floods of *bhakti*, devotion. We may find ourselves staggering and drunk, swept along or tripped up by little deluges of suddenly released emotion. And naturally, we mistake these rushes of joy for the real thing, when the truth is that love has nothing to do with ordinary emotion. Again, Merton warns us against carrying "our passion and our sensible nature along with us like a store of unprotected gasoline." Fire or flood, whatever the figure, the danger is real enough, and I have seen more than a few succumb to it.

But Ma has always come to the rescue, instructing this one to sit with a straighter back, redirecting that one to breathe more easily, scorning professions of devotion when they are confused with emotionalism, scoffing at streams of tears; and always returning her sitters to an original emptiness, the emptiness of persisting failure, without which they will never wear down their pride and find a true quietness, or as Merton calls it, a clean intoxication.

As the years went by, a host of other seductions assailed us. Of these, perhaps the most pernicious deception is that by which impatience disguises itself as patience and convinces the seeker to sit out of habit in a dry regimen and fills him with a false sense of accomplishment at the mere exercise of self-discipline. Because of my long academic training, I fell quickly into this trap, though I was not the worst. There were a few who, even in the midst of busy lives, set aside four or five hours a day for meditation, and who sat going nowhere, enjoying the easy success of undiscriminating effort, shutting out the world when they might have been consuming it. We mistook the quietness which this striving won us for real tranquility, when it was only a kind of numbness. Or if, as sometimes happened, the sense of inner peace was indeed real, we indulged it, exchanging for material pleasure a spiritual indulgence, and putting ourselves at an ever greater distance from God.

Again Ma set us straight, though by different strategies. Some she encouraged to go on sitting, indeed she recommended even longer sessions. She knew the limits of their discipline, and out of earshot predicted more or less accurately when they would run out of steam. Others—the obdurate strivers, the tinder dry, the self-punishing, the spiritual gymnasts—she confronted, one by one, with their essential impatience. "Stop pestering God," she would tell them. "You think because you sit all night, he is going to listen to you! He hears you loud enough. He certainly doesn't want you pulling at his sleeve the whole time!"

And then she would push each of us in whatever direction was needed: to serve, or to attend to livelihood, or to read the Sundarakanda section of the *Ramayana*, or to learn by heart a few lines by the poet Ramprasad, or to mend a broken friendship, or to walk around the pond fifty times—whatever was needed to rescue us from the drought which in our undiscriminating hurry, with such dissembling patience, we contrived for ourselves.

※ ※ ※

Just before noon the wind jumps off the ocean, and running up through the slow and watchful daisies, shouts in my face—or so it seems in such quietness. I open my eyes at the seam of fine low clouds where the water meets the sky, exactly where I closed them, and am not startled to find what was inside is suddenly on the outside, the same unbroken blue where the sky meets the water, unbroken by the wind. It is all unbroken, all blown smooth, all blown away, every blue. There is not a thought in the sky. There is not a cloud in my head. Only a single unbroken blue, and the shouting of the wind.

Beyond the palm tree the shell ridge falls toward the beach, and there, a little out of the salt spray, a small thicket of wild cotton thrives in the dense palm scrub. Not so long ago the federal government hired men and sent them up and down the coast, armed with machetes, to kill the wild cotton, in the hope of keeping down the pink bollworm which infests the homegrown crop. It was all folly. The cotton killers took care not to destroy their livelihood, and their prudent hacking spread the wild cotton, making their work and their pay secure.

So it is with meditation. Thoughts are like wild cotton. However many cotton killers you send out into the thickets of your mind, their hacking will only scatter the seed, and your thoughts will spring up in even denser furrows. Thought cannot kill thought. Only attention, empty of purpose, can kill thought. And only love can empty your attention of purpose, the love which has attention for its substance.

The flower of wild cotton is large, like other flowers of the mallow family, and creamy white with a purple heart. Not even the orange hibiscus, the marsh mallow, is lovelier. And like the hibiscus, if you pick it, it will not last. It is truly wild. Its beauty is so generous, so soft, so large, God must have made it for himself, for his own attention, and we see it only with his eyes.

So it is with meditation. Instead of killing wild cotton, consider the flower and everything you see as seen with his eyes.

* * *

Meditation is the art of dying. After we have safely spurned its early delights, and have begun by repeated failures to understand the relation of spontaneity and constancy in our sitting, then we can settle down to the long hard work of dying, and to the business of embracing our defeat.

Meditation is the art of killing. It is the slow assassination of the self. We are plotting a series of murders! The murder of the senses, the murder of the emotions, the murder of the mind—the murder of all attachments....

But I do not wish to dramatize an undertaking that involves long, arduous labor. Sitting is often very bleak, and it requires an extraordinary tenacity. Once the seeker has survived the first traps and seductions, he often enters a desert, a dark night, where everything becomes cramping and strenuous, dry and mean and baffling. The more his attachments fall away, the more he feels depressed and raw, until by degrees he loses heart. In the end he loses heart altogether, as he must. Then he hates to sit, and with every session all the control he had seemed to win over his mind and his will deserts him, and he finds himself shriveled and stripped, without hope, without faith, without love.

Perhaps that is why monks live in separate cells, and nuns too. At these moments of deracination and despair, which may last months or even years, the pressure of almost any company becomes intolerable. But even that barest luxury of privacy was at first denied us in our ashram life. We were poor and could only afford to live together by cramming into two houses, in crowded bedrooms or sleeping on the floor in the living rooms. After a few years we were able to build a third house, and then we bought the large house next door. But for the first several years we lived cheek to cheek in a pressing and unwanted intimacy; and as, in the regular practice of meditation, our insides were turned out, our private feelings were daily exposed to the unblinking scrutiny of everyone around us. There was no mood too private, no secret too precious, that was not instantly made public. There was no depth of personal despair in which everyone did not trawl. There was no dryness so hidden that was not crumbled through every hand. There was no inner work so intimate that we did not all announce it with busy, brutal gossip.

I have said this was our Kurukshetra, the battlefield of our warring passions. And so it was. Every morning at five when we rose, the battle was freshly engaged, and by noon the field was strewn with corpses. We squealed and snarled and fought for every inch of territory, defending our pride and our anger, assailing each other with jealousy and greed—whatever passions the morning meditation had provoked in us. The carnage was terrific.

But it was also, looking back from quieter times, magnificent. For we came to understand among other things the value of *satsang*, the company of fellow seekers, and how well we served each other in a conspiracy of bloody assassination. You kill me and I kill you. We helped each other to die by a passionate and compelled adversity. And how we loved to murder each other! It was so much more gratifying than murdering oneself. Daily we drew the beam from the eye of our neighbor and knocked him senseless.

All of this would have been, of course, perfectly vindictive and wholly futile without Ma to bear our standard. But she was always there, holding the entire field with all its alarms and diversions in the palm of her hand, raising the vanquished and squashing the victor between thumb and forefinger; and at the end of the day, in an informal class or after another session of sitting, settling the disputes; explaining with limitless patience, dispensing justice, roughly or softly as the occasion demanded, awarding the trophies and patching up the tattered flags.

"Teach me how to live," she would say, "and I will teach you how to die." That was the bargain we struck with her every night. And so she brought us gradually, by a series of rearguard actions, out of the wilderness into which our meditation had led us, at least for the time being, until the next battle, and the next defeat.

* * *

Wherever you find men who are seeking,
and men who are dying, tell this story with love.
When you speak of this deepest mystery,
you make ready to die, you make ready to live.
—Katha Upanishad 3:17

Meditation is the art of living. It is work, a work of dissolution, but it is also recreation. It is play. In its deepest nature it is entirely playful. Why do we sit? When all the religious nonsense has been swept away, all the puffed-up speculation and muscular rituals and flaccid striving, all the fretting over purpose, method and goal, we sit simply to find happiness. We sit in happiness out of happiness, to fulfill our happiness, and to discover with the Buddha how to pull out sorrow's shaft.

And depending on how willing we are to embrace our constant failures, we do become happy. This happiness seems to come when we have more or less given up on it, when meditation moves beyond its own location, beyond sitting, as it must sooner or later. The attention which we develop when we sit counts for nothing unless it reaches farther and deeper into our walking, waking lives, even into our sleep. Slowly, over the years, our activities are overtaken by the ripples of this practiced attention, and then smoothed by the stillness which it brings first to the surface and then to the depths of our daily lives, until, to change the metaphor a little, we are drenched in it: drenched in its tranquility and its wetness. And with this comes a little real happiness, perhaps the first we have felt since childhood.

Dip him in the river who loves water.

Then it is natural to stand in line at the checkout counter and find our attention running on empty, or full of affective prayer, or gathered along the thread of a classical Sanskrit phrase. We find ourselves settling in the present moment. On the road, in the house, at the wheel or the sink, in the field or the office or the factory, we are practicing the presence of God, but without any design or intention. It just happens, and happiness happens with it.

But of what does this purposeless recreation, which comes to occupy our hours and fill our life, consist? What does it have for its object, and what is its subject? The answer must be, *nothing*. The play to which meditation summons us is empty, absolutely empty, and in this it is distinct from ordinary adult pleasures, which are almost always tendentious. When after years of sitting we come to accept our original, natural emptiness, accept that we got nowhere and accomplished nothing, then in our defeat we achieve a childish state, with nothing to do but to play in the hollow at the center of our being, in our heart of hearts. And we fall gladly into it. Thomas Merton describes this marvelous collapse perfectly: "You feel as if you were at last fully born.... And yet you have become nothing. You have sunk to the center of your own poverty, and there you have felt the doors fly open to infinite freedom...."

In this freedom there is exactly that admixture of laughter and gratitude which overtook me at the beginning of my search, when I was finishing my doctorate at Harvard, just as a child laughs and is naturally grateful without the least self-consciousness when he plays. And just as a child hops easily from one game to the next, dropping the passions of the moment as if they never were, so in this marvelous poverty, in which we step forever out of bounds as we had always wished to when young, there is a good deal of detachment—and because we know once and for all how poor we really are, a good deal of humility.

Laughter, gratitude, detachment, humility.

And what are these qualities, compounded, if not the correct prescription for *compassion*?

In this way meditation qualifies us, after a lot of hard work, for true service. The free play of the attentive heart, into which we fall when all the self-interested energies of the mind have sputtered out, involves us in a responsibility that is very far from childish. By fitting us for service, meditation compels us to serve.

Here at Kashi some, by embracing the little way according to Ma's instructions and by a loving constancy in their sitting, have come to deserve in some measure the freedom to serve.

What is most startling about them is not their capacity for ambitious good works but the spontaneity with which they help everyone around them. They rise in the morning, and having seen briefly to their own needs, they attend to the needs of whoever falls in their way, and without hesitation or calculation. They do not look to serve. Their hands reach out in a natural rhythm, out of an unforced attentiveness. They are thoughtless in the sense that they have no thought for themselves. And if they are not thwarted in their helping, they acquire a certain shine. They are very evidently happy! Even at the end of the day, far beyond their bedtime, they are often busy, freely attentive, and bright.

Ma promises us that true service is possible, and she takes care to set each of us the task that will bring us there by the shortest road.

And the shortest road is always the road to Kashi, to the banks of the Ganga. Talk as I may about the ways of sitting, and their failure, and the relation of service and meditation, how some may find quietness through service, and some service through quietness, it is only by sitting on her banks and by dipping in her waters, only by giving ourselves fully to her flowing, that appetite and breath are ever mastered, and the heart is awakened to sit and serve.

In each of us Ma is always attuning the tension between outside and inside, action and contemplation. We resist her with all the ferocious ingenuity of the little self. We are all deaf when it comes to hearing what we need to hear. But Ma perseveres, and step by step, at every step on the road to her river, her love and the love with which her love is returned overwhelm our lagging and our fear.

Step by step, at every step,
We are shown how to take the next step.
—After Patanjali, Yoga Sutras 3.6

* * *

Anyone who sits on a bright day in a patch of winter flowers and closes his eyes for a moment is asking for trouble. If he is still enough and follows his breath out and rests there between the falling and the rising, emptier with every breath and more open, he may find himself by a sea change stranger than the sexual alchemy of a Shakespearean comedy wonderfully translated into a woman. For meditation is a woman's art.

Sitting takes us beyond the masculine urgency of seeking, strips us of the aggression of yearning, and leaves us simply in waiting, our attention ready to be penetrated. After many defeats, our attention empty of thought, activity, desire, will, memory, we are ready at last to draw the breath into the heart as a woman draws her lover into her, awareness penetrated by love, love penetrated by awareness.

Every act of attention, if sitting is practiced with chastity, is tantric. Every time we look at the natural world, it enters us if our observation is open and pure. Whenever we breathe into the heart, we are enjoying God's embrace.

Whether we are contemplating the daisies, yellow and black in the bright winter sun, or God himself, the soul empties itself to embrace the object of its attention. Meditation is this readiness, this vigilant preparation for the single embrace in which we are all gathered, without beginning or end, by the love of attention, and the attention of love.

THOMAS "BILLY" BYROM

The soul empties itself to receive the object of its attention.

> *The way is not in the sky.*
> *The way is in the heart.*
>
> —The Buddha, Dhammapada

* * *

In the evening I walk down to the river, because the forecast is for another frost far heavier than the first and I want to see the great canopies of vine before the north wind turns them overnight into icy sheets of green glass and they splinter and collapse. The water is low from lack of rain, and little black birds fly in under the banks raiding the mud. I sit not far from the boat dock in the shade of a red mulberry tree, which has grown up under the royal sleeves of a single vast live oak, dripping with Spanish moss and lacey epiphytes. The mulberry is the most beautiful tree in the river hammocks, though small and never in any season showy; beautiful, to my eyes, for its leaves alone, which are the size of a child's hand, and oval, and so finely layered that the light falls through them in shallow puddles, like a playful child declining with gestures of innocence the summons to sleep.

The wet light and sweet sifted air of the hammock has clothed the slender arms of the mulberry with a powdery lichen of astonishing loveliness: a smooth coat of gray and pink clay, patched in places with a coarser burlap of green and orange. At first I thought this was the tree's natural bark, but when I brush my fingers along it, I see that it is all bespoke. And lower down, where my head rests, the trunk is greaved with a simple deep red, the color of the fallen sun burning in the palm and oak thickets over the water, where the tawny panther has his lair.

We sit by the river and vanish.

MA & ME

The quietness calls me, but I would be a fool to close my eyes. God has blessed us with so much beauty, even in his low and desolate places, it seems profane ever to shut out the natural world in meditation. Yet many people cannot fully open their eyes until they have first closed them. They cannot see in the light until they have learned to see in the dark. So it has been with me.

We sit by the river and awaken.

9

The Last Degree of Love

Though I have tried hard, there is really no way to describe the singular experience which provoked this strange life of seeking, this absolute dereliction of all worldly responsibility! It is an experience which left me dazed and more than a little ridiculous, and I know it distressed my family very much, for to them I seemed suddenly cold and stiff and remote. "Love has ten degrees," the Sufi proverb goes. "The ninth is silence, and the first, flight from people!" It is all very surprising and awkward. One morning, a morning like any other, you wake up and stretch and look in the mirror, and you see another face there, your own, and yet not your own; and you understand for the first time that all your life you have been in love, crazed with love, drunk with love, and desperate, beyond all despair—in love, and you never knew it! And all that day, and the next, the feeling does not go away, though you hold the door open, but only deepens, till slowly you come to comprehend that you will have lived your life, when it ends, in two halves, the first asleep, and the second, into which you have just now awakened, *awakening*.

And so you fly from people—what else can save you?—because they will not understand. Yet it really does happen! So St. Teresa reassured her nuns, and so St. Catherine protested—"My heart is breaking, but cannot break for the hungry longing it has conceived for you!"

This is my calamity. I fell in love. That's all. And every day my love grew more foolish and complete, exceeding its own folly, exhausting its own fulfillment. But no one would listen to me, and I did not know how to talk, or where to put myself, or whom to embrace.

Until I found You.

*   *   *

A week after winter, a week before spring.

Years ago I found myself in this same emptiness, when the pulse of the seasons misses a beat, watching three blackbirds in an empty field. Strangely fulfilled in the emptiness they left when the light fell from the sky and they flew away, I awoke for the first time to the awkward fact of my infatuation.

This morning I walked down to the river with Ganga. She would not take my hand, so I kept having to run after her like a worried dog or wait for her to have spent her curiosity wherever it alighted—on a stump swarming with fire ants in a grove heavy with marsh white grapefruit, or in a deep burrow under a bush of hog plums. All the while I attended to her breathless, unceasing commentary on her incredible, heroic life, so full of astonishment and self-approval, and so completely managed at every turn. "*You* go this way, *I'll* go this way." For her all company is a following, nothing more, and our expeditions are empty of everything except her happy, imperious now, now, now....

But when we reached the river and sat down on a dry log just above the bend, I noticed that without dropping a stitch Ganga had driven from the mind-crushing tyranny of her chatter, from the terrible treble of her onrushing yarn, a simple word with which for nearly a year she had drubbed and beaten us: the word *why*. It was gone! By some miracle of compassion we were at last spared its drilling insistence. All at once, overnight, it was gone!

She was no longer demanding to know *why*.

This moment comes naturally in the life of every child, and as a relief to every parent—and just as naturally in the life of every seeker, and as a great relief to God, no doubt. One morning or another we stop asking why. We sit down on a dry log in a river meadow a stone's throw above the turn, and for once we sit without questioning.

But there is a difference between child and seeker, the difference between life and death: when the seeker stops asking, he stops once and for all. When his whys have flown away from the empty field, they never return, and the field is forever empty, when the light has fallen from the sky, between winter and spring.

A single scrub jay rises from a cove of spike rushes and flings its way over the water, Ganga claps her hands as if she had created him, and now with careless certainty dismisses him. I wait for the why of it, but she just claps her hands, sure of her own creation.

Now has no why.

Love is now.

Love has no why.

Indeed, in the words of Meister Eckhart, "Love has no why."

I draw this thirsty syllogism from the river which turns at our feet with such easy certainty. Surely there will be more questions, because Ganga is not yet a seeker, just a child. She will pull at my sleeve and demand to know why Denny, the pastor who lives next door, has not yet come down into the meadow to feed his Appaloosa mare, with the sun high in the southern sky.

But for now there is only the careless certainty of the river, wearing by some trick of the midday light a white sheet of uncommon brightness. An extraordinary, soft, luminous white! Reminding me that of all the one hundred and eight names of the ancient river for which Ganga is named, perhaps the loveliest of all is Dhavalambara, "cloth of dazzling white," or Kshirasubha, "white as milk."

All rivers flow from the breasts of the Mother.

My Ganga, milk-white, cloth of dazzling white!

* * *

When you fall in love with God, you fall flat on your face. You pick yourself up, and now that all the questions you had have flown away, you are left with a single, overwhelming question—*how*? How am I to return this love, since that is all that love requires? As Swami Nityananda says in his *The Sky of the Heart*, "He is not a man who does not return what he has been given."

But how?

This question, which began to consume my life, was all the more pressing because it arose from a new comprehension of my absolute incapacity. The more I burned to return the love, the more I felt my own poverty. But at the same time, I began to realize from the very intimacy of these feelings that the answer was entirely my own to find. It was all completely up to me. For how can a lover share or delegate his love? That would be absurd, an utter contradiction of his deepest professions.

At this moment, when I understood the absolute nature both of my responsibility and of my incapacity, I stumbled, like every seeker and lover of God, into the arms of a teacher. And I believe that this stumble, if the seeker truly accepts the singleness and absolute independence of his responsibility and deeply recognizes the fullness of his poverty, is a gift from God.

God sticks out his foot, the seeker trips, and when he picks himself up, the teacher is there to dust him down.

The teacher may not always be his final teacher. Often the seeker must undergo a number of apprenticeships. Nor will the guide always appear in the flesh, on the outside. Sometimes, rather rarely, he shows himself only on the inside, where he truly sits in the heart.

But more often, because we are proud and slow, the guru has to manifest in a human form. In whatever form, the teacher appears.

What then?

The student is summoned to a school of love, and on his first day of instruction a sudden fear stops him dead on the threshold: the fear of losing his freedom.

I have recounted how during my first apprenticeship my heart opened, one day just before noon as I was listening to an ancient Vaishnavite love song and watching the birds playing under the Palisades along the Hudson. My first absurd thought had been for my civil liberties. I felt ravished, snatched up into ecstasy—but also seized against my will. I never believed that such an exaltation of awareness was possible, except by chemical and therefore wholly specious means, and I felt in some comically democratic corner of my being that my permission should have been solicited.

As I have recounted, I picked up the phone and, calling Hilda, demanded to know what she had done to me with her Tibetan mantra out in the chilly woods of Peekskill.

But she had just laughed and told me to take it easy, and I realized that while she had shown me the door, only I had opened it, and that I had been seeking, and ardently for several years, just such an awakening. It was all my own fault, and all God's grace. And I realized also that there is no compulsion in the school of love. The last thing a real teacher can do—and Hilda was in her own way a real teacher—is compel her charges. On the contrary, she will demand of them the utmost independence of mind and spirit and will, to the extent that she is true.

But just as the seeker thinks himself secure in this knowledge, and ready to trust that God will not mislead him, his friends and family, disturbed by his preposterous behavior, may collaborate to convince him that he is being duped and has fallen under the scheming control of a charlatan. Indeed, Hilda's surname was Charlton, and I sometimes heard her cruelly scorned as "Hilda Charlatan." And of course, it does frequently happen that for a while the student of love may be misled by false teachers. How else may he learn discrimination?

But to those whom we leave behind, all teachers are false. And how, if they truly care for us, should they feel otherwise? Their skepticism may arise from a possessive love, but it is love nevertheless, and it is always best received in a spirit of love. The seeker loses nothing by accepting it with its full force and subjecting his trust in his teacher to the impudence of their scrutiny.

A true teacher will only encourage this, because above all he wants the seeker to learn to stand on his own. As Ashtavakra taught King Janaka:

> *By standing on his own*
> *A man finds happiness.*
> *By standing on his own*
> *A man finds freedom.*
> *Only by standing on his own*
> *Will he find the end of the way.*

And he adds by way of reassurance, familiar with the timeless predicament which I am describing, his homely observation echoing over a thousand years and across a score of cultures:

> *Even when his whole family makes fun of him,*
> *He is undismayed.*

So Ma has said to us from the first day in school that her students may be recognized by one thing: "You have nothing of me on you." The true teacher leaves no mark. And true to her word, Ma has always been merciless with those whose devotion becomes slavish or emotional. She never allows us to stagnate. She is forever throwing us in the deep end. And if we are not always learning and growing toward a state of independence, she shows us the door.

Now as long as the student is still serving his first apprenticeship and his teacher is not his guru, he may quickly overcome his fear of losing his freedom. But what if he meets his guru at the schoolhouse door? Then God help him! For the guru is not only teacher and deliverer but also Lover, and, as every lover knows, love is a state not just of giddy freedom but also of abject surrender. It would be foolish to pretend otherwise.

This was what the Persian poet and mystic Rumi discovered, to the ruination of his profession and his sanity. Until his mid-thirties he was a highly respected theologian, an academic and a divine, a man of wisdom and letters, at the height of his fame. Then one day a wandering dervish, unkempt and crazy and profane, came to Konya, where Rumi taught, and at the first sight of him the staid scholar fell madly in love. Abandoning his books and his students, he gave himself over in ecstasy to the service of his beloved, his crazy teacher, his guru, in complete surrender.

This miraculous entrapment overtakes every seeker sooner or later, not always with such violence, but in the same measure—perhaps more steadily but with the same utterly captive exaltation. It is all a matter of temperament and of the seeker's situation in life. Sometimes he needs a real shock, as Rumi did. Sometimes he must be drawn into his infatuation by an appearance of liberal instruction. After all, there are a thousand ways to fall in love.

But once in love, what difference does that make? The lover is trapped in a boundless and completely binding freedom. Trapped! And he comes to understand, usually rather swiftly, that the only way he may realize the true freedom which his love promises him is by an ever deeper submission. When Ashtavakra uses the term *svatantrya*, "independence," to describe the unconditional freedom to which the seeker must always aspire, he understands perfectly well that this freedom is won only by unconditional surrender.

So there is substance to the student's fear, after all, and his apprehension will not be dissolved simply by the intellectual resolution of the paradox: since guru is self, in submitting to his beloved he is only submitting to his true self. That will hardly dispel his fears or disable his selfishness or set him free.

I understood the paradox, and its resolution, well enough the moment I walked into Hilda's living room and saw Ma in her green leotard, dipping her lustrous eyelashes, so fearfully larger than life. But my book learning, for that is all it was, did nothing to rout my fear, and because of it I was not able to accept Ma's help or give her a real place in my life until I had sat at her feet for a couple of years. Hilda was safe because my love for her was not deeply committed, and so I clung to her and shied away from Ma. I could not, I would not, submit.

Like many others I exposed my fears to a hundred challenges. After all, how could I tell if she was true? Perhaps she had appeared as a projection of some baser need of mine, some sly and self-serving compensation? Undoubtedly this often happens, as I have said. The world is full of false teachers, scrabbling to feed those who have not yet emptied their bellies. What, I asked myself, if my hunger was not yet the hunger of Love?

But as always in spiritual life the answer lay in the question. When love is hungry, there is food, and the food is love, and as Christ said, "perfect love casteth out fear." After much trial I learned what I might have learned on the first day of school had I been less slow, that the true teacher brings with her as a sure token of her truth the love that dissolves all fear of being compelled.

But to live in this crazy love requires a constant renewal of trust in oneself and in God and in guru. There must be a constant process of self-renewing trust, in which the seeker asks God to set him once again, moment by moment, on the path of Love. Then whenever the fear arises—how do I know I have not been misled?—he has only to remind himself that *Love knows*. Love always knows itself, and if it is at first or even for a long time blind, in the end it always knows itself. Only love lasts. It is the only thing that endures, outlasting every fear, every doubt, every faltering, every shabby deceit, every spurious discrimination, every form of impatience or spiritual greed. In the end we are never deceived so long as we are in love. Though we are often misled, and most of us suffer imperfect instruction along the way, deceived by those who have deceived themselves into supposing they can help us, yet every misdirection once discovered sets us on the right path, every false prophet is eventually unmasked, and love vanquishes all its adversaries.

Whenever Ma boasts that none of us have anything of her on us, that she has left no mark, and that nothing in love is ever compelled, she adds with a sadness beyond my understanding, and yet not beyond it, that she waits for the day when we are all truly puppets, as she is his puppet. This has always been her loudest, her most vainglorious boast.

But as I say, this lies beyond any understanding I can form of freedom and submission. I hardly dare aspire to such a servitude, or to such release.

> *I have lived on the lip*
> *of insanity, wanting to know reasons,*
> *knocking on a door. It opens.*
> *I've been knocking from the inside!*
>
> —*Rumi*

I was afraid of losing myself, and I would not submit.

But your love was so much stronger than my fear. I should have known I had no chance. There was no turning back! I should have known that my situation was hopeless, that even as my love grew day by day more calamitous, even as I fought you and floundered, never knowing how to talk or where to put myself or whom to embrace, your love was surely wearing down my resistance, until after two or three years, little by little, I began to lose myself in you.

I should have known, once on the path of love there is no turning back.

* * *

To the seeker who has just learned to begin to surrender to his teacher, there is one fear even more harrowing than the fear of losing his freedom. We easily suppose that it is harder to give love than to take it, since we first learn of love at the breast and are forever afterwards looking for other ways to suckle. But to our consternation, the moment we find ourselves face to face with a love larger than our own, we cannot take it! The love we give, we can always measure. But the love we take, especially if it comes from God and not from man, cannot be stemmed or diverted, and once we let it in, we drown.

Love is indeed a calamity, the greatest natural disaster, and its true aspect, when we cannot take it, is one of terror, not confidence.

I first learned this when Ma encouraged a number of us to visit the Banka Bihari temple in Brindavan, the principal seat of devotion to Krishna in the town of his birth. In India there are ten thousand terrible faces of God. I have already described some of the fiercer forms of the mother. But the father is no less ghastly. In order that the demon host never exceed their station, he manifests in forms far uglier and more bestial. But when it suits him, he is also of surpassing beauty and tenderness: as Skanda, for instance, the warrior son of Shiva, most beautiful of all the gods, riding a peacock; or as Dakshinamurti, the golden youth of sixteen who sits under a tree facing south and teaches in silence. But at his most tender and passionately handsome, he is the blue-black Krishna, who plays a flute and makes love to the milkmaids in the moonlit woods and river meadows of Brindavan.

I expected the ceremony in his temple to be joyful and tender, the music mellifluous, and every gesture of devotion graceful and amorous.

Instead, stepping into the inner sanctum, I found a scene of unbridled ferocity. At the end of the hall, raised high above the crowd of worshippers, was a platform with a ragged curtain in front of it. Every few minutes, as the crowd rushed forward with guttural cries, the curtain was hurled apart, and from the interior a giant swing, on which were the savage effigies of Krishna and his consort Radha, was propelled forward with great violence. Those nearest the swing fought to grab it and fling it on its way, and battled wildly for the privilege, clawing at the ropes and the fabric. At the climax of each swing, a crazed shout went up from the crowd, as if they were baying for blood.

I confess I shrank to the back of the hall, stood half behind a pillar, and held tight to the cloth purse which hung around my neck. I expected at any moment to be assaulted and robbed. The whole scene filled me with terror and loathing—the cacophony of the mad drummers, the shrieking of the women devotees, more like harpies than milkmaids, the guttering candles and the acrid smoke of the incense, the wild supplications of the beggars below the steps, and the panic up by the swing over who could make it buck and lurch and swagger on its frayed ropes the more crazily.

I looked around for my friends, and missing them, I was about to go out into the dusty side street to look for them when to my horror I saw Ma, all alone, running up the steps and pushing aside a Brahmin priest and a couple of drunken devotees, grab the sides of the swing and hurl it forward with her eyes flashing and a shout of triumph, which the mob below her answered with redoubling fury. Her black hair streamed out behind her, her sari fell off her shoulder, and when the swing returned, she grabbed it once more out of the hands of the priest and flung it up and out at the crowd, jolting the god and his consort, stamping her bare feet on the stone floor, and wringing her arms as if she was taunting the crowd to fresh excesses.

I felt I had wandered into the very heart of darkness. Slipping out a side door of the temple, I found an old man selling chai. With the clay cup shaking in my hands, I sat down among the beggars on the steps of the temple and reflected that I was a very long way from the evensong of my Anglican childhood.

"Krishna, the God of Love! What has all that bloody hullabaloo to do with love?" I demanded with a poorly dissembled carelessness when Ma at last came out of the temple, her eyes still flashing, flushed with a victory of which I had no comprehension.

"Yes, *love*!" she said. "But how would you know if you don't throw yourself into it?"

But later that evening, back at the guest house where we were staying, she relented a little and suggested that I go up on the roof and sit for a while and consider what it was that so disturbed me.

The view from the roof was calming. There were the river meadows falling away under a full moon toward the banks of the silver Yamuna, and the night air was cool and fresh. One by one the lamps in the nearby bazaar went out, and except for the occasional cries of a few vagabond children playing under the neem trees at the edge of town, there was a sweet and deepening silence.

In this silence I sat and, closing my eyes, I reviewed the pandemonium in the temple. All at once I saw that the panic had been mine and mine alone, and that the darkness and the savagery and barbarous abandon had also been mine—no one else's! They were simply the creatures of my fear. The ceremony had been wild indeed. But when I saw it all again in the open night air above the river meadows, I sensed in its abandon an extraordinary composure.

Even the mad lurching of Krishna's swing now seemed to be graceful, not terrible, and guided by a generous formality. And Ma's full-throated taunting of the mob was instead a marvelous and infectious laughter, a soft and good-humored joy, ravishing and infinitely tender. And at last, feeling the real spirit of the celebration, I was able to ask myself what in all this blissful love-making—for that is all it was—had so terrified me. Why had I not been able to abandon myself to the happy calamity of so exalted a passion?

I realized to my surprise that I was afraid of dying. The temple tasted of death. Now that I could contemplate my feelings without panic, I sensed that if I let this love in, I would surely drown. And remembering Ma's frenzy, I understood too that my fear was precipitated by my deepening commitment to her. For it is the appearance of a spiritual teacher and the student's grateful surrender to the authority of her love that make the possibility of dying real for the first time. I saw that if I let her in, if I succeeded in taking her love, I would be compelled to love myself, and if I loved my true Self, the false self would have to die. I would certainly die to all my habits and opinions and eventually to the petty identity which I had so long and so comfortably mistaken for myself.

The poet Rumi knew from the moment he saw Shams that the touch of love is the touch of death, and he had the courage to sing it from the rooftops of Konya:

> *Die now, die now, in this Love die.*
> *When you have died in this Love,*
> *You will receive new life....*
> *Die now, die now before the beauteous King.*
> *When you have died before the King,*
> *You will all be Kings and renowned....*
> *Die now, die now, and come from behind this cloud.*
> *When you come from behind this cloud*
> *You will all be radiant full moons.*

What is more enthralling, what more fatal, than the kiss of a truly unpossessive, limitless love?

I was afraid because I knew in my heart that the tumult of love in Krishna's temple was Christ's love, God's love, and I was its foremost captive, by a surrender freely undertaken, and that now I must submit in chains of love to my own death.

Ma later told me that she only saw Baba on the swing, and that she was trying to make him lose his balance. She also told me that he used to send his devotees to Banka Bihari temple every day, and she recited Ramprasad's lines:

> *One who has beheld the Mother's swing*
> *Jumps forth from her lap.*
> *Again and again, inebriated, Ramprasad sings:*
> *"Let Mother Kali swing."*

* * *

Over Kashi a river of milk flows across the night sky from the polestar to the first full moon of April. Not long after I fell asleep, I heard myself asking in one of those clearings between dreams, and with the kind of carelessness reserved for the most pressing matters, "Why am I here?" I woke up laughing at the absurd presumption of the question. *"Why am I here at all?"* I heard myself asking, and by way of reproof a great shiver passed over me from my feet to the crown of my head. Laughing and ashamed, I remembered that I was in love and had no more need to pester God with foolish questions.

Unable to fall asleep again, I slipped out the back door and stole under the silk oak a few paces down to the pond. I sat on the bench and shook off my impertinence. And there I saw reflected in the water the milky river washing down the night sky from Dhruva, the polestar, to the bright moon as it fell behind high banks of black clouds in the north and west over Kissimmee.

First there is the calamity of love. Then, when the lover has lost his senses and his bearings, the teacher appears to save him from his panic. And her gift is not a teaching, but a place—a few steps down to the water's edge where the white river, Dhavalambara, runs across the blue-black sky, from the polestar to the bright moon.

> *Like a tree I lift up my hands from the earth*
> *In desire for that one from whom I knew desire.*
>
> —*Rumi*

* * *

Krishna climbs into the high branches of the kadamba tree. He is laughing, and in his arms are long trails of brightly colored cloth, the saris of the cowherd girls, stolen while they were bathing in the river. He hangs them out on the limbs of the tree, far above their reach. Then he takes out his flute, and the river meadows are full of his sweet music.

Even today it is easy to find in the villages around Brindavan a painted effigy of Krishna high in a tree, and the branches flowing with bright streams of cloth. The tree represents a higher state of awareness. The stealing of the clothes is God's way of reminding us that we are all naked in his eyes, free of shame and fear and desire. And when Krishna plays his flute, love consumes desire, and the lover understands the identity of passion and chastity.

But until he hears this divine music, he often feels confused about sexual desire. On the one hand he is assured by almost every tradition that only by a calculating celibacy can he find the kingdom. On the other, he fears that the denial of his sexual nature, which is one of God's greatest gifts, is perverse and dangerous. There is indulgence and there is repression, and no middle path between them.

But when he hears the flute, his heart opens, and then no love making, however burning and pleasurable, will ever again satisfy him. Now he may never find a woman whom he can enter deeply enough. Nor will the woman who is seeking ever find a man who can penetrate her deeply enough. Once they have awoken to the fullness of the heart, how can they ever again prefer the trickle of bliss which till now has been their only experience of ecstasy?

The heart opens, and the lover feels an ecstasy flowing out of him into the world, and flowing back into him. Knowing himself without edges or limitable identity, he also recognizes with complete certainty that this deepest of all intimacies is the true motive of sexuality. That is why he always felt a kind of sadness after making love. To spend our passion in a brief spasm at the base of the body is a waste. It is nearly always self-fascinated, a kind of recoiling from our true nature, which is wholly sexual and wholly spiritual, and should never be limited to what the mystic Gurdjieff called the little sneeze of genital orgasm.

In the music of the flute he hears a summons to undertake a new and sacred responsibility, always to aspire to this true intimacy, to live in the joyful current of the life force. He hears the flute and finds himself naked and shivering in the river with the milkmaids, shivering with delight and free of desire. And above him in the high branches of the tree, Krishna is laughing.

To those still stranded on the banks, this is all very well! Like virgins disputing the pleasures of sex, they would rather disbelieve that such an awakening ever really happens. It is a hallucination, an irregular release of hormones, a compensation for sexual failure—incidental, delusional, even psychotic. And to the fundamentalist, it is simply the work of the Devil.

Yet I have known hundreds to whom this experience is the single, sustaining fact of their seeking. In different measures it has given each of them the composure to survive the tumult of their search. It is the ground of their adventure and the well in which they refresh their thirst when the way becomes too dry.

THOMAS "BILLY" BYROM

But how does it happen?

Only by the accident of perfection, Ma says, and when we are ready to share ourselves. It never happens by design, from striving or calculation, by an enforced celibacy, or by the various strategies of meditation. *The Cloud of Unknowing* warns us: "Fast thou never so much, wake thou never so long, rise thou never so early," every effort to embrace this deepest intimacy of all is bound to fail, until we have been wounded by "the sharp dart of longing love." Then, instead of recoiling from everything around us, we begin to share. We begin to penetrate the world, and the world enters us. Then at last our selfish fascination with sex dissolves of its own accord, and by a natural and spontaneous conservation, all our love is saved in a self-transcending service, and spent in the heart, endlessly.

> *He said: "What is abstinence?"*
> *I said: "The way of salvation."*
> *He said: "Where is calamity?"*
> *I said: "In the street of your love."*
> *He said: "How fare you there?"*
> *I said: "In perfect rectitude."*
>
> —Rumi

* * *

With reckless abstinence, with drunken rectitude, we learn to share. Sharing is the whole curriculum of love. It is simple and natural, and it impresses its own discipline.

But it is also hard to get by heart, even when love has quelled our fear of compulsion. Once we freely accept love's mastery as a daily discipline and not just a sabbatical comfort, we soon come to see that our every gesture has been to grasp or to spurn and hardly ever to share. We have spent our lives snatching at or recoiling from our experience instead of making love. But once God has tripped us up and winded us, and with our first desperate breath we let love in, then we find to our consternation that with our very next breath we must let love out, and let it in again—until sharing, like breathing, is second nature to us and comes easily.

Naturally, but never easily. We are like babies slapped by the midwife. Our first breaths quickly give way to squalls and howls. And as we grow and are nurtured by our parents, what do we learn? When their love is freely given, the breath comes and goes easily, and the self and the sense of love are undivided. But as always happens, even in the most loving family, as soon as love is withheld or sought anxiously in return by the mother or the father, then we learn a game of attraction and aversion, of offering and withholding, of grasping and spurning, abandonment and possession. Until at the heart of the purest and deepest love of all, the love of mother and child, father and child, we learn the power of possession instead of the freedom of love freely shared.

There was a brief period in my life, about five years, when I gave up my Anglican faith, and this came about quite abruptly when I was eighteen and just about to go up to Oxford to begin my studies. I was spending a few months at an Italian university, trying to get Petrarch and Leopardi in the original language, and drunkenly sowing a few wild oats in the local *mensa popolare*. Going to church one morning in the backstreets of Assisi, I heard the priest deliver a homily in which he took for his texts three of the fiercest passages in the Bible: the Abraham and Isaac story; the passages in the Gospels where Christ declares that if you do not hate your brother and sister for his sake, you can never hope to follow him truly; and again where he says that he comes to make trouble in families, with a sword to separate father and son, mother and daughter. Perhaps my Italian was still too stumbling to understand his interpretation, and certainly I had never given much reflection to these very critical teachings, which every lover of Christ must come to terms with.

Anyway, I left the church profoundly shaken.

I had been raised in a large and loving family. We had had our quarrels, and my father had not known how to express his love easily, but it had never been in question, nor our deep caring for each other.

The idea that I must choose, and absolutely, between the love of Christ and the love of family was one I recoiled from so powerfully and completely that I abandoned my faith. I who, raised by a professed atheist and a thoroughly secular family in which the mention of "God" was either embarrassing or laughable, had nevertheless instinctively and uninstructed been praying to Christ from the age of four or five, every morning and night. It was only five or six years after my visit to Assisi, when I had in the natural course of things broken away from my family and gone to study at Harvard, that I was able to reflect, in a half-hearted way, on my sudden revolt, and to suppose that the intention of these Biblical transmissions might not after all be an assault on family love but a challenge to consider that whenever love is deepest and purest, it is also liable to be most possessive; whenever most freely and fully shared, also most liable to be most cruelly withheld and denied.

While I was somewhat reconciled by these thoughts to an older, more instinctive and, as I now know, a deeper view, they were not enough in themselves to restore me to a life of prayer and seeking.

That happened, as I have described in the crazy refrain with which I have now and then interrupted this history of my apprenticeship, more suddenly, and also over the seasons, and with the help of friends along the way, and I suppose when God was once more ready to put up with my stubbornness. Books, as I've said, helped little, except some of the reading I undertook in my study of visionary absurdism for my dissertation. Yet I soaked up Kierkegaard's retelling of the story of Abraham and Isaac, which, as I had heard it in that little church in the backstreets of Assisi, had first driven me from a proper understanding and faith: the part, I mean, where he talks about the need for a leap of faith, a leap beyond the darkness and vanity of an ethical understanding which seeks to justify the ways of God to man, as if we can hold God to account—a leap into the illumination of that love in which the love of family loses all possessiveness as it melts in the radiance of the love of Christ, from whom all love, of philosophy and of family, flows.

To taste this, to perceive it is one thing. To live it is quite another, and only by living it will the seeker ever get it truly by heart.

The truth is, by the time we have broken from our families, however healthy and integrated our personalities, we—even the most deeply loved and loving and the most whole—remain creatures of attraction and aversion. Our breath is so irregular, our appetite is so anxious, we are always fretting over what we approve or disdain, always judging where we cannot love, always offering love in order to gain power by withholding it, so overmastered by our own power that we cannot truly and freely share our hearts.

And it is only when we are at last able to catch ourselves out that we are able, after much labor and suffering, to come to see that we are unlikely to master the curriculum of love without the help of someone—inside or outside—to whom sharing is already second nature, and gotten by heart.

In Ma's houses, once we settled, the arrangements she made for us seemed at first ordinary enough, not unlike the usual rules for contemplatives.

We were celibate. We lived and ate together. We sang and meditated alone and together. We shared expenses and household chores, as I have described, and as in any open order we went out to work every day.

But Ma had a few twists of her own. We lived, men and women, in very close quarters, much closer than monks and nuns. And though there were the usual monastic rules—no sex, drugs, smoking, alcohol—there were no sanctions of any kind. We had to submit to the fiercest rule of all: that "Love cannot compel." From the start we were our own masters, damnably free to disobey, and without redress if anyone wronged us. Thus stripped of privacy and reclusion, we had also to live without the security of an outer discipline—a monastic order of householders, completely open to the outside world, and completely uncompelled.

I was soon suffocating! If I was to undertake a purely religious life, at least give me space and time for myself, and someone to tell me what to do, and, when my will failed, to make sure I did it.

Ma was far too cunning to allow us the luxury of a monastic life. That is reserved for those whose poverty is genuine. Ours was still mostly make-believe, an affectation. So she set about to strip us of much of our private space and time and all our other selfish dependencies, and by throwing us together in an uncompelled chastity, she tricked us into sharing our lives with a sudden candor, a clumsy intimacy, an abrupt and shameless nakedness which, left to ourselves, we would have sought to cover at any cost.

We began to know each other much too well. Living so closely, there was hardly a moment when we could avoid relationship, and yet out of long habit and in constant defense of our privacy, we contrived all kinds of ways of keeping ourselves to ourselves. This recoiling led inevitably to a hundred misunderstandings, and soon we were bickering and backbiting, striking glancing blows; and sometimes, rarely, our quarreling even turned into hand to hand fighting of the kind sometimes provoked between ordinary brothers and sisters.

And all because we could not bear to get close.

But again, something strange and untoward happened.

When we started out, I suppose each of us thought of chastity as a kind of negative force, simply another prohibition. But it soon became clear, even to those of us most fascinated with sex, that it was entirely positive, and that because we were celibate, we were now able to touch and to share physically in ways which we had never imagined. We could hug without hidden expectations and kiss without private desire and hold hands without the reservations of courtship. There were no games, nothing was covert or strategic. If we had secrets, and they were sexual, we were quite unable to keep them. Everyone knew them at once, and because they were known, they had no power or substance. They simply melted away, like ice in a patch of sunlight.

This physical freedom might have meant little by itself. But it expressed, and permitted, an inner relaxation and a deeper intimacy, and bound us together. It was almost tangible, a force, a current rising from the base of the body to the heart and playing there like a fountain. Whatever passion we conserved only drew us closer together. To our surprise we found that by saving ourselves, we were able to open and to give, and not by the denial of passion or its suppression but by spending it as it is always best spent, in the heart. Our passion, by this alchemy, was translated into compassion, and we found ourselves desiring to serve each other, first in small ways and then in larger ones. And when we sat in meditation, after our quarrels were mended, we did not sit apart but in a gathering closeness, merging day by day, year by year, into a common and passionate silence.

Only then after many years of trial and error, was I able to understand in a practical way that the possessiveness imprinted in each of us in our early family life had in some measure been dissolved by chastity. And only then was I able in my imagination to retrace my steps and sit once more in the backstreet church in Assisi and understand why I had fled Christ's words and the staying of Abraham's hand twenty years earlier. Only then, in the common and passionate silence of an uncompelled chastity, my faith restored, was I able at times to share my love without always holding something in reserve. I mean, above all, that sharing became practical and natural.

What had been Baba's first lesson to Ma? "Share me. I am the sharing."

* * *

The school of love has no real curriculum, of course. It has no roof or walls or desks or bells calling you to class. It has only a simple set of steps, one or two, three or four, twenty or thirty, by which we learn to count, depending on our proficiency with the numbers of love and death, our descent to the water's edge; and there we sit, and all our instruction is in our simple attendance at the river's banks, an attendance which only God marks.

So it was that Ma called us to the banks of her river, as unruly a class as ever assembled, and in her fierce patience she taught us the art of *laya yoga*, of "melting into one," the lesson of sharing. *Laya* means melting, and she showed each of us, according to the measure and pace of our understanding, how to begin to dissolve in the waters of her Ganga our desire and pride, fear and judgment, and the possessiveness of a love that holds itself apart.

Little by little, dipping us in the water, she began the long, the lifelong, work of dissolving our little selves, drenching us in the flowing of that constant, single, indivisible Self, where love and awareness are one, flowing in the human heart.

As I have said, we remained unruly—zero for conduct. We still fought, and hid from each other, and dissembled, and hoarded our moments to ourselves, and covered our love with fear and our fear with anger in the universal game of grasping and spurning.

But Ma has always been there, sitting on the banks with timeless patience, unveiled, making us count over and over the steps of our descent into the waters of the heart, and lending us the courage, whenever our own fails, to strip and stand naked and dip in the river.

Of her patience it is easy to speak.

But of her love? That love which melts all our quarrels, melts us with the passion which makes chastity possible—and which chastity makes possible—melts us into a common and passionate and always deepening silence.

MA & ME

How can I describe that love, and how I lost myself in you?

It was my calamity to fall in love, without knowing it, the moment I walked into Hilda's living room, with its wall of holy fools, and saw you sitting there in your green leotards, all two hundred and thirty pounds, daring everyone to suppose with every lustrous dipping of your false eyelashes that you were anything but what you truly are—lovely and noble and slender and purely in love.

And every day my love grew more foolish and complete, exceeding its own folly, exhausting its own fulfillment, betraying its own pretense of perfection, until I let go of my friends, and my family was ashamed and angry. And except for a few who had fallen into the same snare, I had no one who would listen, and I did not know how to talk or where to put myself or whom to embrace.

Until I found You.

* * *

Kashi.
You touch her with your heart, she touches you with her soul. Whoever your guru is, he or she sits there, the same as you, Mother merging with Mother.

Ganga.

She melts your heart. Your soul becomes one with hers. Your eyes see the filth upon her breast, the rats that run so close to her shore, the burning flesh, but you have never seen anything so pure.

For she is you.

She knows her own.

She bows at her children's feet.

There is nothing purer, even filled with the muck of humanity, for she comes from the mountains high above human frailties. She loves all. She represents nothing. She represents everything. She loves all....

THOMAS "BILLY" BYROM

Ganga.

They come down from the mountain, hand in hand, the old woman and the older man. He comes to bring her to Kashi to die. He does not pause to ask why.

The journey is long, the snow is deep. Down the mountain, they follow the river, the river of their heart, knowing not even for a second they will ever part.

She sits by her river, a year and a day, the journey nearly at an end. She sits alone, though he is near.

She need not have lover, father, son or even friend. He is near, and that is enough.

She sits. She watches. She bows before her Mother, Ganga. She does the river's will. She sits for a year and a day. He always sits near, watching the children play. And though there is no space and no time, she begins to rhyme:

Children play by my river

Sadhus stay by my river

Cities old by my river

Temples gold by my river

Cows stray by my river

Night into day by my river

Sadhus yearn by my river

Wise men learn by my river

Ghats burn by my river

How I yearn to return to my river

The sun rises on my river

And when she falls upon my river

She's all alone, so alone

Just a few await the dew

MA & ME

Morning dew, just a few
Down the mountain they walked, hand in hand
Her flesh they will burn
Scatter her ashes upon the river's breast
For it is the river she knows best
Children play, sadhus stay
Cities old, temples gold
Cows stray, sadhus yearn
Wise men learn, ghats burn
Men die, widows cry
All come, saying Ram
The sun falls, the sun rises
The river holds no surprises
Always the same, never the same
The Ganga—that is her name
The black pearl sheds such light
Even in the darkest night
The old woman, the older man
They came down the mountain hand in hand
He takes her to the Ganga to die
He does not ask why
The river
The giver.

—Ma

* * *

We are all dying to love with every breath. It is our nature. From the midwife's first slap, when we first draw breath, we are melting, like ice in a patch of sunlight. With every breath we breathe in the fire of his love, and we begin to dissolve, to lose ourselves altogether, dying with every breath to his love.

I am sitting here still, at my feet the white river falling across the night sky from Dhruva the polestar to the little Milk Dipper in the sign of the Archer, where an hour ago the moon fell below a bank of blue black clouds.

There is only the single flight of love. As the Sufi mystics teach, love has ten degrees. The first is flight from people, and the ninth is silence. But what is the last degree of love?

I look down into the milky river flowing across the face of our pond from the night-blooming water lilies, scarlet and white, to the battered pontoon lopsided in the dark shallows, and I remember that among the one hundred and eight names of the river for which Ganga is named, the simplest and happiest is Nandini, which means simply "happiness."

What is the last degree of love?

In a week the orange trees will drench the roadside and the fields with their heavy and sweet blossoming, but for now everything is fallow. Only the winged sumac and the wax myrtle, bearing a little late winter fruit among the long leaf pine and bluejack oaks, ripen in the darkness of the river hammocks. And in this fallow time, when the pulse of the year misses a measure, there gathers an immense silence, common and passionate and immeasurably deep.

Sitting here, with the river washing over my head among the brilliant stars and at my feet among the night-blooming water lilies, scarlet and white, I reflect that whatever measure I may take of my own love for God, I will never comprehend the immensity of God's love for me. "What heart could keep from breaking!" crazy St. Catherine protests. "Deep well of love, it seems you are so madly in love with your creatures that you could not live without us!"

For countless thousands of years we have looked up at the night sky, or seeing it reflected in the waters at our feet have peered into its depths, and have asked as many questions as there are stars in its immensity. And still we are unable to take the measure of its mysteries, of the spinning of dark matter which holds all created things together, things exotic and invisible, or of the missing mass of the universe. We are still tugging at God's sleeve, pestering him with our impatience.

What folly!

For we have known from the beginning of time, from the first slap of the midwife, from the very first breath we draw, that death is the last degree of love, and love is the spinning of dark matter, holding the universe together. Are we not, all of us, dying to love with every breath? Even at the beginning of time, turning in the darkest and coldest wastes of the night sky, not one of us is ever so far from the sun that we are not melting with every breath we draw, melting in the fire of Christ's love, dissolving, losing ourselves in him, dying with every breath to his love.

10
The Betrayal of Joseph Tillman

It's all sky down here.

Most of Florida is so flat that I can imagine no vaster sky, not in Kansas, not in Texas, not in New Mexico. And this immense dome, crowning and filling our heads, is never as vast as at first light, when, except for the barely visible unfurling of low nimbus clouds rolling in from off the ocean and juggling a late moon on the western horizon, it is all a brightening emptiness, so brightly blank it could only contain, if you spared it a thought, a single cloudless thought.

A thought of freedom.

Here I am, walking around the pond many times, my constitutional two miles, at six in the morning a day past the vernal equinox. As the light climbs, I catch my breath at the cold wetness of the St. Augustine grass under my bare feet, and there is my familiar sentinel, a fly-up-the-creek stockstill in his yellow socks on our lopsided pontoon, attending the first catch which the light will soon deliver him. And as I come fully awake, I am aware of the awakening all around and above me, an infinity of blue without true color dousing my sleepy head with cold draughts of its clear uncolored blue, God's gift of unsmudged awareness, the first of all his morning gifts.

One thought fills immensity.

Living in Florida we may take freely, every morning, season after season, this gift of freedom simply by lifting our eyes and filling them with a limitless elation.

The heron makes his catch, a stippled bass lured by minnows out of the safe shadow of the papyrus.

The ground of every inner life is service, contemplation, and longing.

Its sky is freedom.

Sanskrit has a special word for this sky—*chidakash*. *Chid* in this simple compound means "the heart enlightened," that essential condition of our common nature in which love and awareness are one and the same. *Akash*, the name of one of the five physical elements, is usually translated as "ether," though it has nothing to do with classical science or with anesthetics. Figuratively it means "space" or "sky," and in particular the spaciousness of the inner sky, the roomy heart of awareness, that same blank and colorless sky which fills my head this morning.

Inside, outside.

And here I am walking around the pond in the first light, all by myself, and for all I know I could be on my own in the first light of the first day of creation. But the bird was here before me.

And we are not alone.

As I turn along the northern bank by the border of yellow and magenta jacaranda and green-berried firethorn, I hear a rustling and a banging from Ma's paint studio, a small hut just the other side of the garden fence under its fifty-foot canopy of clumping bamboo. There's the distinct sound of a wooden frame shaken and roughly knocked, and the play of water.

Ma is painting.

For nearly ten years now she has been painting as part of her nightly devotions, privately. She starts at two or three in the morning and paints beyond the first light, until the sun comes over her fence.

Sometimes figurative, sometimes abstract, acrylic and water on soaked canvases, the subject always sacred. And she has had no training except for what the disgraced Mr. Lipschitz gave her at PS 253 so many years ago.

Her latest series is called "The Third Wish," and it celebrates the story of the Katha Upanishad of the Black Yajur Veda, which was written down about a hundred years before Christ. A young boy, Nachiketas, which means "the one who is about to wake up," is distressed that his father tries to fob God off with some stingy gifts. He insists that his father must surrender his most precious possession. But it turns out that his most precious possession is actually Nachiketas! Ashamed and angry, the father refuses and instead sends the child off to the house of Death.

Now in ancient India, Death, Yama, was like Adam the first man. But unlike Adam, instead of falling from grace, he had the purity of heart to discover the secret of life.

When Nachiketas arrived, Death was out, and when he at last came home, to make up for his lack of hospitality, he gave the boy three wishes.

For his third wish the child asked for the secret of life, of "the great crossing," the passage beyond. And though his host tried his best to dissuade him, since not even the gods themselves knew the secret, in the end he had to keep his word; he relented and told the boy, who, true to his name, at last woke up.

And what was the secret?

Death says, if you wish to be free, free as the sky in the heart, you have to surrender everything, you have to give yourself completely away. And this is both the greatest generosity, giving all you have, and also the greatest poverty, since you are left with nothing.

Or are you?

For Death says, if we are all one, then you may give yourself only to yourself, since there is no one, not even God, who is not you. And herein lies the radiant secret of the great passage, the mystery of freedom—we are all one.

This was Baba's single refrain, *sub ek*, all one.

And this is the mystery I hear Ma celebrating, banging the framed canvas on the deck outside her studio, a shower cap covering her pinned-up hair, aproned, and dappled with paint, her sneakers caked with the splatter of a thousand mornings at her art, her devotions.

She is laying out the canvases to dry in the first light as it comes over the fence.

I have done my two miles. Getting my breath back, I sit for a few moments on the bench in the shade of the bamboo, within the banked crescent of prickly shilling holly. Here the sky is all but hidden by the overarching bamboo, blue-green and bulging with new shoots. But I have not lost the gift God gave me when I stepped out this morning, as the morning ascended and filled the sky with blue. An hour later I look up from my desk, where I have been translating the story of Nachiketas from the Sanskrit, and for a few moments there is a bright rain burst from a still cloudless sky.

* * *

Every inner life must be grounded in service, and in serving, the seeker discovers a special freedom, a sky suddenly empty and vast.

Ma has given her time to service since she was a child, and many of us, having worked through our quarrels, began to follow after. But we have to go far afield. Our part of Florida is still too constrained for us to serve it freely. We have tried, but we have been often chased away. And when you have a school with over a hundred children, you cannot safely endure the burning of crosses on the fields where they play, nor the strictures of fundamentalists angry that we will not acknowledge an exclusive path to God nor a hell of eternal torment, nor the attentions of a gutter press quick to cry "cult" for the sake of higher circulation, nor indeed the ordinary politics of the place which have been, up till now at least, too often a matter of self-interested reaction.

So Ma has taken her work ninety miles south to West Palm Beach, and out to Los Angeles every few months, helping abused children, addicted teens, crack babies, and people of all ages with AIDS, bringing care and company and cookies to the dying in the County Home, and working with their caregivers. At present we cook twenty meals a day for local hospice families, just a beginning, but a happy one. And Ma hauls us after her down the turnpike according to our staying power and gifts.

Although she has a special talent for encouraging others to serve, and for getting people to work together (for instance, having her people with AIDS in Los Angeles organize help for AIDS babies' homes like the City of Angels), her own activity is always one to one.

Her service is always a sharing. She never talks about God unless someone asks a question, in the thirst to live or out of the hunger of dying.

And the freedom is all in the one to one, all in the sharing of the secret of the great crossing, that we are all one, and one with God.

Here, to make this plain, and in her own words, is a story about Ma and Mr. Tillman, eighty years old, a brilliant gentleman of the spirit, an old junkie whom she discovered in the AIDS ward of the County Home in West Palm Beach. It is the story of an old man's fearful confinement, and the freedom he won from it.

* * *

So I'm invited to go down to the County Home—baptism by fire, my Bruce, who runs the AIDS coalition, calls it.

Here I go in the front door.

"Hey, look what walked in the door with a dot on her forehead!"

The first people I run into are these five mean guys, really mean, playing dominoes, and it's clear you don't mess with their dominoes.

And Lee, the guy in charge of the place, he's right on top of me to see if I'm going to make trouble, with the dot on my forehead.

So I go up to these tough Black guys and I say, "I'm going to show youse all deep relaxation."

I figure why beat around the bush.

And the main man, real mean, says, without looking up, "Girl, you kiddin' us."

"You got AIDS right? So you gotta relax," I says.

And they say, "White girl, get outta here."

So I say, "Ok! If that's how you want it...."

And I knock down all their dominoes. I wasn't brought up on the streets for nothing.

And the main man says again, "Girl, you kiddin' us?"

And I say, "I don't need you people," and I walk away.

So then Lee who is hovering around still thinks, I'm going to get t his crazy lady. Maybe we can get rid of her. I'm going to give her our very worst patient, the meanest man in the building, who hates everybody.

"How would you like to meet Mr. Tillman?" he says.

And he takes me up to the AIDS ward, the Haney wing, and there's this man, Black, very sick, very old, very handsome, and he doesn't talk to no one.

But I give him a good shove, and he says, "What you do, girl?"

He just needed a shove. And I says, "I do service."

He says, "I don't give a shit, honey." And there's nothing sweet the way he says "honey." "You just lower me down."

See, he's in this chair contraption, buttons and levers and he's stuck full of tubes and he has a bag, and I've been working in hospitals for thirty years but I never saw such a crazy chair.

"You sure?" I says.

"Just lower me down, just a little now," he says. Real mean.

So I push the button.

And suddenly the man's on his head with his feet straight up in the air, the IV bags all over the floor and wrapped around his neck, choking him, and the tubes are coming out of his hands and arms and his nose, and Yashoda is panicking down the hall, shouting for help.

And Mr. T. is choking, "Push that thing, girl, push that other thing!"

And I look at him laying there upside down all over the floor with his chair tipped up on top of him, and I say, "Hey, the last time you said to do that we had a little trouble!"

And he's saying, "The blood's rushing to my head. My feet's bleeding. Get me outta here!"

"So alright," I says, "I'll push the other thing."

I push it—and, so help me God, suddenly Mr. T. is straight upright on his feet, which he hasn't walked on for years, at attention, and now he's standing bolt upright with all the bags and tubes round his neck and his head.

And then he starts laughing, choking and laughing and shaking so much the emergency nurses can't untangle him, and he's fighting them off and cussing away. Cussing and gasping with the tube tight round his neck, and he's laughing.

"White girl," he says, "don't you touch nothing more, don't you touch nothing, I mean it."

His language was worse than mine if you can believe it.

Meantime the nurses slowly get him untangled and slowly they fix up the chair, sticking all the tubes back in the right places, and when they're done I says, "So I'm Ma. What's your name?"

Now he's ready with this line he always uses, "NO TIME FOR CONVERSATION," but he's still dabbing his eyes and shaking with laughter like God himself was tickling him.

And I say, "Well I'm giving you deep relaxation whether you like it or not."

"Now you kiddin' me, girl!"

This is the third time I've been brushed off like that, so I give him a big shove, and I say, "Lay back nice."

And he says, "Just don't touch that button, Ma."

He calls me "Ma!"

Well, I want you to know right then and there I fell in love with him.

Eighty years old with AIDS, a junky forty years on the streets, a powerful womanizer with a wife, a mistress, and two girlfriends, all gone except for the mistress.

No regrets, no remorse, no sorrow. He was just downright mean.

And right there and then I gave him my heart, and my education began all over again. Because what did I know? I had worked with Boozer in the Bowery before the cops ran him over, and with the priest after the Guatemala earthquake picking baby bodies out of the rubble, but what did I know?

I didn't know nothing.

I sat down near him and kept my big mouth shut, and he says, "You sit here so long as you don't say nothing."

But I can't help it, and I say, "Mr. Tillman, don't you know I'm a guru!" I just had to get a rise out of him.

And he says, "Girl, don't you know I'm Mr. Joseph Tillman."

And we both start laughing.

"Yeah," I says, "but I'm more important than you."

And the nurse who had come for the bedpan, her mouth drops open, and she says, "Did I hear you tell him you're more important than him?"

And I say, "Hey I'm just playing. Besides, I am!"

And Mr. T. cuts in real fast, calls her a "dumb n----r" and says, "No, she is. She is more important. Don't you have no sense?"

And the nurse, "What you say?" She is so scandalized she just can't believe it because the old man never showed respect for anyone beside himself.

And, see, this is what Mr. T. and I, Ma, understood. First you respect yourself. You know you are more important. Then you know you're not. That's how it works.

Well, every week I went down to him and as time went by and he didn't have much time left, we became one, him and me. No color. No "you're in the Home and I'm visiting." No "you're dying and I'm living." No life, no death. Just one.

We just held hands and understood each other.

And he was still very mean and jealous. He'd try to tell me who to take care of and who not to, but I didn't pay him any mind.

"Don't you go near that one," he'd say if he didn't like someone. "He's got AIDS."

"And what have you got?" I'd say.

"HIV positive!" But he knew it was all just a matter of time and that names wouldn't hold anything back.

There was a hooker in the ward he wanted to keep me from in the worst way. "Don't you go near that hooker, Ma. She's just trash."

And for me this old man was the essence of Hanuman. He was my Christ. He was the joy of my life. And I couldn't wait to see him.

One day he said, "How come you never talk about God?"

"I don't wanna," I says.

So, "I'll talk about God," he announces. "Just you listen and don't touch no buttons."

"So?" I says.

And he says, "You got him."

"Got who?" I says.

And he says, "God. Any God. Just God. That's what you got, girl." Just like my Mama used to tell me.

This old man suffering such a painful death looks me in the eyes and says, "Ma, your eyes seen more than most."

"A lot less than yours, Mr. T.," I says.

And we just held hands.

And the nurse who didn't like to hear us say how important we were came up to me one day as I was leaving and said, "This old man didn't talk to nobody," and she gave me a big hug, O.K.?

This story is painful to tell because of the joy in it.

Mr. T. took the life he led and had no sorrow or regrets. He lived in the House of Death but he knew it was the House of Life, and he knew he wasn't coming out of it ever.

As for me it was just an honor, Lee letting me in there every week.

And Mr. Tillman and Ma, we were not a couple, we were one.

Until I had to skip a week to go out to L.A. to my AIDS boys there because they were calling out and I told Mr. T. I had to go.

"Girl," he said, "don't you go. I won't be here when you get back."

I thought he was just jealous, and I had to go.

* * *

In this little slapstick in the house of Death there's the same freedom Nachiketas found when Death at last came home, the same tickle of freedom that had Mr. T. bolt upright with bleeding feet, choking with laughter, a freedom so limitless it resists all spiritual glossing. It speaks from a particular stillness of the common roominess of the human heart, which has no text to gloss, no scripture, which is always, however sublime the calligraphy, the scribble of man in the silence of God.

But I can't help observing that Mr. Tillman, bolt upright or upside down, speaks to me in the love he shared with Ma of that essential surrender which Death taught Nachiketas—of that poorest and richest of gifts, the gift of himself, just as he was, mean and without remorse, an old unremarkable junkie brilliant in his dying, shining in the simple giving of himself to the strange, loud, impossible, clumsy Jewish girl half his age who befriended him out of nowhere and wouldn't take no for an answer.

Befriended him out of nowhere, freely, no conditions, just one to one.

One to one.

If we need scripture, there's no better line. It's far from original of course, but it strikes me from the heart of an old man's strict confinement—a spark struck from flint. It is every bit as good a line as *I'm doing service*, which so freely mocks itself, a mockery so deadpan the nurse with the bedpan couldn't at first comprehend that she had been tricked into playing straight man.

Service is only free in the measure that it mocks all virtue. When there is the least righteousness in service, the least smudge of a self-regarding dedication, then it becomes mimicry, a false copy of the heart. So the poet of *The Heart of Awareness* decries the rictus of attachment to *dharma*, the presumption of virtue, as the root of all other attachments: to *kama*, feeling good, and *artha*, feeling safe, and *moksha*, feeling free. In the shams of service there is no freedom, no one to one, and nothing is given or received. Nothing is shared, no one is helped. It is all quite heartless.

THOMAS "BILLY" BYROM

In India one of the darkest forms of the Mother is Bagala, pot-bellied, with the head of a crane. Among other ferocious aspects of the psychology of the separate self, lost as it is in illusion, she represents that power by which we are able to contemplate the suffering of humankind and remain unmoved—the terrible power by which we separate ourselves from each other's sorrows. In this fatal lack of feeling interest in others, Bagala mocks the true detachment of the heart, in which we find the only real staying power to engage our compassion and freely help. And like all dark figures of the Mother, she summons us to consume her, so that we may devour the illusion of the separate self that strives so arduously to keep itself apart, the self that will not be touched, nor touch.

And what is her chief ally if not the presumption of virtue, with whose help she sustains the appearance of service, the counterfeit of good works. But in the exposure of these affectations of kindness, there appears at last the unveiled grace of Bagala who, with all her guiles disgraced, enfolds us in the single embrace in which Mr. T. and Ma became lawlessly one.

* * *

All wonder what happens after death.
Some say you become a ghost,
Some say that you will go to heaven,
Some say that you will live close to God,
And others that you will be united with God.
And the Vedas proclaim that you're a bit of space
Enclosed in a jar fated to shatter.

Prasad says you will be at the end
What you were at the beginning, as a bubble
That appears in water and merges back into it.
—Ramprasad

* * *

After my leukemia diagnosis I spent five weeks in an experimental cancer clinic in Mexico. A group of American physicians had rented a quiet resort on the cliffs of Baja California a couple of hours south of Tijuana.

It was laid out in white stone avenues between desert gray hills of startling desolation and that same boundless friendly Pacific which I had known so intimately as a boy. I had known it then in its southern hemisphere, thousands of miles south and west; yet it was not different here, distinctly hospitable, with its own deep warm blue.

Within the walled grounds there was a small hill pyramid sacred to the indigenous of the place. The staff had reconsecrated it, and they gathered there after nightfall for meditation and prayers.

I had had leukemia for six or seven years by then. The prognosis at the Radcliffe Hospital in Oxford had been clear: I would be fortunate to survive four or five years. But a close family friend in my childhood, Uncle Bunny, an Australian federal judge, had fought the same strain while retaining his seat on the bench for over ten years—not without a remarkable courage—and I had determined to follow his inspiration.

Since no one claimed a cure, I decided to try every going therapy short of obvious quackery. I believed, I still believe strongly, in proper diet and meditation as essential defenses against cancer, and these were two of the many therapies applied at Casa Santa Maria in Baja.

I remember most immediately the coffins lifted through the doors at seven in the morning when I went to get my pint of fresh carrot juice. And then the afternoon conversations in the sunny courtyard where we received chelation therapy: chatting with a retired army officer about his war experiences in Burma; or with a forty-year-old mother of four, an anticlerical Catholic, off a production line in Motown, about her favorite saint of Siena; or with the spectral heiress of a famous candy fortune about the wickedness of refined sugars. And you never knew who might be coming out the door tomorrow in a box, chipping the paint off the lintel, and trundled into the old Studebaker which served as the hospital hearse and which, to its credit, lacked the fatal gloss and shine of hearses north of the border.

When no one was looking, I'd steal a few flowers from the skimpy gardens and stuff them behind the wipers. I knew the wipers were unlikely to work if it rained. I didn't know the names of the Mexican flowers, but before breakfast we all knew the names in the boxes, the ones who had gone in the night—*mrityumukhat pramuktam*, as Death names them for the child in his house, "the ones released from the muzzle of Death." Neither the naming nor the unnaming upset me, but I was distressed by the chipping of the lintels, which had been painted with imaginary flowers, flowers beyond botany, in a childish hand, clumsy and exquisite.

It was my first visit in a house of Death, and I was supposedly one of the dying. But I knew I would not be leaving in a box, chipping the paint, in a dusty limousine with a hoarse transmission. I knew that like Nachiketas I would be returning to the land of the living, and I even hoped that I would leave having learned something, not about therapies since I realized none of them really worked, but about the tricks of life and death, something to help me in my difficult but inevitable return.

After the morning coffins and the afternoon conversations, what I most vividly remember is sitting at sunset about seven in the evening on a small flat bluff halfway down the cliff, out of sight and watching the ocean and the sky. I had done this so often as a child, and with such happiness, that it was easy to reclaim my younger self and his attendant quietness and let myself go into a blue— friendly and nourishing, paler in the sky above, darker in the ocean below—a blue always unbuffeted by doubt or sorrow, the blue of a happy child's reclusion.

Where the sea meets the sky in the Mother's eyes—a place and a moment I had known all my life, though I had often neglected them, the occasion of all solitude and hence of all company, since when I sat in that quietness, with the wind running cold up the cliff face, I was most closely in the presence of my true self, in whose company I am least apart from all the bright beings who lighten my heart—family, lovers, friends, all of us.

One heart, never apart.

It happened that this expedition of mine was undertaken without advice or direction from Ma, except that she gave me without comment a small wooden Bavarian Madonna and Child to take with me, and a silver medallion of Tara, a form of the Mother for both Buddhists and Hindus.

Perched on the bluff overlooking the Pacific at nightfall, I reflected from time to time on the form of Tara and recalled some of the verses by Ramprasad which scold her and pick quarrels with her and adore her. For him she represents, among many other aspects of our spiritual psychology, the hunger to survive. She is at the root of all appetite, all desire, every savage instinct that struggles for life. And of course, here I was, a continent away from home, hungering to survive in the house of Death, teacher of teachers, trying to find in an inner dialogue with him, just as the child Nachiketas had done in his hunger to awaken, an answer to the secret of the crossing, which is, incidentally, what the name Tara means in Sanskrit.

So I meditated on Tara, whose image hung around my neck on a green thread against my breastbone, where the white cells in my marrow were breeding with an unchecked hunger of their own, one that would soon, if it were not sated or transformed, prove fatal to me.

Fixing my eyes on the cloudless sky, then closing them, I felt overtaken by a very simple breath, breathing *in* the middle of my chest where Tara hung, and breathing *out* just above and between my eyes, at the bone of the brow. I did not invent or contrive this exercise. It just came to me out of the blue, out of the sky and the sea as it were, and I let it happen according to its natural rhythm. It was just the natural pulse of the breath.

Every evening for several weeks I sat there in the rising and falling of this unbroken breath.

Then one afternoon, it must have been in my fourth week, toward the end of June, I had a brief conversation in the courtyard with an upholsterer from Far Rockaway who had a liver cancer so advanced his doctors had sent him home from Sloan Kettering to die. His name was Franz, and having survived Bergen-Belsen, he was no stranger to the many hostelries of death. And though a man denied a formal education, he was, even with failing eyes, a greedy reader. I do not say *avid*. Franz was greedy. There was a definite gluttony in his reading; he read always to excess, morbidly, so much so that he had lost some of his powers of expression.

For this reason he wasn't always easy. A curt or faltering conversationalist, he was deeply learned, and sometimes as we sat there in the cold sun with the tubes in our arms, he would reach down into the lining of the deep overstuffed armchair of his book-bulging mind, and pull out an odd, indirect observation upon the situation we shared.

"You never have much of an appetite," he observed.

The nurses were serving us juice and whole-meal cookies, and as usual I turned them away.

"No, I don't," I agreed. "Nor do you."

"No, no, I eat books," he laughed without much humor, reading my mind.

"Yes, I noticed. What's on today's menu?"

"*Bouvard et Pécuchet*," he said, grudgingly.

"Yes, Flaubert," I said. "One of my favorites."

"Yes?" He was clearly alarmed that I might want to borrow it.

"But I no longer read much. I lost my appetite for it."

"Yes!" he agreed, very much relieved.

When Death is close at hand, there is little each of us misses about the other. It's like talking to yourself.

And there I left him to read, brows vexed, holding the margins tight, devouring every word, swallowing hard.

That evening after dinner I made my way down the cliff to the bluff and sat there. The breathing started as usual and rose and fell in its own measure, my head full of the sky. And it came to me that this hunger to survive, Tara's primal hunger, which had brought me to the clinic, was not only the same as any other appetite, more than that, it was identical, like all appetites, with the longing for oneness, for God.

I saw that our basest, most instinctual hunger is entirely the same as our highest, our most exalted. And I felt that the breath that was breathing me was the breath that both feeds and consumes all hungers, the appetite for separate survival and for oneness with God. I understood that it was the bellows which kindles the sacrificial fire of Nachiketas, to which he commits his little self and is reduced to the fine ash of the One Self.

And my thoughts went back to the Shalimar in Queens and the greedy consumption of marbled cheesecake with which Ma had first introduced us to the mastery of breath and the mystery of appetite.

Then the breath stopped of its own accord, and I sat in the stillness between out and in, and perceived, in that moment at least, how the hunger to be fed is also the hunger to feed. I sat in that precise and eternal moment, now and always, when the child, without abandoning the breast, becomes also the mother, Tara, whose fingers express the milk from the nipple even as her arms hold safe the suckling child.

When I opened my eyes the night had taken the sea.

But the sky was still above me, bright and fair, and I felt free in the darkening ashes of the day.

Falling asleep that night, after all my holistic herbal brews and potions, I saw on the windowsill the wooden Madonna and Child, which I had oiled that morning, and I understood why Ma had coupled them with Tara, at whose breast we are all coupled.

Mother, child.

There's not too much more I could say about my trip to Baja. Unlike Nachiketas, I did not of course learn the secret of the great crossing. But like him I was at least restored to my spiritual family, and what I had learned about hunger and longing, breath and appetite, I have tried to put to work.

And I returned in my meditation, with the Pacific sky in my head, a spaciousness unexpectedly reclaimed from my childhood.

There were a few other long afternoons in the courtyard with Franz, and when he wasn't holding too tight to the margins, he confided in me something of his experiences in the camp. But his words were too scarce and laconic, he had a mouthful of death, he was too hungry for his books, and I could not understand.

The day before I left they carried him out of his room in a box. The door jambs were painted a deep aquamarine with yellow and carmine flowers done in that childish, lyrical hand.

The poet of the Upanishad says, "In awe of him, Death rushes to devour us all."

And I called out, "Don't chip the paint."

> *For you are she*
> *Who arises with all life,*
> *Who devours all its forms,*
> *The mother of all powers,*
> *And entering the secret hollow,*
> *There you sit in the heart,*
> *In the heart of all beings,*
> *A child.*
> *One!*
>
> —Katha Upanishad, 4:7

* * *

When I got home, I found a community fully dedicated with Ma's direction to building a house of Life—a school for all our children. The winter before, Mikey, then seven, whose father is Jewish and whose mother is Black, had come home one afternoon from public school and had asked his father, "Dad, what's a n----r?" At that time, this was a word the mayor felt free to use in official meetings.

Ma's response was instant.

We must establish our own school. We all understood that if we did not wish our children to suffer the infection of racism, we would have to take them out of the public system which, though broadly integrated, still had the fevers and chills of a fitful prejudice.

We began with a small red schoolhouse and ran up the flag, pledging allegiance every morning to a nation equal and undivided. The porches and the outdoors had to do for many of our classes at first. Then we built a nursery with a big fenced-in yard. And before long we had a real school, K through 12 as they say, with a few gaps. As for teachers, we had a very large number of postgraduates and people with all sorts of special crafts and skills to draw upon. Our staff was from the start the most highly qualified in the state, with its pool of sixty or seventy university-trained helpers. We were all its faculty, and the whole enterprise was joyful.

We imposed no doctrine in this House of Life, in the shared understanding that life is always fluent, doctrine always fixed. We sing Christmas carols and light the seven candles for Hanukkah, and say a simple grace before lunch, but that's all.

Instead, what has marked our school, apart from a steady scholarship, is the freedom and the inner quietness of the children, and the sense of closeness, a family closeness. I distinguish these three qualities—free, quiet, close—but in truth they are all one. We have secured for our kids a freedom not merely from racism and drugs, but a creative freedom to love and to be themselves, and to share. There arises in the infinitely spacious sky of their childhood a shining stillness that visitors rarely fail to remark on, however misbehaved and rowdy the classroom.

There runs through the school day a curriculum of close and quiet activity.

I spell this out with a certain envy, conscious that, free as my childhood was, I never knew, until I saw it reflected in the eyes of our children, a sky of such particular depth.

* * *

All eyes are on the sky.

A winter morning, a light frost already melted off the bamboo. Hearing the radio countdown, the kids have rushed out of the schoolhouse and stand close together in the field, eyes fixed on the northeast.

Slowly a shaft of purest white rises above the horizon. One of the teens bends his knees, then straightens up, and his younger sister claps her hands silently to her cheeks. The rising spume is scarcely whiter than the flawless sky, the color of finely sifted ash. The radio on the schoolroom windowsill announces a flawless launch.

With a beauty both natural and surprising, the bole divides into three curving branches of flowering chalk-white, and a little way along the lower stem as it unfolds there is a brief burst of orange and black, then the wind disperses the cascading plumes. Even the tallest shaft begins to loop over and fall toward the sea.

Someone turns up the radio, and we all hear what has happened, though we know it already. The shuttle Challenger has exploded.

No one says a word.

And the schoolteacher Christa is dead.

A child clicks the radio off. One by one we sit down on the grass and watch the sky until all the white has been blown away, and it is once again flawless, the color of sifted ash.

*　*　*

However bright the sky of service, however empty the sky of contemplation, there is no sky of such an unbroken blue as the sky of love. But what is love when it is free? Looking back over nearly twenty years of apprenticeship, frequenting once more the houses of life and death in which I have been the lodger of her love, what have I understood?

In India there are many ancient trinities. Beauty in a woman is marked by three folds above the navel. On the forehead of the ascetic there are three horizontal streaks of ash. There are three spices—cinnamon, cardamom, and nutmeg. In the house of Death the seeker is granted three wishes. The holy fire has three flames and must be kindled and stoked three times. Whoever is awakening carries his holy verses in three baskets. And the sacred river Ganga has three currents.

So it is with love. Though it is without conditions, it may be distinguished by three unravelings which unloosen it like a free-flying kite in the sky.

They are grace, dispassion, and surrender.

The first is very simple. Love is all grace, a gift.

In love there can be no manmade doctrine, no law. Like the river which flows through these pages as the essential figure for the presence of God in our lives, love is always flowing. It is never dammed, it never runs dry. No idea, no word, can ever ascertain it. It can never be fixed. And this is a truth which the practice of celibacy reveals in the life of whoever wants to embrace it, as surely as it is revealed in the celebration of sexual love whenever it is fully shared. Blake says, "The cistern contains, the fountain overflows."

There is no letter to love, only spirit. The letter is the nail in Christ's wrist, the letter the spear in his side, the thorn in his brow. Fundamentalisms, literalism of any kind, any fixity, these are the denials of his grace. These are merely the staking out of territory, the nationalisms of the closed heart. So Ma often advises people who have just come to her, "The only time you walk away from anyone is when they say theirs is the only way," and she adds, "walk away, but never put them out of your heart." And this I take as the true meaning of Christ's assurance, his absolute proscription of all sectarian prescriptions, when he says, with Isaiah and the poets of Vedanta, "I am the way and the truth and the life." This is the true meaning of the ancient Indian exclamation *Jaya!*—"victory"—the victory of "I AM," with which he conquers the world.

MA & ME

From the time I first began as a child, unbidden, to pray to Christ, I have never believed that he recognizes any exclusive distinctions of belief. His love dissolves all doctrines, levels all hierarchies. It transgresses all laws, trespasses beyond all boundaries, and tolerates none. He takes all territory. For the victory of his passion is already and always complete. And the only torment a soul may suffer is in the measure that the heart shuts out another. That is our only hell.

As for the second and third unlatchings of love, dispassion and surrender, letting it all be and letting it all go, they are so completely coupled, the closest of all the soul's synonyms, that I can best illustrate the way they complete love's trinity with another of Ma's stories, again in her own words, the last installment, as it happens, of her love affair with Mr. Tillman, in which love finally betrayed him.

*   *   *

I was leaving for LA. And Mr. T. was getting to be scared of dying, just a little, he let on. So he says to me, "What do I gotta do?"

"Well," I said, "before you die, I'll tell you what you gotta do. You just gotta say a certain amount of words to people. You've been quiet too long. No one says you have to talk special or nice, but just talk to people just a certain amount of words, OK?"

He hears me but he says nothing.

The next Thursday when I turn up the big nurse with skin like chocolate says to me, "You know what Mr. T. says to me. He says, "Go fuck yourself!" And he says you told him to, he says Ma said I should talk to you."

So when I catch up to Mr. T. I give him a big shove and he says, "Well, you didn't tell me what to say. You just said talk."

He was so mean, so wonderful.

But I saw he had gotten real tired.

His veins were all collapsing, shooting heroin for years and from all the blood they had to take now to regulate his medicine.

And I saw in his eyes he had had enough, too many sticks and his veins rolling real bad.

"Girl," he said, "I got more sticks than a porcupine."

They'd tried all week to get a vein. And there's this rule in the County Home. If they can't take your blood, they can't give you your medicine, and they have to turn you out. Regulations.

"Ma," he says to me, in so much pain, "no more. I can't. Let me go die in the street. Whatever. I just can't no more."

So I negotiate a deal.

"Look, let's see if I can get you one more week, then I can get someone over from St. Mary's pediatrics."

He shrugs, and we get a week's reprieve.

So the last Thursday before I go out to L.A., Yashoda and her son and me are coming up to the Haney Ward when we hear all this yelling and screaming and the whole AIDS wing is carrying on.

It was Mr. Tillman fighting the needle.

So I see this very straight older nurse with white hair, skinny and brittle, but I can tell she can slide in a needle like into butter.

"Can you get it first shot?" I ask her.

"First shot," she says, "But if he won't let me in...."

And Mr. T. is real wild and mean and cussing.

"No more, Ma. I'm outta here. No way. Too many sticks," and his language is bad even for me. "Too many sticks, girl."

So I look at him and I say, "Mr. T. we had a deal." And my language was worse than his, it had to be.

"No, Ma," he says.

"Mr. T.," I says, "then I'm just going to hold you down." And I know I can because he's gotten so tired, and he will fight the others but maybe he won't fight me. Maybe.

"No you can't!"

"Yes, I can!"

It was his will against mine, whose was stronger.

So the brittle old nurse comes back in, all prim, nerves of steel, a hand like butter, and she says to me, "You have to leave, regulations."

And I says, "Who the fuck's going to hold him down?"

"You don't belong, and mind your language," she says, but she is not unfriendly. This is routine for her.

"The hell I don't," I says. "I'm kin!"

And I held him down, and in one move she slid in and drew his blood. And he was crying out and cussing, but he didn't truly struggle, not truly, and in the doorway Yashoda and her son, who's State Champion Tae Kwon Do 5th Degree Black Belt and tough, they both have tears streaming down their face, but I'm not crying, and neither is Miss Prim and Brittle with her brave needle all butter and steel.

And I ran right after that old bitch of a nurse and I held her so tight, and all she says is, "I guess you really are kin."

Back in the room I kneel down by the wheelchair, and he is madder than mad, and he says, "How could you do that to me?"

I look him in the eye and I say, "I want you to die some place familiar. Because I love you." And I said, "Forgive me please."

He put his huge hand on my head, and I thought he was going to say what I knew he was thinking, which was, "You betrayed me."

But there was no White, no Black, no young, no old, no sick, no well, no man, no woman. There was just this oneness.

And he says, "Why you do that?"

I say, "I love you."

And he keeps his big hand on my head, and looks at me close, you know, and he says, "You really do. You really do." And then a third time, "You really do."

And I had no tears.

And he gave in.

I let it be, and he let it go.

He smiled a smile that, no matter whoever touches me, I'll never forget. Or his hand on my head like a blessing because I betrayed him and he let me.

I don't know why I told Billy this story. He wanted it for his book. I have other stories. But once in a while when it gets really sad and the world is going crazy with wars, and the whole world is crying in anger, or a little baby dies of AIDS in agony, or a child is abused, I can still feel Mr. T.'s hand on my head and he is saying, "You really do," like he's saying my marriage vow for me and I am his bride.

I didn't care if he died thinking I'm a Judas. I had to take that risk.

I had no tears, and he didn't truly fight me, he let go.

And I feel his hand on my head, and on yours too.

MA & ME

* * *

Mr. T. had told Ma not to go out to L.A. "Girl, I won't be here when you get back."

But she had to make it out there to all her boys with AIDS. She had been going regularly for two or three years by then, and there were all those broken bodies and hungry hearts calling out.

The Thursday Ma was away, others went down to the County Home in Ma's place, and Mr. Tillman said, "You tell that white girl when I see her I'm going to beat her butt."

The next day he took a bad turn, and before Ma got back, he was gone.

"You tell that white girl when I see her I'm going to beat her butt." His last words to her, more precious than scripture.

* * *

As morning is breaking, I have already turned five times around the pond. Last night I was rasping a little with some fibrosis in my chest from the chemotherapy. But when I woke, my breathing was easy and free, and passing the little garden consecrated to the risen Christ, I take a few deep clear breaths.

Breathing in the sky.

It would be a great folly to pretend that the pursuit of freedom in the inner life has anything to do with serenity. Quite the contrary. The seeker who has the tenacity, discrimination and grace to follow the right track, to walk the razor's edge as Death told Nachiketas he must, is swiftly overcome with a characteristic panic. And how could it be otherwise? We discover only what we risk, even if we risk betraying ourselves.

Seven times around, and I pause to rest for a spell on the bench between sweet sage and violet myrtle. Leaning back, I lose myself in the deep hollow of the sky.

There is a havoc in the heart of every true seeker, the havoc of freedom. This havoc afflicts her as a natural consequence of her fidelity to herself, and to the radical independence which the true teacher demands of her at every turn. If she really begins to stand on her own, faithfully, she discerns sooner or later that the gift of freedom which God has given her is absolute, constant, and single.

She is confronted after a close and quiet sharing with her teacher by a circumstance from which she may never excuse herself: that she must choose to love herself freely in every moment without the least hesitation or condition. And if she cannot undertake freely this absolute, single, and constant responsibility, there is no other possibility of freedom for her; nor will she ever freely love another unless she first loves herself.

This was the choice Joseph Tillman was able to make in the house of Death, as he made ready to die, making ready to live. He found, as we all must, the space for freedom within the form of his own confinement, and in the happy havoc which Ma brought into his life he recognized his own. He was afraid, he was mean, but in the end he laughed at his fear and his self-importance, and permitted his own betrayal.

Breathing in the sky....

A sky without wind or cloud, without color or the least smudge, without any season. It might be the winter sky of the Himalayas above Annapurna, or the Pacific sky of my boyhood summers, the noon sky over the windy Palisades and the Hudson, the Mexican sky above Casa Santa Maria in late spring, or the quiet autumnal sky over Mary Magdalene and St. Giles in Oxford, shaken by the shivering of a hundred big bells. It might be any and every sky in which I have lost myself these last fifty years.

In its flawless emptiness, its unbroken fullness, I think of the deaths of Franz the upholsterer, bunkered down in his books, and of Christa the schoolteacher, and of Mr. Tillman. And I am made aware with every breath of the constant reprieve of life. We all live to an unannounced deadline. And therefore, like the child who arrived unannounced in Death's household, we must all seek, sooner or later, his counsel and honor him, so we may learn as his guest the secret of the crossing, making ready to die to the separate self, making ready to live in the constant moment of Christ's love, at one.

Passing under the firethorn I hear Ma banging her canvases in the shadow of the blue junipers on her garden deck. She has been painting her River paintings, all of which celebrate the single moment of her own freedom, when Lakshman came down from the snows to claim his child bride on the banks of the Ganga, where the sky is always bright and fair above the cold and turbulent river—there, where we find the space for freedom in the sky of the heart.

11

Anna's Holiday

I found you, black hair in a single braid, where you had wandered off down the beach by yourself, half a mile from the brilliant children shouting in the shallows, a solitary figure, black braid, olive skin, dark eyes searching the white sand under the fallen buttress of a mangrove uprooted in last September's hurricane, searching for shells, sea urchins and heart cockles, marginella and banded tulips, hoarding in a brimless straw hat the unbroken treasures of the storm.

I found you there gathering whatever the wind and the tides have not chipped or shattered, sifting out of the golden salt scrub only the perfect ones, fans and stars and cones, the finished flecks and petals of the Gulf, nutmeg and buttercups, the whorled ears of deaf sailors and drowned ladies, coquina and pear whelks and junonia, sand dollars freshly minted by the storms of spring, calico scallops and egg cockles and the clipped wings of sea angels, fig shells and olive shells, the eyes of sharks and tigers, alphabets from China and bonnets from Scotland, the lace and apple murex.

At last I found you, black hair in a single braid, olive skin, dark eyes scanning the white sand under the toppled buttress of a mangrove bleached black by the sun and wind of a single winter. *I found you there* in your solitary piracy, sieving through your fingers a treasury of perfect shells, the brittle foliage of the deep seabed, fruits and flowers of the mother ocean, thrown up from their fathomless silence by the storms of winter, the storms of spring, scattered in a blazing leafdrift along the endless beach.

MA & ME

There I found you, trackless miles from the nearest path or house, my mother, my child, gathering out of the sea's silence a battered hatful of hollow gold, the empty husks of your own fulfillment.

I found you, and scolded you for wandering off so far out of earshot, and we walked back together on the outer rim of that bright crescent of sand, tipped between the sky and the boundless sea, together and alone, together and one, until we came within sound of the treble shouts of the children in the white distance, and then you stopped to gather a last handful of heart cockles and orange scallops and sunrays, and one perfect shell which you held to my ear, in which I heard the deep pulse of the sea, that rimless silence in the hollow heart, my heart, which you held in your hand.

And for this moment I had driven all night (all the nights of my life) in a caravan of cars and vans across Florida, fifty or a hundred of us—in a buckled Firebird, a blistered pickup, battered Dodges and Buicks and Chevies—all of us hopelessly misaligned, flying westward after midnight, our brakes shot and treads rubbed bare and shocks long gone. We rode through desolate Okeechobee where the ghosts of Black field hands hang at the junction from the dusty live oak, west on 70, outrunning the sun before it rises at our backs, turning south before Arcadia down through Venus and La Belle, and west again toward Cape Coral and Cape Haze. Through sleeping miles of orange groves, and with the first light flooding us at last at Punta Rassa, we reached the causeway to the barrier islands, Sanibel and Captiva, our Sanibel, just as the wind, high, bright, and clear, rose from far out in the Gulf beyond the lighthouse, lifting a scudding argosy of pelicans above the bridges, rose and as suddenly dipped the moment we rolled through the tolls, leaving us breathless with the water beneath us, and the sun climbing behind us, breathless. And the day, just the day before us in all its perfect emptiness, all of us flew into that perfect, empty day.

Once on the island we turned down Periwinkle Way under the high vault of massive red casuarinas and stopped off at Bailey's to refresh the coolers and stock up on sunscreen and zinc and bug spray. We then headed for Bowman's Beach, breakfasting on the move so as not to miss a single moment with her whom we had driven all night to meet at the appointed hour of nine o'clock. Two miles east of the bridge, filling the carpark in the ironweed grove behind the lagoon, we crossed the bridge over the brackish estuary. Finding the trail among the dog fennel and the railroad vines, we struck out west, favoring the scant shade of the feathery pine and tassel trees, for the sun was still climbing and the wind had dropped over the horizon. We were in the unclaimed kingdom of the Calusa Indians, who ruled these woods and shorelines long before the Spanish. Some of the kids raced through the sea oats to the hard wet sand at the water's edge, and a few of the older ones, finding the going easier there, joined them, eyes fixed steadily on the farthest point of the slowly curving crescent of white sand, always on the lookout for the first sight of her whom we had flown through the night to find at the appointed hour, in her kingdom of feathery pines and fallen buttonwood and white sand, on the rim of the deep green Gulf.

Mother, child.

I remember now, shaking your deep silence through the sieve of memory, how we all came upon you out of the woods in a shouting swarm, how we fell on you in a raid of shouting silence, falling into the circle of your great silence, all gathered for the simple love of your attention into that deeper attention for the love of which we had driven westward all night (all the nights of our lives) in a motley caravan, to be gathered here into this astonishing silence; and I remember your amazement, as if you had not seen us coming, had not expected us, as if you had never received so complete and miraculous a surprise, and how, ambushed by the youngest and the oldest swarming up from the wet shoulder below the shell ridge, you gathered each one as a gift, and how our words were caught in the sieve of your startled love, and only the silence sifted through, as only your deep silence is shaken now through the sieve of memory.

Then, like a child, you displayed the treasury inside the brimless straw hat, the priceless loose change of the winter tides, dazzling white and gold contraband, perfect flakes and petals of Gulf fire, and picked out each perfectly finished husk, spilling them into your palm for all to see with an attention so absolute we were all drawn, drawn deeply, drawn under and rolled in those deep, breathless tides which had so turned and polished and perfected each blazing brittle jewel, drawn under and drowned in a silence so breathlessly attentive each shell seemed a wink of eternity—until your palm was loaded with heart cockles and hollow gold tulips, shell kissing shell, and with a sudden cry of *"Here! Look!"* you broke the spell and began to give them all away, the gifts of your joyful emptiness, and with each shell a word or a kiss.

Mother and child.

We scattered and sat around you, the kids conquering the shallows, pelting wet sand and wildly threshing the salt sheaves of morning light, shrill and barbarous, the rest of us pretending not to care how far from you we sat, feigning indifference but measuring with a sweet, secret exactitude the distance between, the measure of our calamitous love, knowing that once we sit with you, near or far, we are forever out of our depth and floundering, with no shallows in which to make a stand, with nothing to conquer, with only the certainty of losing our breath, foundering sooner or later, and drowning.

And Yashoda, sitting behind you, started to let out your hair, releasing the black cordage to fall about your shoulders and down your back, and for a few moments you were wilder than the children in the shallows, and while Yashoda rummaged for the right brush in a beach bag, you sat there unattended, the tarry cordage of your hair spilled wildly over your shoulders, your eyes fixed somewhere out in the unbroken blue of the Gulf.

Where the water meets the sky in the Mother's eyes....

THOMAS "BILLY" BYROM

That unattended wildness!

But it is not your wildness I remember from that day so much as the strange littleness of the shells in your palm—the littleness, yet also the strength and fullness of their perfection, which seemed to be of a making beyond my understanding and yet not beyond it. That was what you showed me. That, and the love with which you kept them in your hand, something in the making and keeping of them which so far exceeded my understanding. And yet I understood, seeing you sitting there unattended, one with the unbroken blue wildness of the Gulf. I understood how we are all shells in your hand, shell kissing shell, each of us held in a perfect making and keeping, until you break the spell and give us all away, the gifts of your bewildering fulfillment, into that happy emptiness.

> *O Mother! You are present in every form*
> *Throughout the whole of creation,*
> *Even in the smallest and least of things.*
> *Wherever I go, wherever I look,*
> *O Mother, it is you I see.*
>
> —*Ramprasad*

* * *

It is a very practical fact, a fact arising from practice, that we only discover how full we are when we are fully empty. Whenever I look back into the brightness of so many long evenings with Ma and see her sitting with us night after night, it is clear to me that all her work has been to empty us, so we may know the simple happiness of our own, natural fullness. I see myself, or someone else, my brother seeker, or sister, gabbing hopelessly in self-defense, hot and lumpish, growing larger with each lie, as she strips our confusion like old paint or tips us upside down like a can of trash and empties us out.

I see her patiently shaking me out night after night, trashing me a thousand nights in a row.

But it is also a practical fact that there is always one thing—one final, obstinate thing—in the way of that complete emptiness in which we find ourselves naturally happy and full. Once stripped of all the self-regarding virtues and self-serving vices—pride and sanity, truth and lust, envy and compassion, sorrow and fortitude, pity and greed, anger and forbearance—there still remains one unyielding thing to be consumed.

Fear.

Who is happy? Who is afraid?

These are essential questions to the seeker, whatever his path to self-mastery, and Ma has been asking them from the moment she began teaching her first students, the Jesuits at Mt. Manresa.

Apprenticed to these same questions, I have been whittled down and hollowed out, and I have found that the last notch to be shaved smooth is always fear. *Nirvana* means literally "blown out," and it signifies that state of perfect emptiness when the pith of fear has been blown out of the reed.

Who is afraid?

In India there are a thousand and eight forms of the Mother, and with one exception they all have two faces, one tender and peaceful, the other savage. Whoever sits at her feet with a true humility is given the grace, the darshan, of her terrible glance, and in meeting her gaze he finds his fears consumed as he surrenders them into the crucible of her implacable rage. Her trembling hands, her love of quarreling, her insatiable hunger, her terrible thirst, the pleasure she takes in the ruin of all human hopes and in the spectacle of human suffering—all these qualities are spelled out in fatal detail in the Dhumavati and Chinnamasta Tantras. Yet as Dhumavati, the Smokey One, it is she who makes possible the luminous joy of Diwali, the Festival of Lights. As Chinnamasta, the Beheaded, who drinks the blood streaming from her own decapitated trunk, she adorns her breasts with blue lotuses, swarming with drunken bees. As Bhairavi, the Fearful, though she represents the power and the night of death, her hands are set in the *mudras*, or sacred gestures, which bestow wisdom and banish fear—the very fear she arouses.

Herein lies the whole meaning of her dark aspects. She scours from the darkest corners of the heart of her devotee his last and most unyielding fears. And she reflects them, so that when he raises his eyes and meets her purifying glance, he sees in her his own terrible image, and held in her furious embrace he offers up all his darkest terrors—just as he discovers in the contemplation of Christ's Passion, that most barbarous of all sacred images, the mysterious reflection of his own torment; or as he finds in the ritual of communion, when he is called to eat the broken body of God, a way to consume the host of his own secret agony.

There is one nameless fear which a thousand fearful images of the Mother cannot consume, however loudly she bays for blood, however greedily she sits by the cremation fires awaiting her midnight feast of blood and ashes. However terrible her form, however passionately the seeker supplicates her, this final fear persists namelessly because it never sees daylight and is buried where he can never by himself find it. Call it the fear of death, or just as well the fear of life, the fear of losing the little self completely, of never again turning back, of drowning, of disappearing forever, the fear of blind abandonment, the same and ultimate fear of which the Katha Upanishad says, "*out of fear the fire burns and the sun shines.*"

It is the fear of love.

Of all the thousand and eight forms of the Mother, there is only one without a savage aspect, only one who is wholly tender, peaceful, and bright. And among the accidents of perfection by which the seeker is released, it is only through her grace that he is delivered from the affliction of this final fear.

She is the river Ganga, white as milk, dazzling white, who is also called Natabhitihrita, "She Who Carries Away Fear," and Bhogyajanani, "She Who Brings Happiness," because she, and she alone, washes away the fear which keeps us from fulfilling the happiness of our true nature, our joyful emptiness.

In this dark age we are released only when we dip in her waters. For the adept following the tantric path, this means bathing in the celestial waters of the *ajna chakra*, the third eye, which is the spiritual confluence, the *triveni*, of the three sacred rivers, Yamuna, Saraswati, and Ganga, within the subtle body. But for the rest of us, the fainthearted, who lack skill and dedication, dipping in the river means abandoning ourselves hopelessly to her love, an abandonment never our own doing but bestowed on us as a gift, a pure accident of that perfection by which we lose ourselves in her.

Shiva, it is said, sent her flowing down to the earth as the most complete expression of compassion, in order that no one is ever left out or behind or alone, so no one is abandoned who has abandoned himself to her. She is indeed the perfect mother, holding, nourishing, forgiving, to whom rage and lust and fear are completely unknown. Only she is wholly good, wholly tender. Her water is mother's milk, and the celestial nectar which confers freedom, and the energy out of which everything is made and unmade. She is consort both to Vishnu, who sustains life, and to Shiva, who destroys it, and she is greater than either of her husbands.

Her influence is above all practical. She needs no mediation. She makes her presence felt immediately, as only a mother can, claiming the seeker as her own, possessively, making him wholly and hopelessly dependent upon her, and childish. She makes him simple, empty and full, and finally happy.

In her milk-white waters our fear of love is washed away.

And her waters are everywhere, inside and out, streaming across the night sky as the Milky Way, cascading from Shiva's knotted hair onto the Himalayas, and flowing out upon the earth in every river, filling the seven oceans. She flows within us too, as one of the channels of the power which rises to open the upturned lotus of the heart, and she is then the tears we shed as she melts our dismay. She is our pond and our river, flowing through these pages, and also, whenever we come to Sanibel, she is the unbroken green waters of the Gulf lapping the shores of the barrier island. In India, Ganga is called Jambhudvipaviharini, "She Who Is Lapping the Shores of Rose Apple Island." India is imagined as a little island, hardly more than a sandbar, held through all time in the gentle embrace of the Mother.

In her waters, who is afraid?

Whenever fear stands in the way, Ma has always driven to where the land runs out, to the Ganga. In the early days in New York she would pack us into her blue van and drive through the night to Montauk in time for the dawn over the ocean. And when we first settled in Florida, from time to time without warning or explanation she would set us on the road in a flotilla of vans and cars and head down to Key West and the Caribbean. But once we discovered Sanibel, a crescent sandbar in the vastness of the Gulf, we knew we had really come to the banks of the Ganga; and dipping in the Gulf waters, we felt at last undismayed, released into her perfect emptiness. And for those few hours the crossing gave up its secret, and we were carried over into that infinite, unfaltering present, into that happy here and now in which she always holds us.

Mother, child.

* * *

When Ma was two or three, her mother Anna gave her the beach. They lived in a cellar on Brighton 8th Street a block and a half from the ocean—Anna and Ma, who was the youngest, and her father Harry, who had done a little soft shoe in vaudeville, her brothers Melvin and Harvey, and her sister Shirley. There was never enough food because Harry was always at the track or out in the alley playing pinochle. They had nothing.

So one day Anna took her daughter to the beach, and showed her the sky and the sand and the sea, and told her it was all hers. "It's yours Joyala, I give it all to you." There was no one else in sight. They had the beach to themselves, so naturally Ma believed her, and when she was older and understood that her mother's gift was not the beach but the belief, she kept both.

Ma always had the beach to herself, whatever the season, however crowded. She always had every beach to herself, sand and sea and sky.

Anna was the daughter of a rabbi from Minsk who brought her over when she was a year old. In those days they still celebrated July 4th by firing off guns in the street. On her first Independence Day Anna was shot in the belly. She lived, but they said she would never have children. Yet she fooled her fate, bearing four children. But she always supposed her life was a kind of gift, like the beach, and believing in her gift, she lived every moment of it.

Anna was never smart or good or beautiful, or gifted in any other way except for her voice. She had a fine singing voice. Five feet tall, three hundred pounds, one dress to wear and one to wash, she couldn't keep house or cook or clean, though she was always spotless on herself. But she loved Harry, loved the gift of her life, and most of all she loved God. And she was always singing show songs or Bessie Smith or Billie Holiday, and her favorite "God Bless the Child."

On Tuesday nights they would sit on the beach and watch the fireworks boat off Coney Island. And I am sure that neither Anna nor Ma ever doubted for a moment that the production was entirely for them. After all, Anna had given Ma the beach. What else was there to celebrate? Those blazing constellations and flaring canopies of shooting stars, all that bright fanfare flooding the beach with shocks of bursting blue and green and gold, in winter when the snow covered the sand, and all summer long, with never an end to the show, and all for them, and them alone.

When Ma was barely ten, Anna got cancer.

She knew she was going to die, so she packed a bag, and without a word of explanation she took off by herself for the Gulf Coast.

She sent Ma two post cards from St. Petersburg, one describing the post office in some detail and another of Silver Springs, where she had taken a tour in a glass-bottom boat. I have both of them before me now on my desk. "Here Joyce Honey...." The second one is dated December 6, 1950. "The Good Lord willing some day dear you'll come here with me. Love Mother."

I have a couple of snapshots too. In one Anna is sitting with a group of women in bathing suits. They are all laughing at some joke she has just made, but above and around the joke there is a kind of quietness, a silence in which they are closely gathered; and in this closeness there is a wild, deep happiness—humor of another kind, and all of it coming from Anna. It is a snapshot of a gift, the gift of joy and wildness which Anna gave wherever she went.

In the other picture she is sitting by herself, in the same floral bathing suit, her fingernails freshly painted and splayed out in the sun to dry with the shameless vanity of a child who has her own.

The second picture explains the first. Anna knew how to love because she loved herself first, and how to give because she took for herself, though all she ever took, between the day she was shot and the day she died, was two weeks on the Gulf in Florida.

When she got home to Brighton 8th Street, she went straight back to work in the typing pool at the Internal Revenue. Whatever wages she brought home Harry gambled away, and Ma's lunch money and carfare too, when he could get it. Ma scavenged for half-eaten pretzels down on the beach under the boardwalk, and Anna put them in the stove and burnt them. And in the evenings Harry taught Ma a little soft shoe while Harvey played the ramshackle piano, and they sang show songs, Ma the loudest though she was always tone deaf.

Harry instructed Ma in some of the arts of the street—"never put your hand in your own pocket if you can put it in someone else's first." But Anna taught Ma the real art of taking for yourself, and how to give it all away.

She worked with both breasts cut off.

Then she lost a lung. Still she went back to work, singing, and whatever she brought home Harry wagered away at the track or at craps or pinochle in the back alley.

Then she lost a kidney. She knew she was dying, but she fought for every hour, every moment.

Ma prayed for her to live. She promised to be good, if God would only let her mother be.

But after her fourth operation, when they wanted to take her legs off, Anna summoned her younger daughter to the ward in Coney Island Hospital and told her, "Scheindele, don't pray for me. I know what I'm doing and who I'm doing it for. God hears *your* prayers. So quit praying for me."

Ma went down to the beach, the beach she owned, and looked out to sea, and said, "Take her."

Where the water meets the sky in the mother's eyes…

There were a hundred others in the ward. Anna kept them all happy with her profane laughter, her dirty mouth and her singing: "Walking down Canal Street, / Knocked on every door, / God damn son of a bitch, / Couldn't find a whore...."

On her way to her fifth operation, wheeled down the ward on a gurney, she was still singing for them. Once again she survived the knife.

Ma turned thirteen.

Anna told her to look after Harry and Shirley and her brothers, though she was the youngest. "They will get lost. But Scheindele, you'll know God." And Ma was not even Anna's favorite. Her favorite was Harvey.

On Friday, July 3rd, Shirley went to sit with her mother after work. She sat with her all evening. Then just before midnight Anna sent her downstairs to get something to eat.

She wanted her last moments for herself. It was her gift to know when to give and when to take. She took her last moments for herself and died a few minutes after midnight, giving it all away, taking it all for herself. It was her gift to know when to live, and when to die.

That Saturday Mel took Ma for a drive. Children were letting off firecrackers in the street. Everywhere people were celebrating their independence. After dark the fireworks boat off Concy Island put on a grand show. The sky was full of bright splinters; bursting constellations spilled into the sea, silver and dark, and floated there, and a shock of broken blue and green washed under the boardwalk. The streets were full of singing, firecrackers like gunshot, and splashing laughter. "They'll be celebrating when I die," Anna had said.

Ma wore a white blouse to the funeral. She could not cry. Walking away, the rabbi told her not to look back, she would turn to stone. Naturally Ma, always defiant, looked back, spitting twice on superstition, spitting three times on unhappiness, spitting with her mother's wildness on her unattended death. Always her mother's daughter.

When she got back to the house, there was a neighbor on the stoop with a basin of water. Ma washed her hands and went in. The mirrors were covered. They sat *shiva* on the orange crates. No need to set aside the furniture; they had none. Ma passed around the honey cakes, and in the morning she took a bus to her aunt's place in Philadelphia.

Her mother's daughter, always looking back.

Mother, child.

* * *

By noon most of us have retreated into the feathery shadows of the pine wood, settling on a fat mattress of pine needles among the yellow flowering cactus and the zigzag tracks of the railroad vine. The children battle in the sea, calling a truce only to let a pack of stingrays fan through the shallows, then falling on each other with a brighter fury. Ma watches them from a few feet above the shell line, from time to time resolving a quarrel, rubbing away tears, or pasting on more sunscreen and lotion. Yashoda sits at her side reading aloud from a pulp romance or pocket thriller. Ma has no patience with deeper books: she likes only the broadest strokes, the highest passions. A child, she likes nothing better than to be startled. A mother, her eyes never shift from the children.

Out in the Gulf, just over the horizon a storm is gathering. Veined with a brittle lightning, a thick smoke of thunder drifts up from the south, too far out to hear but sucking out of the salt marsh behind the woods a low wind. It passes above me, rattling the heart-shaped leaves of the shady mahoe, and runs out to sea, shouting.

The book drops into Yashoda's lap. She has fallen asleep in a moment of terrible passion. The barbarous treble of the children is sucked far out into the Gulf, leaving between the fallen page and the wind's passage a sudden silence in which Ma sits alone, unattended, minding the children yet with her eyes resting always on the thin seam of blue and green where the water touches the sky—where Anna's eyes rested when she ran away to the Gulf half a lifetime ago, rested on the same unbroken seam of blue hemming in the green wildness of the Gulf, where the water meets the sky in the mother's eyes, and mother and child are one, one vanishing into one—where Ma's eyes also rested half a lifetime ago when she ran from her mother's gurney to the beach, rested on the same seamless blue and green wildness, and her heart, falling into its own sudden silence, whispered, "Take her!"

We sit by the water and vanish.

"The Good Lord willing some day dear you'll come here with me."

The wind runs far out to sea, blowing the smoke of thunder back upon itself, and the storm falls below the horizon.

Mother, child.

Above me the yellow flower of the sea hibiscus has deepened to orange. Every hour it deepens. Soon it will be a dark ochre, the color of renunciation. By dusk it will turn a passionate blood red, and fall. It lives only for a day. Tomorrow with the first light a new flower will open in its place, deepen every hour, and fall.

*   *   *

It is hard to be a child, hard to live without shame, hard to be empty and full, and simple and free. It is hard to live in the same unfaltering moment in which children live. It is hard to take it all, and to give it all away.

It is easier, as the Indian saying goes—far easier—to float a stone on water.

In my last years teaching at Oxford, I found the life of a don more and more difficult. Not the intellectual work: that became easier as I understood its limitations. Nor the teaching: that became easier and deeper as I was drawn into its limitless spiritual dimension. But the social labors!

Sometimes at High Table in the medieval hall I found myself quite unable to follow the conversation, and at academic receptions I stammered and fled, bewildered by the Byzantine remarks of the Provost's wife or routed by the Junior Dean's polished small talk.

I needed to find a way for retreat, in the spiritual sense, a daily occasion in which to gather myself and become again the child by the rock pool on the rim of the Pacific, tipped between the sea and the sky, enfolded in your silence, before I had divided and abandoned myself and grown up and become, by a profound irony, a don, an important scholar, a *dominus*, a "master"—I who had no mastery of my true self.

And I found a way.

By five every evening, when my head was usually full of the loose stuffing of university life, I would walk around the corner to St. Mary Magdalene and light a candle in front of a simple wooden statue of Our Lady of Joy, and sit there in the cold nave for an hour and let it all go.

She became my simplicity, before I found Ma.

At the same time, amid all the entanglements of a don's life, I was visited now and then by a strange dream. I say visited because it always arrived like a guest, unexpected but familiar, and established a powerful presence in my life for a day or two and then departed. And I say strange because it was too vivid to be simply a dream. Nowadays I should call it an experience of darshan.

I am sitting on a hillside. The country around me is yellow and stony with patches of green. I must be about fifteen, and I am wearing a simple robe, and I am minding a flock of goats.

From the distance a long avenue lined with cypresses runs to the foot of the hill, and I see a small band of men and women raising the yellow dust as they walk toward me.

A tall dark man leads them.

My heart is suddenly full, and I jump up and start running down the slope. The tall man strides toward me, and I fall into his arms. He holds me tight.

Whenever the life of a scholar cramped or confined me, I fell into the memory of his arms, like a child nursing at the breast. I felt Christ as a father, brother, and friend, but mostly as a mother in whose embrace I could become again the unabandoned, undivided child. Later on I found words for these feelings in Mother Julian of Norwich's *Revelations of Divine Love* when she speaks of Christ as our "true mother in whom we are endlessly born and out of whom we shall never come." And I realized also that this Christ on the dusty avenue was the risen Christ, of whom Luke wrote, "Was not our heart burning within us, while he spake to us in the way?"

He rose in me and became my simplicity, and I became his child; and I lived, whenever I fell into the memory of his embrace, in the same unfaltering moment in which children live, empty and full, free and simple.

He rose in me as the Mother rose in me that morning by the Palisades, a morning when her gift of simplicity gave me back my childhood and set my heart on fire.

Since then I have lived like every seeker, whatever his practice, from one moment of darshan to the next. No matter how broad our independence or deep our courage, it is only by these accidents of perfection, these flashes of grace, that we are able to persevere in our seeking. Without them we lose heart a hundred times. And these moments of brightness fall on us out of the air only when we are simple, like children.

About a month ago I complained to Baba that he only ever gave me his darshan without showing me his human form. I saw him as the empty light above a rock high in the mountains, or as the wind in the palm and scrub hammocks running out into the river, or an oak tree with seven sinuous bends pointing to the wide bend in the river where it flows north like the Ganga at Kashi. But since the train ride to Guntakal thirty years ago, I had never encountered his human form. And so I asked.

That night, deep in my sleep, I found myself sitting with friends in a small house in the foothills of the Himalayas. A jeep drew up, and Baba bundled out of it and strode into the hut. He was wearing a simple white cloth around his waist, nothing more. He sat down in a corner of the hut and looked around, beaming with pride. I was distressed that people were still talking among themselves. I felt it was disrespectful. But he only beamed with a deep and unqualified love, like a proud mother. So I gave up my distress, and the moment I did so, I felt my gaze drawn into his huge breast, white and hairy, and all at once I recognized that everything that I loved or understood, the only truth or reality in my entire life's experience, was here in the massive breadth of his breast.

It was as if the whole world was drawn into his heart and made larger there and more abundant, and I felt that I had not lived or breathed before this moment and that there was no longer any possibility of life or breath after it. I felt a complete happiness. I felt full to the brim of my being.

Everything came down to this—the fullness of his breast, in which I had all my wholeness.

In all our love, in all our schooling, there is only one Mother, from whom we are never weaned. Ma had many teachers and mothers—Nityananda, Anna, and two of whom I have not had the space or occasion to speak: Shirdi Sai Baba and Ramana Maharshi. But she had only one Mother—her Christ who brought her to her Hanuman, her Baba, in whom she discovered not only their essential identity, but her own true nature as the Mother who suckles herself, the one true Mother in whom she found herself, empty and full, simple and free, with the freedom of the child who has her own.

Ma always had her own.

Child and mother.

When at last, abandoning ourselves to the arms of love, we are drawn into his breast, when at last we dip in her river, then our final fear—the fear of unconditional love—is washed away like the last spit of black sand when the monsoon rains swell the Ganga. Then at last we are children again, and it is easy to be simple and free, empty and full; easy to float a stone on water; easy to take it all, as children do shamelessly, and give it all away.

> *When you strip without being ashamed and you take your clothes and put them under your feet like little children and trample them, then [you] will see the child of the living one and you will not be afraid.*
>
> —*Gospel of Thomas 37*

* * *

It is hard to be a mother, hard to live without judgment or possession, hard to be empty and full, and simple and free. It is hard to have it all, and to give it all away.

Now Kim is calling for Ma.

MA & ME

It was hardly more than a year ago when she first heard she was stricken. She was in the middle of writing a letter to Ma, bewildered by her sudden debility and seeking help, when her physician called to tell her she had AIDS. And it made no sense, since she was young and chaste and had never taken drugs, a devout Catholic.

Suddenly, inexplicably stricken.

She came to see us, and it was love at first sight. Ma stoked her brightness and encouraged her to fight. Everything in her wanted to live.

The Centers for Disease Control in Atlanta singled her out for special study because there was no reason for her infection. They interviewed hundreds of people in her life and turned up nothing.

It was hard not to be angry at the injustice of it, as it always is, but the more so with her: there was such love of life in her, and her bewilderment was so troubling. But Ma always fanned the blaze of her bewilderment into a brighter light, the fire to fight for life, for the gift and honor of it.

It took the CDC many months to discover that Kim's dentist had died of AIDS, and tissue typing seemed to confirm the transmission. Against prejudice and disbelief, Kim fought for a settlement, not for money but for the principle, for others at risk. And she won.

But now her strength is ebbing, and she is calling for Ma.

We arrive a little after dusk at the house, just off A1A, a minute from the ocean.

She is lying on a couch in the day room by the pool, and her family—her two sisters, her mother and her father—a house full of animals and birds, and her best friend from Tampa have wrapped themselves around her.

She is failing but still shining, her body wasted to nothing but her face with her fine bones and brow still full and flushed from the sun. Yesterday her friend had wheeled her down to the beach. When I take her hand, she opens her eyes and looks at me from very near and from very far. The disease has invaded her brain, but her awareness is as fully and brightly present as ever. She makes ready to die, she makes ready to live.

But she has been disturbed by a smell of burning.

Her family shares her fear. Good Catholics, they are naturally afraid. They have not known what Ma is now able to tell them, that in the East a smell of burning is for the dying a special sign of grace. Shiva and Christ have committed to the flame the dross of her life, and she is smelling the fire which consumes the broken kindling and flawed tinder of her life. There's little enough to burn, she has lived so purely.

Hearing Ma's assurance, Kim eases into a deeper rest. She is no longer vexed. I feel her whole being falling into a deeper stillness. And yet she has lived life so fully, and has fought for her settlement so ardently, she cannot now easily let go.

She stays with us, luminous and full, her frail form on the day bed quietly failing. Her distress has been eased, but still she blazes.

And sitting at her side, I find myself sitting once again beside Ma just below the highest step of the burning ghats of Manikarnika on the Ganges.

* * *

It is October, a day after the Festival of the Mother. We are in Varanasi, the ancient city whose oldest name is Kashi.

We had arrived the previous evening at dusk just in time to see the huge statues of Durga hauled on palanquins from every temple, every quarter of the city, converging where we come upon them on the main road to the principal ghat. Torches everywhere dipping and smearing hot long arcs in the dark, everywhere the dense crowd in a frenzy of happiness, shouting the Mother's name, invoking her victory over the forces of darkness. They tip and roll the palanquins from side to side, lurch forward, quarrel for precedence. The pride of each temple is at stake, and the greatest devotion and care has been lavished on each flower-laden *murti* and its crazy carriage.

Ma plunges into the throng, wildly crying out with the crowd in adoration of the Mother, and we follow after her, alarmed and swept along against our better judgment, and then jubilant as we surrender to the general joy and let it fill us, casting off the superstitions of Western reserve.

Ma's hair streams wildly over her sari, she grabs one of the struts bearing up the goddess, a privilege that is denied women, but the temple priests see she is drenched in God, God-intoxicated as they say, and they dare not push her off. Some of them *pranam* and touch her feet, others clap their hands and shout for joy.

For this is the night when all women are holy.

Forty or fifty forms of the Mother are swept down the wide avenue to the steep steps of the ghat, then are tilted down to the river and straddled across the broad low hulls, and pushed out onto the breast of the river. Torches sizzle and flare on the water.

The crowd is shouting "Jaya! Jaya! Jaya!"—"She wins! She wins! It's her victory!" A night of victory for all women, when all women are the Mother.

Midstream an amazing play is enacted. Astride the boats, huge cream and ruby images of the Mother stream with silken pennons and colored tassels and cloth of gold and purple and white. Slowly at first, then with a gathering abandon, the crews who have punted them out onto the river's breast now rock them from side to side, singing and shouting, until one by one the Mothers are tipped and hurled into the water, where they float for a moment and then sink, leaving little eddies of flowers where they went under.

So many Mothers, yet she is One Mother, and she sinks into herself, the river, one with herself.

The river turns in large slow eddies, bearing on its shaken black breast a thousand flowers, and the temple crews pole back to the shore, dousing their torches in her flow. The crowd mills on the steps, gazing out into the dark midstream where she went under, taking all their troubles with her.

At dawn the next morning we accompany Ma to Manikarnika, where the bodies are brought for burning, and we sit just below a tall stack of shaved and broken timber in the thickest part of the sweet smoke, letting it soak into our pores. The acrid smell smarts in our nostrils, we taste the ash on our tongues, it settles in our hair. We are smudged with death.

For an hour and more we sit there in silence, watching the first litters of the day issue from the narrow streets, bodies bound in white, the color of mourning; watching how fire devours the human form, peeling back the flesh off the bone, smelting bone and gristle, till the charred skull is ready to crack. The skull is always the last to go, and when it cracks, the oldest son, whose task it is to set and tend the fire with the untouchables who supervise the cremation grounds, knows that the soul is at last released.

In this way the whole family lets go of its grief, acknowledging that the body is nothing and the soul is free.

It is astonishing, this ceremony, in its intimacy, this never-ceasing dance with Death which every devout believer undertakes for his gift of freedom, making way for the way over, the beyond the beyond, the great crossing.

Below us an eddy has snared in its backwater a great sludge of last night's floating flowers, drizzled with ash from the flaming terraces.

I wipe the soot of burnt flesh from my eyes, and I am conscious of the purity of these unceasing gestures of feeding and stoking.

And I realize that Ma has brought me here to help me devour the fear of the crab crawling in my blood, to smoke out my fear of leukemia. And now I am ready to defy the doctors' prognosis, now I know I am by no means ready to make ready to die.

Sitting in the sweet stench of the slag of human kindling, I am making ready to live. Against the odds, I *shall* live!

The river burns in my heart.

The river says, all women are holy.

Before we leave, we descend the steps to the water's edge and scoop up a palmful of life from the flow and dribble it on our brows and the crown of our heads, in her honor.

* * *

And back beside Kim's bed, I smell again the burning, her special sign of grace, and I see she is sitting with Ma, holding hands in silence, on the bank of the river.

Kim's eyes never leave Ma's.

They sit there for a moment, for a year and a day, and the river turns in slow silent eddies, her shaken black breast sprinkled with a thousand white flowers, the color of mourning.

But we have nothing to mourn. The quiet joy of the family suffuses the day room. The family has wrapped around her like a tabby cat.

And now we all feel the fear flowing out of Kim, leaving her happy just to let it all be, just to let it all go.

Mother, child, sitting by the river for a moment, for a year and a day.

As yet I can form no comprehension of this surrender, though I feel Kim's speechless composure, and Ma's. I can form no comprehension of the fearful independence and complete responsibility which is the only end of this unbidden surrender of mother and child.

Who is the mother? And who is daughter?

After these many long years of arduous and joyful apprenticeship, it is still so hard for me, bound as I am in daily denial, the bondservant of my fear of love, to conceive of that whole and accomplishing love which Christ promises casts out all fear; so hard to imagine that I may ever master breath and desire; ever melt in his fire, ever dissolve in her waters; ever find in her emptiness my own fulfillment; ever let it all go; ever let it all be, and abandon myself to that constant abandonment in which everything is for once and always fully possessed and relinquished.

Yet here I am, sitting every day with her, a year and a day by the river.

Kim has fallen asleep, easily.

My Ganga, Dhavalambara, "Cloth of Dazzling White...."

Every moment I am summoned to the moment of her sacrifice, when she gives herself back to the river, losing him for our sakes, to share him with us, and bring us all home to Kashi.

Dip him in the river who loves water.

All things, she says, begin and end in Christ.

Mother and child.

But for me the sacrifice of the way of the Mother is as yet too hard. And out of my struggle there arise still the necessity of her sacrifice, the mystery of his silence, the passion of their sharing.

* * *

A faint rasp of thunder out of the emptiness of the Gulf, then a roll of black smoke curls swiftly above the horizon, an army mustering in the south, then as swiftly falls below the green ledge and vanishes.

It is four in the afternoon, and the children have not flagged in their conquest of the shallows or tired of battling for shells along the ridge. From the splintered shade of the pinewood I hear their animal cries, full of the happy brutality of love, spirits naturally generous, naturally careless, frail bodies burned dark by the day's fire, sudden and natural in the bright shallows. They will never be broken.

A little after five the storm deploys its artillery once more below the horizon, and the wind drops. In one undivided moment everyone looks out to sea. Nothing. And then again, muffled shellbursts carried over the copper green water in a colossal silence.

But the children quickly renew their warfare, reckless as the sapping wind digs deeper trenches in the waves, folding in the thunder, until looking up they see legs of stalk lightning burn on the water, and the sky palled in a pearl black smoke, and the water lifting all around them and darkening.

Then they are hauled protesting from the sea, still hurling the high, sharp imprecations of their love at each other. They will never be broken.

We swarm out of the pinewoods, gather on the beach, and watch the storm rush toward us. Our attention draws it on. The stillness of our attention raises the sea, sucks in the first breath of the storm, and in a moment blackens the sky from east to west, drawing the dark sky over us and filling the woods and the salt lagoon. With a common and reckless stillness we draw on the storm, we pull down its pure violence.

Who is happy? Who is afraid?

Before it breaks, I turn back into the woods and gather up my clothes. The flower of the sea hibiscus has darkened to a deep blood red. I wanted to catch it the moment it fell. But we are packing to leave before the storm breaks, and in the moment of its falling we shall be gone.

Brushfires of lightning burn closer over the purple water, the wind spatters the first fat pits of rain along the shell ridge and shouts out behind us in the salt lagoon, under the roots of the black mangroves. And yet we do not hurry to pack. There is no panic. Our attention is steadfast. Even as we draw on the storm, we hold it off till we are ready to go.

Returning to the beach, I see you sitting there, black hair in a single braid, for a moment unattended, your eyes still turned far out to sea, beyond the smoke of the storm, resting on the blue and green wildness of the Gulf with a composure so breathless, so absolute, you seem to have shut up the wind and the thunder, the rising sea and the lightning in the hollow shell of that common and passionate silence which has always been your gift to us.

In the attention of this love, and in the love of this attention, what things are not possible? It is hardly strange that we should hold back the storm, or draw it on. For we are the shells in whom you have confided and enclosed the storm and your joyful composure.

I see you sitting there, dark eyes far out in the Gulf, and for an instant all fear is taken from me. For an instant I am free.

And then we let out our breath, the storm's breath, and it breaks.

It breaks in solid sheets, drenching us before we can draw the next breath, and shakes us with gusts of laughter and dismay out of the woods and into a single ragged file along the twisting path. Now we are a nearly naked expedition, striking east, the rain dousing the sun's fire in the children's hair and running in great gunnels over shoulders and sandy haunches. Now we are animals, sudden and natural in the bright deluge, brutally happy. Now we are the tussling spirits of the storm, released into its fury, fearless and happy.

Catching my breath at a turn in the path, where the wind crumples the dog fennel, I see you walking quietly at the head of the file, a captive of the children on each side of you, tugging you on, black hair in a single braid, captive yet utterly free. And looking back I see a hundred and more—creatures of the drenching wind and the scorched rain—trailing after you, ragged and free, like shells you have scattered along the path, chips of rose, a litter of kindling.

We reach the ironwood grove a little after seven, as the storm flies over the barrier islands and passes inland.

The falling sun tips the feathers of the tall pines, and in the storm's wake an evening wind low off the water warms the shadows. We shake out our wet rags, stuff the cars, slam the trunks, then drift back toward the bridge over the lagoon, milling in the red shade of the casuarinas, hardly talking, just a word, here and there. Smoldering with the day's fire, we hesitate in the deep shadows like happy ghosts, fulfilled, yet reluctant, still burning....

Burning now with a single flame, which has consumed all other desires—the flame which burns at the crown of the head, where all desires and fears are consumed, in whose brightness even the fear of love is stoked to ash.

How is it possible now to be afraid of love, or to turn aside the happiness with which you have filled us? For now we burn with the fire of a perfect, empty day. Now we burn with an endless longing in the fiery love of your attention, and in the unfailing attention of your love our longing is endlessly consumed.

And what is this flame at the crown of the head?

It is the fire of his passion, which you have shared with us, the passion of Hanuman's torn heart, the passion of Christ's purpose, constantly blazing, "that my joy may be in you and that your joy may be made full." And it is the fire of Manikarnika, of the charring slag of skulls at the sweet and sooty ghats by the river, Ganga, in whose constant, joyful incandescence all our desires are consumed, even the desolation of the separate self. The skull cracks open at last, releasing us fearlessly into her infinite happiness.

Who is happy? Who is afraid?

Ma's van draws out, and we follow.

The sun has fallen into the water as we turn onto the causeway into the bright dusk. The sky is vast and cloudless over Punta Rassa. Black skimmers fly under the bridges, scooping silver out of the evening swell. A heavy wind tramples the black water at our backs in the long shadow of Pine Island Sound, and to the south, far out in the shining emptiness of the dark Gulf, beyond Naples and the Ten Thousand Islands, the night has already scattered the searing ashes of the day—the perfect, empty day.

Ahead I see a few early stars low in the sky, and I think of the blood-red flower of the sea mallow darkening in the pine wood. I wanted to catch it the moment it fell, but in the moment of its falling we are gone.

We pass into the night, fifty or a hundred of us, a threadbare caravan of buckled compacts.

And somewhere up ahead you are flying before us on silent rushing wheels in a van loaded down with drowsy children, the sun still smoldering in the tangled cordage of their hair, flying into the deep night which has swallowed up their barbarous treble and swept into the starry sky the ashes of a perfect empty day, flying toward midnight through miles of orange grove, flying home to Kashi, city of love and death, home to Ganga, river of life and death.

And we are flying after you, breathless, still amazed, and burning—burning in the fire of your love, dying with every breath to your amazing, crazy love, as you lose yourself in him.

Mother, child.

In a half sleep, slumped in the back seat, I hear thunder and the first fat pits of rain spattering and rattling the heart-shaped leaves of the sea mallow. Drawn under, I see its darkening flower that I wanted to catch in the moment it fell, but we are flying home, and in the moment of its falling we are gone.

Gaté	*Gone*
Gaté	*Gone*
Paragaté	*Gone beyond*
Parasamgaté	*Gone beyond beyond*
Bodhi, swaha!	*Lover, awake!*

– Heart Sutra, translation by Thomas Byrom

About the Author

Dr. Thomas "Billy" Byrom (1941-1991) earned his Master's degree in English Literature at Baillol College, Oxford University, and his PhD at Harvard. He taught at Harvard, Bennington, and Oxford, where he held the J.R.R Tolkein chair in English Language and Literature.

His life changed dramatically when he met his guru, Ma Jaya Sati Bhagavati, in 1974. Billy had studied the great mystics of many traditions, but now he was face to face with a genuine modern mystic who quickly set him on a path of direct experience. After some hesitation, he committed to what he calls his "apprenticeship." Besides absorbing spiritual practices, he assisted Ma Jaya in developing a spiritual community, founding a school, developing AIDS service organizations, engaging in interfaith networking, and supporting her work as an author and artist.

He is the author of published books including *Dhammapada: The Sayings of the Buddha*, and *The Heart of Awareness: A Translation of the Ashtavakra Gita*, a classic of nondualistic Indian philosophy. At his death he was working on a translation of the Katha Upanishad to be entitled *The Third Wish: The Disquisition of Death*.

Billy often accompanied Ma Jaya in her work with people with AIDS. She taught about AIDS internationally, and offered deep and personal teachings to thousands who were dying. Meanwhile, he was facing his own diagnosis of terminal leukemia. He died at Kashi Ashram, with Ma Jaya by his side.

Endnotes

Prologue

p. vi "Love has ten degrees": Sufi proverb (attributed).

p. vii "My heart is breaking": St. Catherine of Siena, *The Dialogue (Classics of Western Spirituality Series)*, trans. and intro. Suzanne Noffke, O.P. (New York: Paulist Press, 1980). Copyright © Paulist Press, Inc., New York/Mahwah, NJ. Used with permission. www.paulistpress.com

Chapter 1

p. 5 "That my joy may be": John 15:11, *Holy Bible, American Standard Version* (New York: Thomas Nelson & Sons, 1901).

p. 10 "You who tell the truth": *The Thunder, Perfect Mind*, in *The Nag Hammadi Scriptures* by Marvin W. Meyer and James M. Robinson (San Francisco: HarperCollins, 1990). Copyright © 2007 by Marvin W. Meyer. Used by permission of HarperCollins Publishers. *The Thunder, Perfect Mind* is one of the ancient documents discovered and unearthed in Egypt in 1945, often referred to as the Gnostic Gospels.

p. 12 "Who is lazier": *The Heart of Awareness: A Translation of the Ashtavakra Gita*, trans. Thomas Byrom (Boston: Shambala Publications, 1990).

p. 13 "Inside the seed": Thomas Byrom, after Rumi. Jalal ad-Din Muhammad Rumi (c 1207-1273) was an Islamic jurist, scholar, poet, and mystic, generally associated with the Sufi order, a mystical branch of Islam.

p. 15 "I am foolish": *The Thunder, Perfect Mind*, in *The Nag Hammadi Scriptures* by Marvin W. Meyer and James M. Robinson (San Francisco: HarperCollins, 1990). Copyright © 2007 by Marvin W. Meyer. Used by permission of HarperCollins Publishers.

p. 17 "His mind is cool": *The Heart of Awareness: A Translation of the Ashtavakra Gita*, Chapter 18, Verse 81, trans. Thomas Byrom (Boston: Shambala Publications, 1990).

p. 18 "Our true mother": Julian of Norwich, *Revelations of Divine Love*, ed. Grace Harriet Warrack (London: Methuen Company, 1901). Mother Julian of Norwich (1342-1416) was the first woman to write in English. While deathly ill, she experienced 16 visions of Christ. After a miraculous recovery, she wrote this account. There are many editions, under a variety of titles, some in the original Middle English, some in modern English.

Chapter 2

p. 22 "This is my body": Luke 22:19, *Holy Bible, American Standard Version* (New York: Thomas Nelson & Sons, 1901).

p. 22 "God comes to the hungry": attributed to Mahatma Gandhi.

p. 24 "O Sadhu!": *Songs of Kabir*, 1.13, trans. Rabindranath Tagore, intro. Evelyn Underhill (New York: The Macmillan Company, 1915). Kabir was a 15th-century Indian poet and mystic who is honored by both Hindus and Sikhs.

p. 32 "Rabbi, eat!": John 4:31-34, *Holy Bible, American Standard Version* (New York: Thomas Nelson & Sons, 1901).

pp. 32-33 "On a dark night": St. John of the Cross, *Dark Night of the Soul*, 3rd rev. ed., trans. & ed., with an intro., by

E. Allison Peers, from the critical edition of P. Silverio de Santa Teresa, C.D. (Garden City, NY: Image Books, a division of Doubleday & Company, Inc., 1959; by special arrangement with The Newman Press). Electronic edition scanned by Harry Plantinga, 1994. This electronic text is in the public domain. https://www.jesus-passion.com/DarkNightSoul.htm

p. 34   "In the happy night": Ibid.

p. 35   "This light guided me": Ibid.

p. 36   "Oh, night that guided me": Ibid.

p. 38   "I remained, lost in oblivion;": Ibid.

Chapter 3

p. 41   "Was not our heart": Luke 24:32, *Holy Bible, American Standard Version* (New York: Thomas Nelson & Sons, 1901).

p. 43   "That my joy may be": John 15:11, *Holy Bible, American Standard Version* (New York: Thomas Nelson & Sons, 1901).

p. 48   "With all its heart": *Songs of Kabir,* LIII I. 122, trans. Rabindranath Tagore, intro. Evelyn Underhill (New York: The Macmillan Company, 1915).

p. 51   "Some say that the soul": St. Teresa of Avila, ed. Benedict Zimmerman, *The Interior Castle* or *The Mansions,* 3rd ed. (Grand Rapids, MI: Christian Classics Ethereal Library/London: Thomas Baker, 1921).

p. 52   "Knock, and it shall be opened": Matthew 7:7, *Holy Bible, American Standard Version* (New York: Thomas Nelson & Sons, 1901).

p. 53   "Dip him in the river": William Blake, *The Marriage of Heaven and Hell* (Boston: John W. Luce & Co., 1906). Although he was a Christian, William Blake (1757-1827) rejected organized religion. Contemporaries often ignored him or dismissed him as mad, but he is now recognized as a major figure in the Romantic period in both literature and art.

p. 53   "How hard it is": *Songs of Kabir,* : LXIV I. 117, trans. Rabindranath Tagore, intro. Evelyn Underhill (New York: The Macmillan Company, 1915).

p. 60   "I marvelled more": Richard Rolle, Hermit of Hampole, trans. Richard Misyn, ed. Frances M. Comper, intro. Evelyn Underhill, *The Fire of Love* or *Melody of Love and the Mending of Life* or *Rule of Living* (from *Incendium Amoris* and *De Emendatione Vitae*) (London: Methuen, 1914, 1920).

p. 60   "The mind...wanders hither": St. Teresa of Avila, ed. Benedict Zimmerman, *The Interior Castle* or *The Mansions*, 3rd ed. (Grand Rapids, MI: Christian Classics Ethereal Library / London: Thomas Baker, 1921).

p. 61   "He who sits": Sufi saying (attributed).

p. 62   "in the hands of God": St. Teresa of Avila, ed. Benedict Zimmerman, *The Interior Castle* or *The Mansions*, 3rd ed. (Grand Rapids, MI: Christian Classics Ethereal Library/ London: Thomas Baker, 1921).

p. 63   "Near the breastbone": *Kabir: Ecstatic Poems*, versions by Robert Bly, © 2004, used with permission of Beacon Press, permission conveyed through Copyright Clearance Center, Inc.

p. 66   "If the world hateth you": John 15:18, *Holy Bible, American Standard Version* (New York: Thomas Nelson & Sons, 1901).

p. 67   "like divine consolations": St. Teresa of Avila, ed. Benedict Zimmerman, *The Interior Castle or The Mansions*, 3rd ed. (Grand Rapids, MI: Christian Classics Ethereal Library/ London: Thomas Baker, 1921).

Chapter 4

p. 70   "We are all condemned": Victor Hugo, *The Last Day of a Condemned Man*, trans. Sir P. Hesketh-Fleetwood, 1829/1840. Victor Hugo published this novella after witnessing an execution by guillotine. It became popular as an argument against capital punishment.

p. 70   "His disciples said": Gospel of Thomas 113, in *The Nag Hammadi Scriptures* by Marvin W. Meyer and James M. Robinson (San Francisco: HarperCollins, 1990). Copyright © 2007 by Marvin W. Meyer. Used by permission of HarperCollins Publishers. The Gospel of Thomas was found buried at Nag Hammadi, Egypt, in 1945, and purports to be the words of Jesus.

p. 71   "Console thyself": Blaise Pascal, *Pensées* 167, translated from the text of M. Auguste Molinier by C. Kegan Paul, *The Thoughts of Blaise Pascal* (London: George Bell and Sons, 1901).

p. 79   "This time I shall devour": Ram Prasad, *The Gospel of Sri Ramakrishna*, translated into English by Swami Nikhilananda, copyright 1942, reprinted by permission of the Ramakrishna-Vivekananda Center.

p. 83   "Ever since I have been separated": Ramayana, trans. Devadatta Kali. The *Ramayana* is one of the great Sanskrit epics of ancient India, telling the story of Rama and Sita's exile, Sita's kidnapping by the demon Ravanna, and her rescue by the monkey Hanuman. It was originally composed by Maharishi Valmiki as early as the 7th century BCE.

p. 93 "He (Christ) never died": Neem Karoli Baba, *Miracle of Love: Stories About Neem Karoli Baba*, as compiled by Ram Dass, copyright © Hanuman Foundation, all rights reserved. Neem Karoli Baba (?-1973) was Ma Jaya's guru.

p. 95-96 "I will tell you a secret": Ma, by permission of the Ma Jaya Bhagavati Trust. Unpublished talk, archived at Kashi Ashram, Sebastian, Florida. Date between 1975 and 1990.

p. 98 "Christ is the population": Rumi, from *The Essential Rumi*, Chapter 19, trans. Coleman Barks, published by Harper San Francisco, 1995 © Coleman Barks. (Although the publication date of this collection is later than Thomas Byrom's death, he would have been familiar with earlier editions of Coleman Barks' renderings, available since the 1970s.)

p. 102-103 "How do you think of me?": Ramayana, trans. Devadatta Kali. This passage from the *Ramayana* can be found in *The Gospel of Sri Ramakrishna*.

Chapter 5

p. 116 "I came to cast fire": Luke 12:49-53, *Holy Bible, American Standard Version* (New York: Thomas Nelson & Sons, 1901).

p. 123-124 "I am silence": *The Thunder, Perfect Mind*, in *The Nag Hammadi Scriptures* by Marvin W. Meyer and James M. Robinson (San Francisco: HarperCollins, 1990). Copyright © 2007 by Marvin W. Meyer. Used by permission of HarperCollins Publishers.

p. 131 "My blood...which is poured": Luke 22:20, *Holy Bible, American Standard Version* (New York: Thomas Nelson & Sons, 1901).

Chapter 6

p. 155 "This is our Kashi": Ma, by permission of the Ma Jaya Bhagavati Trust. Ma Jaya Sati Bhagavati often recited this poem. A version can be found in her book, *The River* (Sebastian, Florida: Ganga Press, 1993).

p. 157 "Before you can straighten": Thomas Byrom, *The Dhammapada: The Sayings of the Buddha*, trans. Thomas Byrom (New York: Vintage Books, 1976).

p. 158-160 "*Children play by my river*": Ma, by permission of the Ma Jaya Bhagavati Trust. The River (Sebastian, Florida: Ganga Press, 1993).

p. 161 "Ever since I have been separated": Ramayana, trans. Devadatta Kali.

p. 163 "Let the lover be": Rumi, from *The Essential Rumi*, trans. Coleman Barks, published by Harper San Francisco, 1995 © Coleman Barks. Another version can be found at found online at "Votica Poetry Spoken," with no translator or other publisher listed.

p. 165 "Any man who has": Plato, *Phaedo: The Death of Socrates*. https://ethicsofsuicide.lib.utah.edu/selections/plato/

p. 167 "There are hundreds": Rumi, from *The Essential Rumi*, trans. Coleman Barks, published by Harper San Francisco, 1995 © Coleman Barks.

p. 167 "Mad is my Father": Ramprasad, trans. Devadatta Kali. Ramprasad Sen (ca. 1718-75) was a Bengali poet and devotee of the goddess Kali.

p. 169 "I have lived on the lip": Rumi, from *The Essential Rumi*, trans. Coleman Barks, published by Harper San Francisco, 1995 © Coleman Barks.

p. 170 "This is our Kashi": Ma, by permission of the Ma Jaya Bhagavati Trust.

p. 171 "Nothing succeeds like excess": Oscar Wilde, *A Woman of No Importance*, Act 3, 1893 (London: Methuen and Co., 1908).

p. 171 "The road of excess": William Blake, *The Marriage of Heaven and Hell* (Boston: John W. Luce & Co., 1906). Although he was a Christian, William Blake (1757-1827) rejected organized religion. Contemporaries often ignored him or dismissed him as mad, but he is now recognized as a major figure in the Romantic period in both literature and art.

p. 173 "It may be that in all her phrases": Wallace Stevens, "The Idea of Order at Key West," *The Collected Poems of Wallace Stevens*, copyright © 1936 by Wallace Stevens, copyright renewed 1964 by Holly Stevens, used by permission of Alfred A. Knopf, an imprint of the Knopf Doubleday Publishing Group, a division of Penguin Random House LLC, all rights reserved.

p. 175 "Don't run away": Rumi, from *The Essential Rumi*, trans. Coleman Barks, published by Harper San Francisco, 1995 © Coleman Barks.

p. 177 "But Kashi is the sky": Swami Chetanananda, *The Sky of the Heart: Jewels of Wisdom from Nityananda*, republished with permission of Rudra Press, copyright 1996. Swami Bhagawan Nityananda (1897-1961) was an important teacher to both Ma Jaya and Thomas Byrom.

Chapter 7

p. 181 "Striving is the root": *The Heart of Awareness: A Translation of the Ashtavakra Gita*, Chapter 16, Verse 3, trans. Thomas Byrom (Boston: Shambala Publications, 1990).

p. 185 "Seeking or striving": *The Heart of Awareness: A Translation of the Ashtavakra Gita*, Chapter 10, Verse 1, trans. Thomas Byrom (Boston: Shambala Publications, 1990).

p. 188 "Who sweeps a room": George Herbert, "The Elixir," *The Temple*, 1633.

p. 189 "Before kingdoms change": attributed to John the Baptist, an intinerant preacher who baptized Jesus at the start of his ministry. Very few of his words were recorded. There is no scriptural authority for this quote.

p. 197 "Service is from the heart": Ma, by permission of the Ma Jaya Bhagavati Trust.

p. 201 "For I was hungry": Matthew 25:35-36, *Holy Bible, American Standard Version* (New York: Thomas Nelson & Sons, 1901).

p. 201 "O my Beloved": Ramayana, trans. Devadatta Kali.

p. 202 "Now pray the prayer": St. Catherine of Siena, *The Dialogue (Classics of Western Spirituality Series)*, trans. and intro. Suzanne Noffke, O.P. (New York: Paulist Press, 1980). Copyright © Paulist Press, Inc., New York/Mahwah, NJ. Used with permission. www.paulistpress.com

p. 204 "That my joy may be": John 15:11, *Holy Bible, American Standard Version* (New York: Thomas Nelson & Sons, 1901).

Chapter 8

p. 207 "All water is the Ganga": Neem Karoli Baba, *Miracle of Love: Stories About Neem Karoli Baba*, as compiled by Ram Dass, copyright © Hanuman Foundation, all rights reserved. These words are often credited to Mahatma Ghandi, who said something very similar in *Young India* magazine in 1913. One or both were not speaking English, so correct attribution is difficult.

p. 208 "I am the way": John 14:6, *Holy Bible, American Standard Version* (New York: Thomas Nelson & Sons, 1901).

p. 209 "this bafflement," Thomas Merton, 29 "Mental Prayer," *New Seeds of Contemplation*, copyright © 1961 by The Abbey of Gethsemani, Inc., reprinted by permission of New Directions Publishing Corp. for the United States, its terrotories, and Canada.

p. 209 "Wanting nothing": Thomas Byrom, *The Dhammapada: The Sayings of the Buddha*, trans. Thomas Byrom (New York: Vintage Books, 1976).

p. 212 "The size of a thumb": Thomas Byrom, *The Third Wish: The Disquisition of Death, A translation of the Katha Upanishad of the Black Yajur Veda*, 4:13, © Thomas Byrom, 1991, unpublished manuscript.

p. 213 "the miserable little consolations": Thomas Merton, *New Seeds of Contemplation*, copyright © 1961 by The Abbey of Gethsemani, Inc., reprinted by permission of New Directions Publishing Corp. for the United States, its terrotories, and Canada.

p. 214 "our passion and our sensible": Thomas Merton, 34 "The Wrong Flame," *New Seeds of Contemplation*, copyright © 1961 by The Abbey of Gethsemani, Inc., reprinted by permission of New Directions Publishing Corp. for the United States, its terrotories, and Canada.

p. 219 "Wherever you find": Thomas Byrom, *The Third Wish: The Disquisition of Death, A translation of the Katha Upanishad of the Black Yajur Veda*, 3:17, © Thomas Byrom, 1991, unpublished manuscript.

p. 219 "Dip him in the river": William Blake, *The Marriage of Heaven and Hell* (Boston: John W. Luce & Co., 1906).

p. 220 "You feel as if": Thomas Merton, 29 "Mental Prayer," *New Seeds of Contemplation*, copyright © 1961 by The Abbey of Gethsemani, Inc., reprinted by permission of New Directions Publishing Corp. for the United States, its terrotories, and Canada.

p. 222 "Step by step": after Patanjali, *Yoga Sutras* 3:6.

p. 223 "The way is not": Thomas Byrom, 18 "Impurity," *The Dhammapada: The Sayings of the Buddha*, trans. Thomas Byrom (New York: Vintage Books, 1976).

Chapter 9

p. 225 "Love has ten degrees": Sufi proverb (attributed).

p. 225 "My heart is breaking": St. Catherine of Siena, *The Dialogue (Classics of Western Spirituality Series)*, trans. and intro. Suzanne Noffke, O.P. (New York: Paulist Press, 1980). Copyright © Paulist Press, Inc., New York/Mahwah, NJ. Used with permission. www.paulistpress.com

p. 227 "Love has no why": Meister Eckhart, ed. Paul E. Szarmach, *An Introduction to the Medieval Mystics of Europe*, (Albany: State University of New York Press, 1984). Meister Eckhart (c. 1260–c. 1328) was a German Catholic theologian, philosopher, and mystic.

p. 228 "He is not a man": Swami Chetanananda, *The Sky of the Heart: Jewels of Wisdom from Nityananda*, republished with permission of Rudra Press, copyright 1996.

p. 230 "By standing on his own": Thomas Byrom, *The Heart of Awareness: A Translation of the Ashtavakra Gita*, Chapter 18, Verse 50, 55; trans. Thomas Byrom (Boston: Shambala Publications, 1990).

p. 232 "perfect love casteth out fear": 1 John 4:18, *Holy Bible, American Standard Version* (New York: Thomas Nelson & Sons, 1901).

p. 233 "I have lived on the lip": Rumi, from *The Essential Rumi*, Chapter 27, trans. Coleman Barks, published by Harper San Francisco, 1995 © Coleman Barks.

p. 237 "Die now, die now": Rumi, Jalal al-Din, *Mystical Poems of Rumi*, trans. A. J. Arbery, © 1968, republished with permission of The University of Chicago Press, permission conveyed through Copyright Clearance Center, Inc.

p. 238 "One who has beheld": Ramprasad, trans. Devadatta Kali.

p. 239 "Like a tree": Rumi, Jalal al-Din, *Mystical Poems of Rumi*, trans. A. J. Arbery, © 1968, republished with permission of The University of Chicago Press, permission conveyed through Copyright Clearance Center, Inc.

p. 241 "Fast thou never so much": Anonymous, *A Book of Contemplation The Which Is Called The Cloud Of Unknowing, in the Which a Soul Is Oned With God*, 2nd ed., Edited from the British Museum MS. Harl. 674, intro. Evelyn Underhill (London: John M. Watkins, 1922), p. 37.

p. 241 "He said: 'What is abstinence?'": Rumi, Jalal al-Din, *Mystical Poems of Rumi*, trans. A. J. Arbery, © 1968, republished with permission of The University of Chicago Press, permission conveyed through Copyright Clearance Center, Inc.

p. 246 "Share me": Ma, quoting Neem Karoli Baba, by permission of the Ma Jaya Bhagavati Trust.

p. 251 "What heart could keep": St. Catherine of Siena, *The Dialogue (Classics of Western Spirituality Series)*, trans. and intro. Suzanne Noffke, O.P. (New York: Paulist Press, 1980). Copyright © Paulist Press, Inc., New York/Mahwah, NJ. Used with permission. www.paulistpress.com

Chapter 10

p. 265 "All wonder what happens": Ramprasad, trans. Devadatta Kali.

p. 272 "In awe of him...For you are she": Thomas Byrom, *The Third Wish: The Disquisition of Death, A translation of the Katha Upanishad of the Black Yajur Veda*, Katha Unipanishad, 4:7, © Thomas Byrom, 1991, unpublished manuscript.

p. 275 "The cistern contains": William Blake, *The Marriage of Heaven and Hell* (Boston: John W. Luce & Co., 1906).

p. 275 "I am the way": John 14:6, *Holy Bible, American Standard Version* (New York: Thomas Nelson & Sons, 1901).

Chapter 11

p. 287 "O Mother!": Ramprasad, trans. Devadatta Kali.

p. 289 "out of fear": Thomas Byrom, *The Third Wish: The Disquisition of Death, A translation of the Katha Upanishad of the Black Yajur Veda*, © Thomas Byrom, 1991, unpublished manuscript.

p. 299 "true mother in whom...": Mother Julian of Norwich, *Revelations of Divine Love,* ed. Grace Harriet Warrack (London: Methuen Company, 1901).

p. 299 "Was not our heart": Luke 24:32, *Holy Bible, American Standard Version* (New York: Thomas Nelson & Sons, 1901).

p. 301 "When you strip": Gospel of Thomas, 37, in *The Nag Hammadi Scriptures* by Marvin W. Meyer and James M. Robinson (San Francisco: HarperCollins, 1990). Copyright © 2007 by Marvin W. Meyer. Used by permission of HarperCollins Publishers.

p. 307 "Dip him in the river": William Blake, *The Marriage of Heaven and Hell* (Boston: John W. Luce & Co., 1906).

p. 311 "that my joy may be": John 15:11, *Holy Bible, American Standard Version* (New York: Thomas Nelson & Sons, 1901).

p. 312 "Gaté / Gone Gaté / Gone": The Buddha, *Heart Sutra,* trans. Thomas Byrom.